The Process of Counseling and Psychotherapy

Matters of Skill

Ira David Welch
Gannon University
David M. Gonzalez
University of Northern Colorado

Brooks/Cole Publishing Company
I(T)P® An International Thomson Publishing Company

Pacific Grove • Albany • Belmont • Bonn • Boston • Cincinnati • Detroit • Johannesburg
London • Madrid • Melbourne • Mexico City • New York • Paris • Singapore
Tokyo • Toronto • Washington

Sponsoring Editor: *Lisa Gebo*
Editorial Assistant: *Susan Carlson*
Marketing Team: *Steve Catalano,*
Aaron Eden, and Kyrrha Sevco
Manuscript Editor: *Rebecca Glenister*
Production Editor: *Mary Vezilich*
Permissions Editor: *May Clark*

Design Editor: *Roy Neuhaus*
Interior and Cover Design: *Geri Davis*
Cover Illustration: *Jose Ortega/*
The Stock Illustration Source, Inc.
Art Editor: *Jennifer Mackres*
Typesetting: *The Cowans*
Printing and Binding: *Webcom*

For more information contact:

BROOKS/COLE PUBLISHING COMPANY
511 Forest Lodge Road
Pacific Grove, CA 93950
USA

International Thomson Editores
Seneca 53
Col. Polanco
11560 México, D.F., México

International Thomson Publishing Europe
Berkshire House 168-173
High Holborn
London WC1V 7AA
England

International Thomson Publishing GmbH
Königswinterer Strasse 418
53227 Bonn
Germany

Thomas Nelson Australia
102 Dodds Street
South Melbourne, 3205
Victoria, Australia

International Thomson Publishing Asia
60 Albert Street
#15-01 Albert Complex
Singapore 189969

Nelson Canada
1120 Birchmount Road
Scarborough, Ontario
Canada M1K 5G4

International Thomson Publishing Japan
Hirakawacho Kyowa Building, 3F
2-2-1 Hirakawacho
Chiyoda-ku, Tokyo 102
Japan

Printed in Canada

10 9 8 7 6 5 4 3 2 1

Library of Congress Cataloging-in-Publication Data
Welch, I. David (Ira David), [date]
    The process of counseling and psychotherapy: matters of skill /
Ira David Welch, David M. Gonzalez.
        p.   cm.
    Includes index.
    ISBN 0-534-34413-5 (pbk.)
    1. Psychotherapy.   2. Mental health counseling.   I. Gonzalez,
David M.   II. Title.
RC480.W379 1998
616.89' 14—dc21

98-19881
CIP

Dedication

To Marie, my wife, with whom I have spent a lifetime and anticipate another yet and to David and Daniel, our sons, who have made the world a beautiful place for us.

IDW

To Sherri, my beloved wife, and our son, Nicholas, who every day reminds us of the importance and joy of living in the moment.

DMG

About the Authors

DAVID WELCH (left) is a psychologist. He is recognized as a Diplomate in Counseling Psychology by the American Board of Professional Psychology (ABPP) and is a Professor at Gannon University.

His practice includes the young and the old, the well and the infirm, rich and poor—in fact, people from all walks of life who, like himself, struggle to make meaning from the sometimes (often?) puzzling mysteries of living.

DAVID GONZALEZ (right) is an Associate Professor and Director of Training for Counseling Psychology at the University of Northern Colorado. He received his doctorate from the University of Colorado, Boulder, in 1988 and is a licensed psychologist in the state of Colorado. He is a new father, and the birth of his first child, Nicholas, has served as reinforcement to him of the importance of the helping professions as a means to provide a more humane and loving environment for all the world's beings.

Contents

Section One

The Essence of Counseling and Psychotherapy

Section Two

The Foundation of Counseling and Psychotherapy

Section Three

The Skill of Counseling and Psychotherapy

Section Four

The Practice of Counseling and Psychotherapy

Appendices

Aids for More Effective Practice

Index

Preface

❧

Skills provide the surest path to the realization of our intentions. A pure heart is a lovely possession and is often a restorative gift to others. A prepared, educated, and skilled pure heart is a consistent healing gift to others. The purpose of this book is to give our readers the skills to translate their good intentions into the reality of effective therapeutic relationships with those who come to them for assistance. It often has been said that good intentions are not enough, and although this is true, we fear this pronouncement implies a degree of cynicism that undervalues good intentions. Skills without good intentions do not bode well for the target of their application. Thus, we hope that this book can match clients with those of good intent who need skills to actualize their hope of being an effective helper. To accompany the skills presented here, helping professionals may want to read Dr. Welch's companion book, *The Path of Psychotherapy: Matters of the Heart* (Brooks/Cole, 1998). Here you will find a description of how a psychotherapist works—the personal philosophy and variety of experiences that have come with years of practice. More importantly, the "Heart" book should stimulate thought, discussion, and guidance for the helper who must ponder the meaning and impact of his or her own work with clients.

We are psychologists, psychotherapists, educators and supervisors of clinical experience. We literally have spent thousands of hours in the practice, observation, supervision, and instruction of counselors in training. This book is a product of that experience—an attempt to communicate what we have learned not only from our own counseling experience but from teaching that experience to others. Our students have taught us again and again what is difficult and what needs a new word, a new metaphor, and a new way of instruction. They have given us insights into what must be taught firmly and unwaveringly and what must be approached with gentleness and subtlety. Our years of observation, feedback, and instruction have taught us what must be stressed and what might be assumed (little, we discovered). We have sought to provide the reader with the attitudinal conditions of effective counseling and psychotherapy while providing concrete, step-by-step procedures when we believed that such a tangible approach would better suit the needs of a developing counselor.

The terms *counseling* and *psychotherapy* are used interchangeably throughout this book. There was a time, perhaps, when these terms may have had different meanings, but that time has passed, for us at least. We have tried to communicate that in the context of the counseling relationship a variety of words carry the same message. For us psychotherapy, counseling, and therapy all mean essentially the same thing; they are merely different words for the same process.

We must also mention that although we separate the phenomenon of individual differences into a separate chapter (7), we have tried to communicate throughout the book, that cultural, gender, lifestyle, religious, and national differences are an ongoing part of the therapy process. Counseling is grounded in the desire to understand clients in their uniqueness. Honoring that uniqueness must not be obvious only intellectually or academically, but it must also translate into effective practice. It is crucial that psychotherapists "walk the walk" as well as "talk the talk" of respecting people's individuality.

We invite each reader to walk the path from the introduction of the counseling profession and its fundamental values through the need for a guiding philosophy to the formulation of a plan for working with others. Along the way, we offer tools to make the therapeutic encounter a more effective and a more enriching one. This book will aid the reader from the first client encounter to the final meeting. We offer a counseling model as well as a plan for developing one's own counseling model. Finally, the appendices provides the reader with guidelines for developing an affective vocabulary (the language of the emotions), selected counseling techniques, and a sampling of the forms most often used in the counseling profession.

We would like to take a moment to thank those who helped us in the development of this book. We have already thanked our students, but perhaps it would be wise to say another word. All good teachers are instructed by their students. This book would not exist if it weren't for the relationships and interactions between and among our students. They have struggled. They have profited from our instruction and have taught us what was helpful and what was not. How can we thank them adequately? Our colleagues, those who have also argued and struggled with us as we sought more effective ways to teach the counseling process, continue to enrich us and stimulate us to put on paper what we teach verbally every day. You will find yourself here and there, throughout the text.

We wish to thank the libraries at the University of Northern Colorado and at Gannon University. Their assistance and guidance helped steer us through the sometimes rocky path of references and sources. Thank you. We would also like to acknowledge the helpful comments and suggestions of the book's reviewers: John Bowers, Northwest Missouri State University; Patricia Emilie Hudson, George Washington University; Linda P. Keel, Northeastern Illinois University; Mary Kay Kreider, St. Louis Community College–Meramec; and Kevin Peterson, Frostburg State University.

The folks at Brooks/Cole could not have been more helpful. In what some describe as the rough and exacting world of academic publishing, it is probably expected that one's individual concerns and wishes might be stepped on or ignored. We do not know how it has been for others, but we could not have been better treated and respected had our parents been our publishers! We cannot say enough about how much we enjoyed working with Lisa Gebo. We wish her on everyone. Our production editor, Mary Vezilich, who is as patient and understanding an editor as one can hope for, treats our words as if they were her own. We appreciate the early work of Susan Carlson, who guided us through the review process, and we wish her well as she moves on to other experiences.

We wish each reader well as you take your initial steps on this path to becoming a helper of others. We know it is a path that seems to be continually uphill and that only infrequently permits one to rest along the side, but also we know the personal rewards that come from walking it well. Although counselors who create the conditions of psychotherapeutic change within their clients are not awarded "lifesaving badges," we think they should be.

Ira David Welch
David M. Gonzalez

The Essence of Counseling and Psychotherapy

*T*his section provides information and perspectives on why people seek counseling and looks at the essential ingredients that make helping others possible. The reasons people seek help can be straightforward or complex. To become experts, psychotherapists need to develop a keen awareness about the possible meanings and motives that clients bring into the therapeutic process. This section also looks closely at the characteristics of a therapeutic relationship—that is, what attributes allow it to become an environment that fosters healing and change? Empathy, which is one of those attributes, is the focus of an entire chapter because we regard it as the foundation for all effective psychotherapy. Actually attaining the capacity for empathy can be quite challenging. Being empathic requires us to see well beyond the confines of our own individual and ethnocentric experiences; it requires a nonjudgmental appreciation for other cultures and for other experiences of gender and sexual orientation. In this section we strive to create an awareness in our readers for all the factors involved in the empathy process, and we hope this awareness will result in more therapeutic understanding and fewer empathic failures by therapists.

Later in this section we look further at the nature of the therapeutic relationship by exploring the importance of achieving and maintaining a healthy therapeutic distance. It is common for therapists in training to overidentify with their clientele, which ultimately makes them less able to be of service to their clients.

1

~

The Goals of Counseling and Psychotherapy

*W*hy do clients come to counseling? What is the counselor's or psychotherapist's role in helping clients achieve their purposes? Answers to these questions are important for a number of reasons. Much of what you will do as a therapist will be based on what you consider your purpose or role to be. If you are to help other people, then it is important to understand the nature of human beings. When clients seek the help of a counselor, what are they seeking? What are the forces operating within and around people that influence their perceptions?

Understanding the Nature of Persons

It is in the very nature of the human organism to move toward health and away from illness. Some have called this an organismic valuing tendency. Maslow (1970) postulated that humans experience a hierarchy of needs ranging from physiological needs, such as the need for food, water, and air, to the need for self-actualization.

Level 1. Physiological needs such as the need for food, water, and air.

Level 2. Safety needs such as security, stability, freedom from fear, and the need for structure and limits.

Level 3. Belonging and love needs such as affectionate relationships with people and the feeling that one belongs in some social context.

Level 4. Self-esteem needs such as reputation, recognition, achievement, adequacy, or mastery.

Level 5. Self-actualization needs such as self-fulfillment, to actualize one's potential.

Rogers's Fully Functioning Person

Rogers (1962) described people as having a kind of internal gyroscope. This process can be disrupted by experiences of "conditions of worth." Rogers hypothesized that if negative conditions changed toward more open, productive ones, and the new conditions lasted long enough, then the person would experience a renewed drive toward a more healthful way of being. Rogers proposed a concept called the fully functioning person. In this description Rogers said a fully functioning person has a variety of characteristics. They are:

4

1. Aversion to facades—the person ceases the struggle to be what he or she is not.
2. Aversion to "oughts and shoulds"—the person ceases to guide his or her conduct in terms of what he or she "ought" to become or "ought" to be.
3. Movement away from meeting others' expectations—the person stops trying to compulsively please others at his or her own expense.
4. Movement toward self-direction—the person chooses his or her own behavior in a responsible fashion.
5. Acceptance of self—one accepts the self as a person in the process of becoming.
6. Being open to one's own experiences—the person does not blot out thoughts, feelings, perceptions, or memories that might be unpleasant.
7. Acceptance—the person accepts others and trusts the self.

Combs's Adequate Personality

Combs (1989) described the human organism's need to maintain and enhance itself. "The existence of a fundamental drive toward health and fulfillment rooted in protoplasm itself means the human organism is essentially trustworthy. It can, it will, it must move toward health and fulfillment *if the way seems open to do so* [italics added]" (Combs, 1989, p. 21). In other words, in broad conceptual terms people seek therapy to correct the things that are blocking their growth. It is in their nature not to just remain resigned to their struggles, but to resolve and move past their problems as they head toward fulfillment, self-actualization, or becoming more fully functioning.

Sometimes notions of self-actualization and self-fulfillment are misunderstood as selfish, while in fact people with higher levels of fulfillment and self-actualization often are deeply concerned about others. They are freer to care about other people because their energy is not spent compensating for feelings of inadequacy. Their capacity to identify with greater numbers of people as well as to realize the interdependent nature of all people is enhanced. These factors combine to make a self-actualized person one who is deeply concerned about others and one who acts responsibly toward his or her fellow human beings. Thus, the motivation and drive for clients entering psychotherapy is not merely an intrapsychic, self-centered one, but often is driven by the client's desire to interact more effectively in an interpersonal relationship or even to become a better citizen in some larger community.

Those who enter the therapeutic professions have an idea that they want to help. However, the form that such help will take depends largely on the conceptualization of counseling formulated by a therapist. (See Chapter 6 on developing a theoretical orientation.)

Reasons for Seeking Counseling

Clients may seek counseling for a variety of reasons. They may be at their wit's end from struggling with a particular problem. They may be in a state of incongruence. They may be confused and need clarification.

5

They may be desperate. They may have lost confidence in themselves. They may be exasperated. They may be afraid or scared. They may be fearful not just of the past, but of the present and the future. They may be afraid that they are going crazy. They may feel they have lost control of their lives. Yet no matter how circumscribed the difficulty, seldom is it simply a matter just of "fixing" that particular problem. Effective helping usually requires understanding how the presenting problem fits within an overall life pattern. For example, a client may come in requesting help managing anger with his or her co-workers; however, exploration reveals that the client doesn't deal well with anger in any situation and that possibly the source of anger is an experienced personal hurt. The therapeutic model provided in Chapter 2 respects the client's initial issues while acknowledging that clients often do not fully know the source of the discontent that brought them to counseling. Clients want to feel better about themselves; we call this a striving for health or fulfillment.

Client Goals

Clients come in because they want something better. The fact that they seek the assistance of a counselor is an indication that they think such an outcome is possible. The hope that is an inextricable part of this process provides an impetus to solve one's problems.

Specific Goals

Clients may be dealing with advancing age and the associated changes in health and abilities. They may feel betrayed by their bodies as they find that that they can no longer do activities that used to be important to them. They may be struggling with how others now treat them differently—as if to be older is to be diminished somehow.

A terminal illness can prompt people to seek counseling, not only to talk about the illness but because such an event leads to a reevaluation of what is important. Existential questions about the meaning of life and what to do with one's remaining time smack the client in the face, and the need to find an answer can be overwhelming.

The stress of a relationship between spouses/partners can bring people seeking to find ways to communicate or to resolve deep-seated resentments that have grown over the years. Perhaps the whole family will seek therapy to become a better functioning family unit.

Presenting problems may be of a developmental nature. For example, college-age clients, away from home for the first time, often struggle with separation and individuation. They need assistance with the transition of being on their own and becoming confident adults. Likewise, young teenagers may need help moving from being a child to dealing with the myriad challenges that come with adolescence.

Sometimes clients will seek help to solve a problem that has troubled them for years and they have finally decided to do something about it. For example, a person who lacks confidence may decide to resolve the struggle to believe in himself or herself once and for all.

Perhaps a problem is making people feel like life is passing them by and they want to resolve this issue before life gets away from them. At various times throughout their lives people reach moments where the need to resolve nagging concerns becomes more pressing. For example, milestone birthdays such as reaching 40 or 50 can spur people to seek counseling.

Sometimes people seek therapy for professional development reasons. For example, as a future or current therapist they may want to be a more effective helper. They recognize a number of their own unresolved struggles, and they seek to resolve them in order to be a healthier, more aware therapist.

Clients often express a wish to resolve a specific problem such as marital distress, depression, or low self-esteem. But seldom is it simply a matter of solving a specific problem. That problem is usually one piece or manifestation of a larger picture or puzzle. For example, if a client comes in describing trouble communicating in his or her marriage, chances are that communication has been a problem for this person in other contexts, too. If we only look at that discrete piece of behavior, then we will see it as somehow disconnected from the person. Clients often talk about a variety of problems that really seem to reflect a struggle to find self-fulfillment. The presenting problems are real and serious; however, if we do not understand how the problem fits in as a part of the client's overall behavior, then we may miss the greater significance.

The list of reasons for clients seeking counseling could go on for pages. Welch (1998) provides a look at how life concerns can be seen with different degrees of significance—as issues, problems, or dilemmas. Each person is unique and each must be appreciated and understood in his or her uniqueness.

Respect for Client Goals

Respecting client goals may seem easy at first glance. If clients come in, tell you their struggles, and specify the problems and changes that they desire, there is usually no difficulty respecting their goals. However, the first session does not always go like you would expect. Clients can present a variety of goals, some that may take us off guard. Sometimes the client's goal is to get Social Services off his or her back. Such a goal is real and pressing for the client, and we must respect it as such if we expect the client to trust us. The difficulty is, of course, that some client goals lie outside our range of competence, and our role becomes one of referral or redirection. Often, however, what initially seems to be an inappropriate goal can, in a climate of respect and growing trust, be seen to have psychological meaning.

In the case of children, remember that usually they are not willing customers. They are in the therapist's office because adults have brought them there. A child's goal may be to stop coming in for therapy or to please a parent. It is important to honor the goals of the child too. This of course can be the basis for a mutual working relationship (e.g., "Let's figure out what has to happen so you will not have to come in anymore").

Clients who are court ordered or pressured by Social Services to seek counseling may be trying to please those agencies. If that is their goal, we must respect it as being important to those clients. It does not matter how much we wish that they would say, "I am here because I need to change some important things about myself"; they are there because someone else said they have to be. Such clients usually are threatened with the custodial loss of a child or jail time. Resistance can be a major factor for clients who come to counseling under duress. Just consider how anyone feels when forced to do something against his or her will. Remember the underdog slogan, "You can make me do it, but you can't make me like it or do it right." (Ossorio, personal communication, 1986). If clients say something to the effect that they are in counseling only because the court ordered them there, it is your job to find a way to work constructively together. For example, identifying what behaviors got the client into trouble with the court system and helping the client to change the troublesome behaviors can be a reasonable and attainable goal.

The Changing Nature of Goals

Goals may change over time. As persons begin to understand themselves better, they may have a clearer idea of the problems that plague them than they did when they first sought help. Sometimes clients' journeys to the therapist's office happen in cycles. The first visit may be to get their feet wet and check out what it is like to be in a therapeutic relationship, and each time they may go deeper. A client came to see one of us with a clear goal. She planned to deal with some "self-esteem" issues for four sessions and "just needed to clear them up." She remained in therapy for 18 months. Each session unfolded deeper concerns and more profound life issues. And, as her life changed, she encountered other life crises, and she was able to use therapy as a place to more securely cope with new life pressures.

With time clients learn how to better use therapy—that is, they get better at coping with their problems and at working effectively in the session to maximize their time. The process of introspection is not an easy one. Therapy is hard work. Consider your own experience of how difficult it is to change. Change can be painful and painfully slow.

Ability to Express and Describe Goals

Clients' abilities to describe their problems vary greatly. Some clients have a remarkably rich capacity to characterize their problems, complete with stories, feelings, and key experiences in their lives. Others are able initially to offer only a skeleton view. One of our clients had a limited affective vocabulary. He literally could only describe his experiences and feelings by saying something was a good experience or

9

a bad experience, and even that rudimentary description was provided with great difficulty. He was unable to describe or express any other feelings. As the therapy progressed, his understanding and recognition of feelings grew. As he struggled through both the recognition of feelings and the effort to label them, his vocabulary grew as well. He spoke with more sensitivity and authority as he was able to more accurately name the emotional experiences of his life. There is power in words, and sometimes the lack of the proper word can present clients with one more obstacle to overcome.

Inappropriate Goals

Sometimes a client may present with an inappropriate goal. For example, a parent involved in a custody battle may have an initial goal of showing you that he or she is the better parent, with an eventual goal of having you, as the counselor, side with him or her in the custody battle. Beginning counselors are sometimes afraid to be direct about the inappropriate nature of such a goal and instead try to figure out how to help the client achieve that goal. In another example, a prospective client called an inexperienced therapist and asked to be hypnotized to find out if she had been sexually molested as a child. The therapist initially agreed to the client's request, but after having second thoughts the therapist consulted with a supervisor to determine the appropriateness of such a goal. After that discussion it became clear to the therapist that such a course of action was fraught with major pitfalls and was an inappropriate goal. The counselor was able to give the client a clear message that the concerns she was having were perhaps more suited for psychotherapy than for hypnosis alone. As we mature as counselors, we must be clear about our roles and be confident enough to tell clients when a goal is inappropriate.

Cultural, Gender, and Lifestyle Factors

Clients may seek counseling to find some comfort around their cultural, gender, and lifestyle identities. They may seek counseling to try to heal from the wounds of discrimination. Multiple barriers block minority groups from full participation in society. Some of these barriers are visible while others are institutionalized and are more difficult for someone in the "majority" culture to discern. Counselors are expected to create an environment that is safe, welcoming, and understanding for all clients. A person of color first may want to determine whether the therapist can understand the experience of a "minority" or a person different in a variety of ways from the counselor's background, beliefs, culture, or ethnicity before talking further about a therapy goal. It also may be important that the therapist understand and accept that many life issues do not have intrapsychic origins and that the pressures, struggles, and barriers to effective living can well lie outside the client. This is especially true for clients who come from backgrounds of discrimination.

The Goal-Less Client

On occasion, counselors will encounter clients who seem to be without a goal. No matter what direction or topic is explored the clients remain vague and indefinite as to what they wish to work on. The client can describe general feelings of dissatisfaction or discomfort yet cannot seem to pinpoint a central problem. In such cases the therapist may end up working harder than the client. The client continues therapy but struggles to specify the problem. Although it may prove challenging, it usually is possible to help the client more clearly define the problem. In our experience, such clients may be depressed, and their lack of a clear counseling goal may be symptomatic of the lack of a clear life goal. They lack meaning. This is the situation for which the model presented in Chapter 2 becomes most important. The initial phase of psychotherapy—exploration—is most crucial with clients who present with vague and undifferentiated goals. Exploring their life experiences and vague meanings lays the foundation for effective and lasting psychotherapeutic change. The goals that emerge can be trusted to have come genuinely from the clients and not to have been led or influenced by the counselor.

Counselor Goals

Counselors operate with some general goals that apply to any counseling or psychotherapy session.

1. One goal is to have a well-grounded and internally consistent guiding philosophy or theoretical orientation for the therapist to use in his or her work with the client and to aid in understanding the nature of psychological functioning. (See Chapter 6 for a discussion on developing a personal theory.)

2. Another goal is to establish a therapeutic relationship. Such a relationship should be characterized by empathy, authenticity, respect, courage, collaboration, and therapeutic perspective. (See Chapter 4 for a discussion of these relationship issues.)

3. An obvious goal is to explore and clarify the problem. You must achieve an adequate understanding of the problem before deciding on solutions. Clarification of the problem usually does not occur without exploration. (See Chapter 2 for a discussion of a model of psychotherapy.)

4. Another goal is to move toward problem resolution. Clients would not be seeking our assistance if they did not want to resolve the problem or take some kind of action to move toward that end. (See Chapter 8 for a discussion of this phase of therapy.)

5. A therapist goal is to make the experience palatable or safe for the client. Initially some clients are reluctant to engage in the therapy process. They may be unfamiliar with the process, and its intimate nature can be quite threatening for some. Such clients need the therapist to create an atmosphere that allows them to engage further in the process.

6. In the case of children, a counselor's goal should include helping them understand why they were brought in for counseling. It is not unusual for children to say that they are not sure why their parents or guardians think they need counseling. Children may need repeated clarification.

7. "Above all do no harm" is a therapeutic Hippocratic oath that should be a part of every therapist's conceptualization. Among the ways a client might be harmed by the therapist are moving to solutions without understanding the problem, sexual exploitation, and judging clients. (See Chapter 9 on ethics.)

Barriers to Accomplishing Counselor Goals

Oftentimes, discussions of empathy, congruence, and positive regard, which are the *core conditions* of effective psychotherapy, get mixed in with factors such as listening and attending, which are sometimes called "microskills." It is almost as if these factors are assumed to be something that every counselor or psychotherapist will be able to achieve or attributes that one will, of course, have. This is a misleading message. First of all, to regard the central features of therapy as "micro" does not accurately convey their importance. Secondly, such a label does not adequately communicate that these conditions are not usually achieved merely by regarding them as important. Therapists exert considerable effort—both in time and energy—to develop the capacity to be empathic, authentic, and respectful in the therapeutic sense.

13

Empathy. Therapists in training are quick to recognize that empathy is important and usually consider themselves sensitive and empathic. Developing true empathy, however, can be a significant challenge. Barriers to being able to understand can come in a variety of forms. Values, traditions, culture, language, fear, and background can all interfere. Such things can create worldviews and paradigms that render the attainment of empathy a monumental task. The barriers can lie outside awareness so that a counselor may not realize that he or she does not understand the client. There is also the difficulty of describing personal experience. Sometimes no words can adequately describe all the factors involved in one's experience. (See Chapter 3 for an expanded discussion of empathy.)

Authenticity. Being authentic can be enormously difficult. Although no one is likely to say that they want to be inauthentic, to actually be oneself can be a frightening prospect. In one advanced counseling practicum, the students developed a class motto as they struggled to improve their counseling competence: "Why is it so difficult to be simply and naturally who we are?" They were directly confronting their struggles with authenticity. So many messages from early life make it seem that if we don't hide our true selves we will somehow be seen as unacceptable or deficient. Our fears and the defenses we develop to protect ourselves can have a sneaky way of altering our behavior, thus making us not ourselves.

Respect. Feeling respect is difficult enough; demonstrating respect is even more difficult. It is easy to *say* that you respect your clients, but to *show* respect is more of a challenge. For example, what happens when a client has values that differ significantly from your central values? What if you hold antigay and antilesbian sentiments, yet your client is gay or lesbian? What if you are deeply religious and are presented with an atheist? Our tolerance and respect for differences is directly challenged in the process of becoming a helper.

Sometimes people in training strenuously object to the notion that respect is a necessary condition for effective therapy. They cite some of the client's "offensive" behaviors that prevent them from feeling respect. However, this is a misunderstanding of what is meant by the word. Respect in therapeutic terms is for the person, not the behavior. Sometimes it is necessary to engage in a form of "age regression" to recognize that every bigot was once a person free of prejudice. Even the most disgusting clients were once innocent and malleable children whose life experiences and, perhaps, personal decisions have contributed to their present state. Somehow, effective counselors find a way to view clients as persons of worth in spite of their socially destructive actions.

Personal Values. What to do with one's personal values is an important challenge for therapists. Inevitably counselors will find themselves dealing with clients whose value systems are different from their own. If the counselor sees the client as somehow less than respectable because of those values or if the counselor feels a huge abyss between client and counselor because of them, then effective work cannot take place. The counselor may find himself or herself trying to revamp the client's values rather than listening to and allowing the client to explore and move to his or her own healthier way of being. To illustrate how values may be used inappropriately in therapy, consider a therapist who advertises therapeutic services by saying, "Professional counseling services available for depression, self-esteem, and addictions, unless I do not agree with your values. If you have values different from mine, then you will have to go elsewhere for help." As ridiculous as this sounds, the net effect is the same when a therapist judges a client's values rather than being available to assist the client in his or her struggles.

Thus far, we have discussed the goals of counseling and psychotherapy for both clients and counselors. The following sections will address and explore the amazing and challenging process of becoming a counselor, one who is able to facilitate the achievement of such goals.

Becoming a Counselor

Becoming an effective counselor or psychotherapist is a unique endeavor. It does not consist merely of going to school, gaining a knowledge base, and learning particular techniques or methods. Even though beginning therapists will be taught proven techniques and methods for helping others, this knowledge alone is not what makes an effective counselor or psychotherapist. The process extends beyond the training needed for most occupations. "It calls for the very personal construction of a complex system of beliefs capable of providing trustworthy guidelines to professional thought and practice" (Combs & Gonzalez, 1994, p. 203). "Prepare to meet yourself" would be a fair caveat in programs that train counselors and psychotherapists. Becoming a counselor or psychotherapist requires a commitment to a process of change in you as the therapist. Hence, the word *becoming* is important, because the word implies a process. Therapists who are unwilling to change or *become* are unlikely to be effective helpers. How can therapists help a client's growth process if they are unwilling or unable to participate in their own growth process? Therapists must be willing to straightforwardly face themselves if they are to have any hope of being able to help clients do the same.

15

Counselors and psychotherapists need to have accurate, realistic views of themselves. They need to recognize who they are, complete with both their strengths and their weaknesses. Part of becoming a counselor is accepting that your values and beliefs will inevitably be challenged. Learning to tolerate differences and other points of view is a difficult yet essential part of knowing the self. A helper without an accurate conception of one's self is likely to play out his or her own issues in the therapy process and at times may be unable to be empathic with others.

Therapy for the Therapist

In the process of becoming a helper, a person might be advised to see a counselor or therapist for himself or herself. Oftentimes, counselors are reluctant to participate in the therapeutic process from the client's chair. They feel as if they should be above needing help, or perhaps they define themselves as helpers and have difficulty asking for help for themselves even when it would be in their best interest to do so. It is like a physician who says that he or she would never go to a doctor. The therapist is challenged with demonstrating faith in what he or she wishes to offer others. Being a client can significantly enhance one's understanding of the process and therefore increase one's effectiveness. Therapists who see themselves as above ordinary persons are unable to remain in touch with their clients' needs and therefore are unable to help them. For example, how can a counselor help someone who is frightened or depressed if he or she denies ever experiencing these emotional states? Welch (1998, pp. 73–79) describes the concept of the "wounded healer," which says that a counselor or psychotherapist does not have to be a perfect human being in order to be an effective therapist.

Learning to Say No or to Set Limits

Those who see themselves as helpers may struggle with being able to say no. No matter how much is asked of them, they keep saying yes rather than having to feel guilty for saying no to someone in need. Agreeing to extremely inconvenient appointment times or taking on more clients than you could reasonably handle are just some of the ways this happens. In small towns where most people know one another, you, as the counselor or therapist, may be expected to fulfill that role even in social situations. Learning to take care of your own needs is critical. Not doing so almost assures an early burnout. By taking care of your own needs, you will have more energy and vitality for your clients and you will become a role model for setting limits.

Others' Discomfort with Counselors

Socially, becoming a counselor can be a double-edged sword. One edge gives a counselor a degree of recognition and status, whereas, the other edge carries a degree of suspicion and rejection. Psychotherapists tell endless stories of innocent conversations coming to a screeching halt once the other person asks, "What do you do for a living?" People often react negatively when you admit that you are a psychologist, counselor, or psychotherapist, fearing that you have been "analyzing" them. Some mental health professionals avoid explaining what they do for a living and still others go so far as to give a false answer. Some say that they usually only attend social gatherings consisting of mostly psychologists and counselors to avoid the problem. Regardless of how counselors deal with this issue, it is real and something with which helpers must cope.

Summary

The goals of therapy for clients are best described on two levels. On the global level, clients are trying to solve their problems because it is human nature to maintain and enhance themselves. On a specific level, clients are seeking to resolve various issues such as how to express feelings more adequately or how to resolve a marital problem. These specific problems, which need to be addressed because clients directly feel their impact, are best understood by discovering how they fit into an overall life pattern or struggle.

Becoming counselors and psychotherapists is both a unique and an enormous challenge. The process of becoming a skilled helper takes time, commitment, and a willingness to participate in an ongoing process of growth as a person and as a helper. You cannot become a skilled helping professional without facing your own struggles along the way.

Thus, the process of becoming a counselor is not only one of mastering a set of techniques or skills but rather one of coming to terms with who you are as a person and learning to use that self as an instrument of help for others. Training counselors and psychotherapists includes not only mastering skills but facing yourself and developing the attitudes and personal knowledge necessary to strive to understand others, to enter the relationship honestly and without guile, and to suspend moralistic judgment.

References and for Further Reading

Combs, A. W. (1989). *A theory of therapy: Guidelines for counseling practice*. Newbury Park, CA: Sage Publications.

Combs, A. W., & Gonzalez, D. M. (1994). *Helping relationships: Basic concepts for the helping professions* (4th ed.). Boston: Allyn & Bacon.

Doherty, W. J. (1995). *Soul searching: Why psychotherapy must promote moral responsibility*. New York: Basic Books.

Dryden, W., & Spurling, L. (Eds.). (1989). *On becoming a psychotherapist*. London: Tavistock/Routledge.

Goldberg, C. (1991). *On being a psychotherapist*. Northvale, NJ: Jason Aronson.

Karasu, T. B. (1992). *Wisdom in the practice of psychotherapy*. New York: Basic Books.

Klein, J. (1995). *Doubts and certainties in the practice of psychotherapy*. London: Karnac Books.

Kottler, J. A. (1986). *On being a therapist*. San Francisco: Jossey-Bass.

Maslow, A. H. (1970). *Motivation and personality*. New York: Harper & Row.

Rogers, C. R. (1962). Toward becoming a fully functioning person. In A. W. Combs (Ed.), *Perceiving, behaving, becoming: A new focus for education*. Alexandria, VA: Association for Supervision and Curriculum Development.

Storr, A. (1990). *The art of psychotherapy* (2nd ed.). London: Routledge.

Sussman, M. B. (Ed.). (1995). *A perilous calling: The hazards of psychotherapy practice*. New York: Wiley.

Symington, N. (1996). *The making of a psychotherapist*. London: Karnac Books.

Welch, I. D. (1998). *The path of psychotherapy: Matters of the heart*. Pacific Grove, CA: Brooks/Cole.

Zeig, J. K. (Ed.). (1990). *What is psychotherapy?: Contemporary perspectives*. San Francisco: Jossey-Bass.

2

~

A Model for the Counseling Process

*P*sychotherapy is an often misunderstood process with much of the misunderstanding caused by a few simple confusions. For example, many beginning psychotherapists assume, have read, or have been taught that they should not guide, lead, or direct the client. They believe that for psychotherapy to be effective, the issues, concerns, insights, and ultimate solutions of the process should come mainly from the clients themselves. While this is, in the main, accurate and helpful, it also may cause beginning psychotherapists to be awkward, vague, and indecisive in both describing their procedures and in implementing them. This indecisiveness may stem from a confusion between directing the client and managing the process. Directing the client involves common mistakes of psychotherapy that Gordon (1974) labeled *communication roadblocks* (see Box 2.1). These include moralizing, giving advice, persuading, praising, and making suggestions. Managing the process is decidedly different. The rate and content of the issues, problems, or dilemmas the client brings to psychotherapy remain, primarily, with the client. The purposes of the psychotherapist and the client, however, may not initially be the same. The purposes of the client may well revolve around immediate alleviation of presently felt stressors. The purposes of the psychotherapist would include clarifying issues, understanding emotions, and directing an attitudinal shift

Box 2.1
Communication Roadblocks

When another person owns (is experiencing) a problem and you have decided to help, you may consider approaches like "giving good advice" or "asking key questions." However, as the following 12 descriptions indicate, these common helping attempts generally do more harm than good and impede the flow of communication from the troubled person.

It is important to note that most of these 12 helping attempts only become roadblocks when they are delivered in a problem area. When a relationship is in the no-problem area, many of the "roadblocks" (e.g., asking questions or giving job directions or advice) are both appropriate and productive. Expressions that "put down" and demean are always roadblocks to an effective working relationship.

(Based on Gordon, 1974)

Solution Messages

These roadblocks all take responsibility away from the other person and tend to put the person under external control. Solution messages secretly say: "You're too dumb to figure out the problem, so I have to do it for you."

1. *Ordering, Directing, Commanding*. Telling the other person to do something, giving an order or command.

2. *Warning, Admonishing, Threatening*. Alluding to the use of your power by telling the other person what consequences will occur.

3. *Moralizing, Preaching, Obliging*. Telling another what should or ought to be correct behavior.

4. *Advising, Giving Suggestions or Solutions*. Telling the other person how to solve his or her problems.

5. *Persuading with Logic, Arguing, Instructing, Lecturing*. Trying to influence the other person with facts, counterarguments, logic, information, or your own opinions.

Judgment Messages

These roadblocks diminish the self-worth and integrity of the other person, saying in effect, "There is something wrong (bad) about you that needs to be fixed."

6. *Judging, Criticizing, Disagreeing, Blaming*. Making negative judgments or evaluations of the other person.

7. *Praising, Agreeing, Evaluating Positively, Approving*. Manipulating the other through flattery or implied promise of reward.

8. *Name-Calling, Ridiculing, Shaming*. Making the other person appear foolish; stereotyping or categorizing the person in negative ways.

9. *Interpreting, Analyzing, Diagnosing*. Analyzing the other's motives and behavior; communicating that you have the other person figured out or "diagnosed."

10. *Reassuring, Sympathizing, Consoling, Supporting*. Trying to make the other person feel better; talking the person out of strong feelings; trying to make the feelings go away; denying the strength of the feelings.

11. *Probing, Questioning, Interrogating*. Trying to find reasons, motives, causes; searching for more information to help you solve the problem.

Denial Messages

12. *Withdrawing, Distracting, Humoring*. Trying to get the other person away from the problem; withdrawing from the problem yourself; distracting the person; kidding the person out of strong feelings; pushing the problem aside.

toward personal client coping. The purposes of psychotherapists do not dramatically change across modalities, between theories, or by client issue. In order for psychotherapy to proceed effectively and efficiently, psychotherapists must understand the process before even seeing their first client.

A Model

While there are a number of ways to understand the process of psychotherapy, this model has three stages. The first stage of psychotherapy is considered to be exploratory. The primary purpose of the exploration phase is to help the client clarify and isolate the issues, problems, and/or dilemmas in his or her life. The second stage is understanding. The goal of understanding is to determine with the client the reasons underlying the emotions that accompany the issues, problems, and/or dilemmas the client brings to psychotherapy. The third stage is resolution. The best outcome for psychotherapy—and the goal of the resolution stage—is for the client to recognize that coping with life concerns lies within his or her coping skills.

Exploration

The exploration phase has two clear purposes: to establish a therapeutic relationship with the client and to clarify the issue, problem, or dilemma.

The Relationship. The quality of the relationship between the psychotherapist and the client has proven itself time and again to be the best predictor of successful outcome in psychotherapy. In 1957, Rogers outlined what he labeled the necessary and sufficient conditions of effective psychotherapy. Over the years, many challenges to Rogers's conditions have been made, yet they remain stable and predictive qualities of a therapeutic relationship. The descriptions of that relationship continue to reflect Rogers's metatheoretical statement that identified empathy, authenticity, and respect as central to a positive outcome from psychotherapy. These attitudinal conditions are discussed in greater detail in Chapter 4. The psychotherapist who is able to create a climate incorporating these characteristics has a greater chance of realistically being of service to clients.

Clarification. When clients come to psychotherapy a number of things are true. First, they come because they are in pain and are vulnerable. Second, they come because the common solutions to their felt concerns are not working, and the advice they have sought has not produced any additional, helpful solutions. Third, they frequently believe that they know what the problem is but do not know what to do about it. Fourth, paradoxically, they frequently do not know what the problem is. The purpose of establishing a relationship characterized by understanding, genuineness, and nonjudgmentalism is, of course, to let clients know that their pain and vulnerability will be treated with respect and tenderness. The purpose of clarification goes somewhat deeper. Whether clients know or do not know what the problem is, they come prepared to tell a story (one aspect of clarification is narration). The stories clients initially tell are called the presenting problem.

The Presenting Problem. The presenting problem plays a role for both the client and the psychotherapist. For the client it serves to "test the waters." Clients often come to psychotherapy uncertain of what specifically to talk about and how. If the psychotherapist proves to be understanding, nonjudgmental, and respectful, then other more deeply held concerns may be expressed. At a university counseling center, for example, a student may request counseling because of a reported roommate conflict. In listening and responding, the client and the psychotherapist may discover that homesickness and loneliness are more pressing concerns. Another client may come to psychotherapy concerned over self-esteem issues, only to discover that the client's marriage is in trouble, and he or she is on the verge of asking for a divorce and is struggling with the fears and embarrassment that may entail. Yet another client may come concerned with interpersonal relationships only to report after a few meetings that the real issue is a lingering and emerging feeling of homosexuality. As the therapeutic relationship strengthens, more painful issues can be revealed.

If, however, the psychotherapist proves to be unhelpful, then no deep vulnerability has been exposed and clients must move on to seek help elsewhere or continue with their own counsel. It needs to be said that the client is not being disingenuous and we are not suggesting that a presenting problem is false. It is merely that the presenting problem is less threatening than other concerns that might be expressed once the presenting problem is sensitively and genuinely understood by the psychotherapist.

The presenting problem allows the psychotherapist to demonstrate the difference between clients' prior relationships and the one they will experience in psychotherapy. In psychotherapy, clients will interact with a person who is respectful, concerned, and attentive and who will not quickly jump to judgments or solutions. Their therapist will not withdraw when the going gets tough and will stick with them through deepening involvement and will struggle with them until some resolution is achieved. They will find themselves in a relationship in which they are at the center and in which the psychotherapist continually takes the role of an adjutant—a person who will help them with their affairs but who will not take over their lives.

The Presenting Symptom. Often clients will come to psychotherapy with a description of their symptoms rather than with a narrative of their situation, and what clients frequently want is to alleviate the symptom. They believe, for example, that if they are depressed, then depression is the problem and the solution is becoming undepressed. In this situation clients believe that they know what the problem is when actually depression, anxiety, anger, and despair are not *problems*, in and of themselves, but *solutions*.

The role of exploration is not only to help the client cope with the presenting symptom, but to delve into the situations, circumstances, events, and relationships of life to identify its source. It takes some time for people to recognize that the pain they are experiencing is not the problem but their response to some unidentified issue, problem, or dilemma. The most ready analogy is the common cold. Many of us assume that the problem with the common cold is a runny nose, body aches, a sore throat, and a cough. We are sometimes surprised to discover that these symptoms are evidence of the body's immune system doing battle with the actual problem, which is a virus. It may bring temporary relief to deal with the symptoms, but it does nothing to prevent the recurrence of a future cold. It is just so in psychotherapy. If all psychotherapy offers is the temporary relief of symptoms, then nothing has happened to prevent the reoccurrence of the symptoms in the future. More accurately, the client has not learned more effective skills to deal with future problems so that the assistance of a psychotherapist is not needed.

The issues of the presenting problem and the presenting symptom go to the heart of the necessity of exploration in psychotherapy. The goal of the exploration phase is to clarify, for both the client and the psychotherapist, the problem, which is not always obvious, as we have seen above. One aspect of respect is the recognition that clients are not stupid which is one of the reasons that effective psychotherapists resist the temptation to give advice. Clients have, in all likelihood, already tried the readily apparent solutions. They are in psychotherapy precisely because the ordinary solutions have not worked and, more to the point, because they do not know what the problem is. If they actually knew the source of their discontent, with clarity and without misleading feedback from others, then they would be able to arrive at a satisfactory resolution for themselves. Because they do not know the problem and its sources, the resolutions they attempt are unsatisfying. It also may be the case that even when they do know the problem and its sources they are still prevented from arriving at a good resolution for themselves, which brings us to the second phase of psychotherapy.

Understanding

In this three-phase model of psychotherapy, the next task is understanding. Once the issue, problem, or dilemma has been clarified another question presents itself to both the client and the psychotherapist: *Why* is this a problem? The answer may seem self-evident because people often believe that any traumatic event in a person's life results in psychological or emotional problems; however, this is not the case.

A 13-year-old girl had been raped. Her parents were justifiably concerned that this traumatic experience would carry with it psychological as well as physical injuries. They brought her to a psychotherapist for an evaluation and psychotherapy. During the initial interview the psychotherapist wanted to assess the girl's emotional response to her attack. The therapist looked for guilt, shame, fear, embarrassment, and other expected emotions, but none of these seemed present. In explaining her reactions, the girl said, "I know I didn't do anything wrong. I wish it hadn't happened, and I know I was hurt but that wasn't my fault either. But I didn't do anything wrong, and so I'm not ashamed or guilty or anything like that. And I know that my Mom and Dad love me, and I know they don't think I did anything wrong either." The psychotherapist explained to the parents that psychotherapy appeared unnecessary; they should watch for any warning signs, but it appeared their daughter understood that what had happened to her was an awful, unplanned accident of life. She appeared able to deal with that experience and felt supported by them, so they should continue to give the love and support they had obviously been giving. And, as it turned out, that was the case. The girl checked in after a month, and it was the last time the psychotherapist needed to see her.

This is an example of a young girl who, in a resolution far beyond her years, was able to suffer through a traumatic event and not attribute to it any personally damaging implications. What is a problem for so many was not for this adolescent. Some people are troubled more deeply by their experiences than others. Some children are deeply affected by their parents' divorce, while some are affected only peripherally. If a

25

client comes to psychotherapy and exploration reveals that the source of the emotional pain is divorce, then it becomes important to understand why the divorce is a painful episode in the person's life. For some, divorce may violate some deeply held personal value. For others, it may mean public embarrassment or guilt over fears that they somehow contributed to the divorce. Still other clients may be anticipating financial problems and may feel secondary guilt over focusing on money rather than family relationships. Or perhaps they feel selfish for concentrating on their personal losses rather than their parents' losses. Each of these reasons may be the source of discontent and each may have a different resolution. Coping with divorce is not a single problem nor is any issue, problem, or dilemma explored in psychotherapy. *Why* it is a problem leads the way toward resolution.

When both the client and the psychotherapist perceive and comprehend the significance of the reasons an event is a problem, then it is time to actively seek strategies, techniques, and means for coping with those reasons. *Why* is answered in understanding and moves psychotherapy into the next phase.

Resolution

The third phase of psychotherapy is resolution. Once clients have clarified the issue, problem, or dilemma and understood why it is painful and disconcerting in their lives, another question arises: *How* do I cope with this? *How* do I live with this reason and its meaning in my life? The goal of the resolution phase of psychotherapy is to move, if possible, toward some accommodation or transcendence of this distress. Maybe tangible outcomes present themselves for the first time and the client is now working toward some material end. Psychotherapy has moved into psychological treatment.

Treatment Versus Therapy. Managing stress, alleviating depression, conquering panic, dealing with anxiety, and improving interpersonal relationships represent specific symptomatic goals of psychological treatment. Symptom relief is a legitimate goal of psychological treatment and may precede other, more significant changes. Seeking life meaning, redefining the self, examining life values, and setting a new life course are more profound psychological outcomes of psychotherapy. In this model the first two phases of the therapeutic process are viewed as "psychotherapy" and the resolution phase is seen as "treatment." This conceptualization helps one understand that problem solving must follow clarification and understanding and can help the psychotherapist from rushing too quickly into it. Problem solving in the absence of clarification and understanding has no better chance of helping a client than trial and error.

There are two important differences between psychotherapy and treatment. First, the purpose of psychotherapy is to provide a climate in which clarifying exploration and understanding of life problems can occur. The purpose of psychological treatment is to arrive at a predetermined outcome or objective. Second, at the beginning of psychotherapy both the problem and the outcome are unknown. At the beginning of treatment, however, whether the source of the problems are known or not, the outcome is identified and success is considered the accomplishment or movement toward this goal. Some psychological treatment programs are well-known and accepted, such as alcohol treatment. The goal of alcohol treatment is to stop drinking. Another common treatment program involves physically abusive spouses (batterers), and the goal of those programs is for the batterers to stop hitting. Why the alcoholic drinks or why the batterer hits may or may not be important in treatment. In this model the treatment of depression, in which assignments may be given and tasks undertaken with the purpose of alleviating the depression, is considered treatment. *What* and *why* are important questions and would precede treatment in the case of depression.

Two Forms of Change. The resolutions arrived at in psychotherapy more often than not result in some form of change. Change may take two forms. First, behavior may change. Clients may be forced to stop doing something that has significantly contributed to their life distress, or they may be forced to start doing something to significantly reduce or help manage their life distress. Second, beliefs, attitudes, or values may change. Behaviors may not shift dramatically, but what clients believe about their behavior may be radically altered.

Behavior changes that may occur during the resolution phase include the hoped for outcomes of alcohol and battering treatment programs. As another example, a client who was sexually acting out was not only sexually promiscuous but sought out punishing sexual partners. This particular client selected men who were dirty, crude, and often violent and who forced her into humiliating sexual practices. In this case, the presenting symptom was the client's personal shame at her behavior. The exploration phase revealed several underlying difficulties. She used sex to attract and hold men. She needed men to feel worthwhile. Sex attracted men. She did not use seductiveness in her other relationships. Her need for men related to a general desire to be loved, yet she perceived herself to be essentially unlovable. Her feelings of unloveableness translated into feelings of worthlessness. If she was worthless, then she must be bad. And, because she was bad, she needed to be punished, hence the punishing sexual behavior.

On the surface, it would seem clear why her behavior was troubling. Yet, her behavior was only partially troubling to her. She recognized that her selection of men was dangerous. However, she actually enjoyed her sexual behavior and was troubled by it not because of any personal concerns but because *she believed that she should be ashamed of her behavior.* She also realized that she had no difficulty attracting men or establishing relationships with a wide variety of people and that even though she enjoyed sex she did not need to use it to attract and hold men. Once the problem was clarified and understood, she realized that in order to live without shame she needed to change her selection of men, not necessarily her sexual behavior. The resolution in this case represented both a change of behavior and a change of belief.

Here is one final example regarding how a change of belief can resolve life issues for some clients. Difficulties between children and their parents are not an uncommon theme in psychotherapy. Many adults report lingering disappointments over how they were treated as children by their parents. Some parents are unloving, distant, aloof, and even cold. Clients with this history often resolve that the flaw rested with their parents and not with them. Just because some parents are not able to easily demonstrate their love does not mean that the child was unlovable. Even in cases where the parent was cruel, clients come to recognize that the failing was in the parent and not in themselves. Once this is recognized, then the client can hold feelings other than guilt or resentment toward unsatisfying parents. It is in this change of attitude that the client can begin to live a life more focused on the present and the future than on the past.

Summary

This chapter presented a three-phase model of psychotherapy. Exploration is a necessary first phase that allows clients to tell their story and provides psychotherapists with time to build a relationship with the client before delving into deeply significant material. Exploration helps both the client and the psychotherapist define what the issue, problem, or dilemma is for the client.

The second phase of psychotherapy seeks to answer the question of why the issue, problem, or dilemma is disconcerting for the client. Understanding leads the way to the third phase of psychotherapy.

In the third phase, resolution, the client comes to a change in behavior or in belief. Behavioral change may involve stopping the behavior that is causing the client's discontent or acting differently than in the past. A change in belief is often an outcome of psychotherapy when clients discover that the problem is not in what they have been doing but in what they believe.

All psychotherapy begins in empathy, the best tool of exploration. Any psychotherapy that doesn't take the time to clarify and understand client concerns may help only by chance. Psychotherapy that is grounded in exploration and understanding increases the probability that the ultimate resolution will be long lasting and helpful.

29

References and for Further Reading

Andrews, J. D. W. (1993). The active self model: A paradigm for psychotherapy integration. In G. Stricker & J. R. Gold (Eds.), *Comprehensive handbook of psychotherapy integration* (pp. 165–183). New York: Plenum Press.

Burke, J. F. (1989). *Contemporary approaches to psychotherapy and counseling: The self-regulation and maturity model.* Pacific Grove, CA: Brooks/Cole.

Combs, A. W. (1989). *A theory of therapy: Guidelines for counseling practice.* Newbury Park, CA: Sage Publications.

Fine, C. G. (1996). Models of helping: The role of responsibility. In J. L. Spira & I. D. Yalom (Eds.), *Treating dissociative identity disorder.* San Francisco: Jossey-Bass.

Gold, J. R. (1996). *Key concepts in psychotherapy integration.* New York: Plenum Press.

Gordon, T. E. (1974). *T.E.T.: Teacher Effectiveness Training.* New York: P. H. Wyden.

Jackson, A. M. (1992). A theoretical model for the practice of psychotherapy with black populations. In A. K. H. Burlew, W. C. Banks, H. P. McAdoo, & D. A. ya Azibo (Eds.), *African American psychology: Theory, research, and practice.* Newbury Park, CA: Sage Publications.

Jordan, J. V. (1995). Female therapists and the search for a new paradigm. In M. B. Sussman (Ed.), *A perilous calling: The hazards of psychotherapy practice.* New York: Wiley.

Kleinke, C. L. (1994). *Common principles of psychotherapy.* Pacific Grove, CA: Brooks/Cole.

Norcross, J. C., & Goldfried, M. R. (Eds.). (1992). *Handbook of psychotherapy integration.* New York: Basic Books.

Rogers, C. R. (1957). The necessary and sufficient conditions of therapeutic personality change. *Journal of Consulting Psychology, 21*(4), pp. 95–103.

Rogers, C. R., Rychlak, J. F., Packer, M. J., Jennings, J. L., May, R., Wertheimer, M., & Bergin, A. E. (1992). Philosophical issues of the phenomenological and existential approaches. In R. B. Miller (Ed.), *The restoration of dialogue: Readings in the philosophy of clinical psychology.* Washington, DC: American Psychological Association.

Walborn, F. S. (1996). *Process variables: Four common elements of counseling and psychotherapy.* Pacific Grove, CA: Brooks/Cole.

3

Empathy: The Foundation for All Psychotherapy

The importance of empathy in counseling and psychotherapy is unmistakable. Who among you would likely revisit a counselor who did not understand your thoughts, feelings, and the meaning of your experience? Clearly, "the helper needs accurate conceptions of the ways his or her clients are thinking, feeling and perceiving themselves in their worlds" (Combs & Gonzalez, 1994, p. 167). Most people have developed a certain level of sensitivity to how other people are feeling. As children, we learn early on by necessity the importance of being aware of how others are feeling. Being sensitive to others enables us to interact with them in a more graceful, sensitive, and effective manner. Over time we realize that it is not necessary to be sensitive to everyone on an empathic level—that would be too cumbersome. Instead, we become more sensitive to those who are important to us.

Thus, being empathic does not usually involve having to learn a new or foreign skill. Rather, for counselors and psychotherapists who seek to further develop their empathy skills, "it is a matter of learning to do explicitly and frequently what we naturally do implicitly and occasionally" (Combs & Gonzalez, 1994, p. 168). Also, in counseling it is necessary to articulate our understanding of the client's thoughts, feelings, and meaning rather than merely "sensing" them. As we shall see, developing our existing empathy skills to a much more refined level involves many factors.

Understanding Is Not a Common Experience

Most of us have had many times when our feelings or experiences were not understood, recognized, or validated. For example, after telling someone how a family member said something that was painful, you are likely to hear a response such as, "I'm sure that person did not mean to hurt your feelings." Something in us wants to help right away, like putting a Band-Aid on a child's knee and saying, "There, there, everything is going to be all right." We want everything to be okay; we want to be soothing and helpful. We want people to feel better right now. In the process, we may unwittingly try to talk people out of their experiences or feelings. The message to the person in distress is that "you should not be feeling what you are feeling; feel a different way and you will feel better."

In fact, when we tell someone to not feel a certain way, we inadvertently mean that if the person will just feel this way instead of that way, *we* will feel better. It is akin to the old notion of telling people who are weeping to stop crying and they will feel better, when what we mean is please stop crying and we will feel better. A good friend is someone who understands and respects your feelings without cross-examining you as to whether or not they are the "right" feelings. The simple experience of being understood without being told how you should actually be feeling is in itself therapeutic. It is important for a client to be able to say, *this is how I feel*, not how I should or should not feel, *just plain how I feel*; being understood and accepted by the therapist can lead to understanding and accepting oneself. Clients then have the opportunity to further clarify their feelings and experiences. Also, if having certain feelings carried negative consequences clients may have spent years learning to deny or curtail those feelings. For example, anger or frustration at a parent or a deep disagreement with a parent's values may leave clients afraid to have such feelings, almost as if they are being disloyal. The result may be confusion and uncertainty. In an empathic counseling session such clients can have their feelings without anyone trying to tell them how they should or should not feel. They are free to experience, explore, clarify, and understand their feelings without having to distort or hide them.

Accurate Empathy

Accurate empathy allows us to understand what other people are saying and feeling as well as some of the reasons behind these things. For example, if a lion entered a room and the people inside ran out, we could be pretty sure that they did so because they were afraid of the lion and they did not want to be killed. We can trust our inference because we can look at the situation and understand the factors involved. It was not a matter of subjective interpretation. This is exactly how accurate empathy works and why it is possible for us to understand our clients without getting caught up in our own subjective interpretations. If our empathy is not accurate, our conceptualizations of the client's world might be full of our projections and shaky conjectures.

The Selective Nature of Perceiving

As counselors, recognizing the importance of being sensitive to the client's world is critical. We have to *have a belief* that it is important to do so. Otherwise, being able to see and hear what is important will be a hit-or-miss process. Helpers must do better than that. Consider how common it is to not notice a new building down the street, only to discover it has been there for over a year, or to see the neighbors' "new" flower garden that they planted last spring. Perhaps a friend shaved off his beard after 20 years, but you were not sure what was different about him. Or perhaps the beauty of a painting leaves you awestruck as you notice it for the first time, even though you may have looked at it many times without really seeing it. We ask ourselves how could we not have noticed!? The same missed perceptions can occur in the therapeutic process. As counselors, if we want to understand someone, or notice all aspects of them, we have to want to do so. Wanting to do so or fully believing that being sensitive is important makes it possible to see and hear the details that may be significant in understanding our clients.

We must believe that other people's realities are important, otherwise we are unlikely to pay attention to the very things that will permit us to understand them. Consider the case of a client diagnosed with paranoid schizophrenia. This client often heard voices threatening to kill him. While his primary therapist was out of town, he had a crisis and went to the hospital to see the backup therapist. Even though he was in crisis, the client came in only once. When the primary therapist returned, the client said he really needed to talk with somebody, but he realized that the backup therapist did not believe what he was telling him. The client said, "I tried to tell him about the voices and the scary things they were saying to me, but I could tell right away he did not believe me. He looked at me as though I was crazy and I felt no trust between us, so it did not make sense to come back to see him again. I knew he did not understand what I was saying. I decided to wait until you returned. I suffered a lot by myself." Clearly, the backup therapist failed to be sensitive to the client's experience. It is important that if we as therapists are going to be empathic with our clients we appreciate that other people's realities are just as real for them as ours are to us. Equally important is the concept that what is being believed is the client's experience, not necessarily the content or facts as they are described. The backup therapist's failure was just that. By focusing on content, and its unlikely occurrences, the therapist failed to recognize and acknowledge the client's fear.

34

Early in training a therapist had a client who described having a drug problem in the past but declared that she was not currently using. The client indicated with many hints and clues that she was still having a problem with cocaine, but she could not or would not say so directly. The therapist could not or would not recognize the hints and clues. A colleague said to him, "If it looks like a duck, walks like a duck, and quacks like a duck, it is usually a duck. It sure seems like your client still has a serious problem with cocaine." The therapist did not want to believe that such a nice young woman could have a drug problem. The sessions seemed to be going nowhere, until the therapist heard the client more completely. The client was terrified of facing the reality of her drug problem, so she was pretending it was something of the past. Once the therapist more fully recognized the client's problem and helped her to vocalize it, the therapy began to progress more rapidly. In this case, the therapist was innocent and had never worked with anyone with a drug problem, so his own naiveté interfered with his effectiveness. Also, he had a client who could not face her own truth alone and needed the therapist to help her do so. Once an empathic understanding was reached, the client and therapist successfully dealt with the client's drug addiction.

Listening

Listening is a skill. So often, when other people are talking to us, competing thoughts interfere with our ability to hear what they are saying. For example, look how often you have someone introduced to you only to immediately forget that person's name. You had to remember only two words (first and last name) and yet sometimes you cannot. Counselors and psychotherapists have to learn to pay attention to what is being said in order to truly listen. Empathic listening means that we quiet ourselves so that we can get a sense of the whole person. That includes listening to the client's words without passing judgment or otherwise letting our values and opinions get in the way. If we do not learn to listen well, the chances of our understanding and responding being empathic are not great. See Chapter 10 for an expanded discussion on listening.

Observing the Whole Person

Empathy includes empathic observing. For example, an empathic helper notices when a client's anxiety is moving to a nonproductive level and knows when to lessen the intensity of the moment or at least when not to push the client to any higher level of anxiety. The anxiety is not always verbal, but it certainly can be felt or seen by someone who is sensitive and pays attention.

Observing also means being aware of many aspects of the person, including his or her choices. As Combs and Gonzalez (1994) state,

"The choices that people make are not haphazard. They have meaning. The kind of cars people drive, the sort of houses they build, the care they give their yards, the clothes they wear, and the pictures they paint all have something to say about them" (p. 176). We can increase our level of understanding of our clients by sensitively observing them. Listening to what a client tells us gives us some information, but empathy means gathering information in other ways too. Paying attention to the choices that clients make tells us important things about them and about what is meaningful to them. (See Chapter 12 for a deeper discussion of nonverbal understanding.)

Using One's Own Self and Experience

You can use your own self as the basis for accurate empathy. An important part of our understanding of others comes from our own experiences. In our lives we learn firsthand what it means to be sad, angry, or disappointed. We know how our whole worldview can change when grieving the loss of a loved one. It is not necessary to have shared another person's exact experience to understand that person. For example, maybe a client was mugged at gunpoint and you as the therapist have never had such an experience. Yet, by imagining yourself in that circumstance you can probably gain a good sense of what the client went through, whether it was terror, anger, or a fear of death. Thus, your own experience with feelings and accompanying thoughts provide a rich source of information to help you understand your clients.

36

Consider the case of a 19-year-old woman with a schizophrenic mother. For the most part, she was raised primarily by her mother. Her grandmother lived nearby and helped to care for her occasionally. Her father had abandoned the family when this young woman was born and drifted into a life as a homeless alcoholic. One day, while she was riding in a car with relatives, her aunt pointed and said, "That's your father over there." The man was apparently drunk, was dressed in dirty and tattered clothing, and was staggering down the street. The young woman said that she ducked down in the car, not wanting him to see her. It was the first time she had ever seen her father and she felt overwhelmed by a variety of feelings. Even though you probably have not had the same experience, you could ask yourself how you would feel if you were her. If you considered it deeply you might have some idea of how awful that experience was and how bad she feels about it. Her sense of loss and regret were tainted by feelings of disgust, embarrassment, and revulsion. These are feelings each of us can understand and that seem appropriate when we put ourselves in her situation.

However, empathy is not always that simple. Some people may have a similar or even a shared experience, yet have remarkably different reactions and descriptions. One person may react to a difficult experience by becoming wiser and warmer. Another person may respond by becoming hostile or distrustful of others. In life, most of us have had painful experiences, and how we react to them has important implications for our psychological health and certainly for our effectiveness as therapists. People who react by building walls to protect themselves from future hurts are in effect constructing a prison in which to live. For example, a client who had been deeply hurt in the breakup of a significant relationship recalled making a vow to himself, "Never again will I let myself be in a position in which someone could hurt me this much." In the process of constructing walls to protect himself from being vulnerable, many of his subsequent life experiences were not fully lived; instead they were defended against. He built a wall to keep others out without recognizing that the same wall kept him in.

37

The Self as a Reliable Instrument

For both clients and psychotherapists, remaining open to experience is an important factor for continued growth. Otherwise, new experiences remain unprocessed, unfinished, or incomplete. For a person who is not open to experience, or who has not resolved his or her own pain, using the self may not be a reliable source of information. How can someone full of turbulence accurately reflect what comes in? To borrow a metaphor from Buddhist teachings, just as a turbulent body of water cannot accurately reflect the moon above, the same is true of a person full of turmoil. The information that comes in will be filtered through the therapist's distortions and defenses and will be misread. Whereas, a calm lake can accurately reflect the image of the mountains, trees, or moon above. Its calmness allows it to receive the incoming images without distortion. For accurate empathy, helpers need a calm center. Think of times you have been angry, sad, or depressed and consider how dramatically your perception of the world is altered. Using the self to help understand others can either be a tremendous asset or can result in a lack of understanding. The difference is in the inner calmness of the therapist.

Needs of the Helper

Being empathic means that often, for the benefit of the clients, we have to postpone our own needs for satisfaction. We may be so sure of our ways that we want to "get the client to see the light." Ways of being and perceiving that fit for each of us have a feeling of rightness, hence that is why we have adopted them. But just as we needed to find these ways for ourselves, so do our clients. This process can be frustrating for therapists because we sometimes think "this works so well for me and I feel so good about it, it will be good for you too." Take the case of a therapist who believes strongly in egalitarian marital relationships. A couple with a patriarchal marital structure comes in to see the therapist. If the therapist is unable to let go of the need to get people to be like him or her, empathy is unlikely. No matter how well intentioned, this approach is just not going to work for obvious reasons. What does work is setting aside our personal need to create clients in our own image and instead to assist them in finding their own best way. By doing so, we are free to really listen and understand what the client is trying to tell us.

A Humble Approach

The therapist also must have a genuine recognition or realization that he or she could be wrong. By acknowledging such a possibility, the helper keeps open the chance of having accurate empathic understanding. Once a therapist assumes that he or she is always "right" in perceiving how others feel, the important process of listening and questioning one's understanding stops. Acknowledging the possibility of being wrong can be difficult. When placed in the role of expert helpers, we find it compelling to provide "right" answers. The need to provide expert direction to a client in distress or our need to be competent can make it challenging to remember that we too can be wrong.

An interesting study by Temerlin (1970) illustrated how easily the accuracy of our perceptions can be affected. In that study, Temerlin gave several groups the "prestige suggestion" that a respected mental health professional said he knew the man being interviewed and that he was interesting because he appeared neurotic but was actually psychotic. The man was really an actor portraying someone with good mental health. Of 25 psychiatrists who received the suggestion, not a single one rated him as having good mental health; all 25 diagnosed him as psychotic or neurotic. Out of the 25 clinical psychologists given the suggestion, only 3 diagnosed the man as having good mental health. An overwhelming number of members of various control groups in the study that did not receive the suggestion of mental illness saw the man as healthy. Thus, a humble attitude toward your abilities can greatly enhance their quality and strength by keeping you alert and open to searching and questioning.

Countertransference

The therapist's unresolved issues that arise in therapy are sometimes termed *countertransference issues*. For example, perhaps the therapist grew up with a harsh parent and he or she has not yet dealt with the impact of that experience. At some point a client may remind the therapist of that parent, causing the therapist to feel intimidated or angry in relation to the client, without understanding that these strong feelings are the therapist's problem, not the client's. As a second example, imagine that a therapist felt unattended to or neglected as a child and that he or she has not dealt with the emotional ramifications of that experience. When a client comes in for therapy with a similar background, the therapist may overidentify with the client's pain and suffering and may want to "save" the client by trying to provide all the things the client (and the therapist) did not get in childhood, rather than being able to be empathic and objective. Whatever the case, an important part of a therapist's training includes an intimate knowledge of one's own countertransference issues. Without such information, not only will empathy be difficult to achieve, but the likelihood of wreaking havoc in the client's life becomes a real possibility.

The Importance of Meaning

A client is not going to feel understood if the therapist does not grasp the meaning of events to the client. Meaning gives the behavior a context within which the person can be better understood. For example, take the case of a client who considered himself to be clumsy. Upon entering the therapist's office, the client knocked over a plant stand, breaking the pot and sending plant soil all over the carpet. The client was profoundly apologetic and embarrassed. After calming down, the client spilled a glass of water 5 minutes later, ruining some papers and damaging some electronic equipment. The client began to weep. For the client, being clumsy meant difficulty forming important relationships such as those with a potential marriage partner, difficulty forming good relationships at work, and difficulty being promoted in his career. The client experienced each "clumsy" event as corroboration of his ineptness as a person. His perception of his whole being as worthy or not worthy had become intertwined with each event of tripping or spilling or breaking something. The depth of his weeping went beyond what might seem the case upon first glance. One of the most important aspects of the therapist's treatment was to treat the person with dignity, respect, and patience. Empathic understanding helped the therapist realize that the client felt he was without dignity, respect, and worthiness. After a few sessions in which the client experienced himself as a person of worth, his "clumsiness" diminished as did his berating of himself for the occasional slips that still occurred.

Another case that illustrates the importance of understanding meaning involved a traditional Hispanic male whose wife had passed away three weeks prior. When he returned home one evening and found his children dancing and playing records, he grew furious and began screaming at them, then turned silent, wept, and fell into a deep sadness. He was taken to a mental health clinic where the intake worker diagnosed him with major depression with psychotic features. The next day, a counselor asked him what led to his being brought to the clinic. The client explained his wife had passed away and that in his cultural tradition, a period of mourning should be observed with no celebrating, playing records, or dancing. When he saw his children engaging in such fun-filled activities, he was deeply saddened and heartbroken that they were not showing respect for their mother. The process of mourning or "luto" was important to him and he found the loss of that practice in the family deeply painful. Without understanding the meaning of the client's behavior, any attempt at diagnosis had limited utility. The new information about the personal life and the cultural, gender, and lifestyle background of the client allowed the counselor to consider a diagnosis of normal grief rather than psychotic reaction.

41

Summary

A relationship without empathy is likely to be more adversarial in nature than therapeutic. Rogers considered empathy to be the most important of the three core conditions of therapy (the other two are authenticity and respect). Empathy makes all other aspects of therapy possible and allows them to move forward in a helpful and skillful fashion. Providing an atmosphere of deep and accurate understanding of our clients' world can be challenging because of the variety of potential barriers to connecting at an empathic level, yet such an atmosphere increases the possibility for clients to resolve their difficulties and creates the probability of positive change.

References and for Further Reading

Berger, D. M. (1987). *Clinical empathy*. Northvale, NJ: Jason Aronson.

Bozarth, J. D. (1984). Beyond reflection: Emergent modes of empathy. In R. F. Levant & J. M. Shlien (Eds.), *Client-centered therapy and the person-centered approach: New directions in theory, research, and practice*. New York: Praeger/Greenwood Publishing Group.

Brazier, D. (Ed.). (1993). *Beyond Carl Rogers*. London: Constable.

Castillo, R. J. (1997). *Culture and mental illness*. Pacific Grove, CA: Brooks/Cole.

Chin, J. L., Liem, J. H., Ham, M. D. C., & Hong, G. K. (1993). *Transference and empathy in Asian American psychotherapy: Cultural values and treatment needs*. Westport, CT: Praeger/Greenwood Publishing Group.

Combs, A. W., & Gonzalez, D. M. (1994). *Helping relationships: Basic concepts for the helping professions* (4th ed.). Boston: Allyn & Bacon.

Eisenberg, N., & Strayer, J. (Eds.). (1990). *Empathy and its development*. New York: Cambridge University Press.

Marcia, J. (1987). Empathy and psychotherapy. In N. Eisenberg & J. Strayer (Eds.), *Empathy and its development* (pp. 81–102). New York: Cambridge University Press.

Margulies, A. (1989). *The empathic imagination*. New York: W. W. Norton.

Rogers, C. R. (1951). *Client-centered therapy*. Boston: Houghton Mifflin.

Sharma, R. M. (1992). Empathy: A retrospective on its development in psychotherapy. *Australian and New Zealand Journal of Psychiatry, 26,* 377–390.

Temerlin, M. K. (1970). Diagnostic bias in community mental health. *Community Mental Health Journal, 6,* 110–117.

4

❦

The Qualities of the Therapeutic Relationship

*W*hat unique or special characteristics make a relationship therapeutic? A look in the dictionary at the descriptor *therapeutic* reveals a number of meanings such as "curative, beneficial, restorative, healthful, corrective, and constructive." Such characteristics are readily recognizable as desirable aspects of a helping relationship. Antonyms of the term *therapeutic*—detrimental, harmful, damaging, and destructive—are characteristics easily discerned as antithetical to a helping relationship. What are the actual components of a therapeutic relationship? Table 4.1 summarizes some of the key factors inextricably involved in creating and maintaining a therapeutic relationship. The opposites of the helpful characteristics are also presented to emphasize the importance of each condition or characteristic.

Empathy

Of course, empathy is the sine qua non of therapy. Welch (1998) states this clearly and pointedly: "All psychotherapy begins in empathy. Any psychotherapy that does not have this origin is, at best, predictably unhelpful and, at worst, harmful (p. 6). In a therapeutic relationship, the counselor or psychotherapist has the capacity for an empathic understanding of the client's phenomenology. This includes not only

---

Table 4.1   *Summary of Therapeutic and Antitherapeutic Conditions*

Therapeutic Conditions	*Anti-therapeutic Conditions*
Empathy	Failure to Understand
Authenticity	Pretentiousness, Phoniness
Respect	Disrespect/Lack of Belief in Clients
Acceptance	Nonacceptance
Collaboration	Noncollaboration
Courage	Fear
Healthy Distance	Overidentification
Limits and Boundaries	Unstable Boundaries
Atmosphere of Challenge	Atmosphere of Threat

NOTE: We invite the reader to consider how each of these dimensions is affected when working with clients from diverse backgrounds.

---

how a client feels and thinks, but also the meaning that he or she attaches to whatever is being presented. The helper also has the ability to put his or her understanding into words so that the client clearly feels understood in the truest sense of the word. If the counselor or psychotherapist does not understand the client, how can he or she be consistently helpful? Furthermore, a client who does not feel understood is unlikely to share any deep concerns. This only makes sense. Why would a client share significant personal material with someone who does not seem to understand?

Authenticity

In a therapeutic relationship the counselor or psychotherapist must be authentic. The effective helper is without pretense—the more authentic the therapist, the more powerful the potential for a therapeutic experience. In the presence of an authentic therapist, the client has a unique opportunity to be more himself or herself. Because many clients struggle with feeling that it is somehow not alright to be themselves, that somehow they are not fundamentally okay, the need for therapist authenticity is all the more important. How could a client resolve his or her problems in the presence of a therapist who is afraid of being himself or herself?

Authenticity and Training

Therapist authenticity is a much more important factor than adopting any particular method or theoretical orientation toward helping. This is a particularly difficult aspect of training for those seeking advanced degrees in counseling and psychotherapy. As trainees learn various approaches to helping, they often feel like they are "wearing someone else's coat," like they are not being themselves when their supervisor gives them ideas about how to be more helpful to their clients. New therapists can feel like these are other people's ideas, other people's ways of helping. However, what supervisors and trainers are trying to do is to help the new counselor weave a coat or a way of helping that fits him or her. And, at the same time, that way of helping has to be grounded in a consistent theoretical system that incorporates proven methods of helping clients resolve their problems.

Beginning therapists also have to learn which parts of their personalities are not helpful to the therapeutic process, so their supervisors sometimes ask them to refrain from certain behaviors that are detrimental to helping their clients. This can make new therapists feel like they are being asked to give up part of their personality, but this is usually not the case. It is more a matter of learning to leave those characteristics out of the therapy room. For example, someone with a quick wit who is good at making people laugh must learn when humor is and is not appropriate in therapy. Ill-timed humor can greatly interfere with the process. If a client is talking about a significant loss and the counselor is good at making people feel better by making them laugh, the temptation to proceed with this maneuver may be great. The result, however, would be that the client did not have the opportunity to work through his or her pain. Laughing the pain away for the moment does not mean it is gone. In this case, the therapist's tendency to use humor would likely interfere with healing rather than enhance it. Consider a counselor who often gives long-winded responses. A supervisor would point out that the therapist is doing most of the talking and that anything important is probably lost in the sheer volume of words. The trainee may feel uncomfortable being significantly quieter, but adopting this behavior is important for effective therapy. It is perfectly alright for the therapist to remain long-winded out of the counseling session.

Respect

Respect refers to the therapist's belief in the client. It is crucial that the helper believe in the capacity of the client to find healthy answers to his or her dilemmas. Think of times in your own life when someone with whom you were interacting did not believe in you. How did you feel? How did it affect your relationship with that person? It is safe to assume that you probably did not seek out that person when you needed help. At some level, clients will sense your belief or lack of belief in them. To have someone truly respect your capacity to get better is in itself therapeutic, just as being around people who do not respect you or believe in you is potentially damaging.

As counselors and psychotherapists we hold ourselves out as helpers, and to not respect and believe in our clients can be devastating to them. It is doubtful that one would declare he or she does not respect clients, so how might a lack of respect happen or play itself out? Examining what you find yourself saying about your clients can be a clue. For example, saying that you need to "convince" your client or "get your client to . . ." may be signs that you do not believe in your client's capacity to grow. Other signs are making disparaging remarks like, "They can't do it" or "They will never change." Counselors and psychotherapists who respect their clients use words such as "assisting," "facilitating," or "encouraging" when discussing clients. One of us was employed at a clinic where an experienced therapist would work with clients for only four sessions regardless of the client or the presenting problem. When queried about this stance the therapist declared, "I've seen just about every kind of problem in my years of practice. I know what the client is going to say and do. Why prolong it? I pretty much know who is going to change and who is not going to change. I know how it is going to turn out the day the client walks in the door." In this case, the therapist's cynicism and lack of belief in the clients' capacity to change in their own unique ways probably created the conditions for lack of change.

Acceptance

Acceptance is of primary importance in creating a therapeutic environment. A relationship characterized by nonjudgment or acceptance makes it possible for concerns, fears, embarrassments, and confusions to be discussed and explored without the fear of someone passing judgment. How could you be expected to face your own weaknesses if you knew someone was judging them as unworthy, defective, or somehow "less than"? Thus, the condition of acceptance adds a crucial element to what makes a relationship therapeutic. To know that you can maintain a sense of dignity no matter what is revealed is a powerful therapeutic condition. The effective therapist demonstrates a continued atmosphere of respect even when the client talks about aspects of shame, embarrassment, and disgust. When a helper makes it possible to discuss the very things that previously were not discussable (because of shame or embarrassment), then the therapist has already been helpful. Clearly, when talking about acceptance, we do not mean approval or disapproval.

Acceptance and Patience

Another aspect of acceptance is patience. Clients often need time to discover answers to their problems. It is very difficult to see clients in pain. The temptation is to tell them the answer (as if we really knew) or to "fix them." No matter how much we feel compelled to hurry the client along, no amount of pushing can circumvent the experience needed by the client to make sense of the problem. Many counselors and psychotherapists have rendered themselves ineffective by their attempts to hurry along the process. Remember that if helping were simply a matter of telling people what they should do, their problems would have been solved long ago. Chances are that clients have been told what to do many times by people they know without effect. Obviously, something more has to happen in order to effect change, and that process usually takes time. As Galileo observed, "You cannot teach a person anything, you can only help someone discover it for oneself."

Of course we have a responsibility to assist our clients as quickly as possible, but that is different from saying that the client must get better by today. The pressure to hurry the counseling process has become even greater with the growing influence of managed care. It is not unusual to discover settings in which clients are limited to four to six sessions. Trusting that clients will move expeditiously toward a more healthful way of being in the world when they are truly provided with the opportunity to do so (in a therapeutic atmosphere) is part of acceptance. Clients will and do discover new answers and options to problems when they feel free to explore and clarify; they do not need to be coerced or manipulated into a course of action. Clients need to be accepted where they are, not where we would like them to be. As Combs and Gonzalez (1994) state, "Growth cannot proceed from where people are not; it can only begin from where people are" (p. 121).

48

The Effect of Acceptance: A Story

One of us attended a Christmas party at which an extraordinary event occurred. A few hours into the party, sleigh bells were ringing outside the window and Santa was heard commanding his reindeer. The host was dressed in full regalia as Santa Claus. The children were beyond excitement at the appearance of Santa who was portrayed in a lively and convincing fashion. Santa began talking to the children who listened intently to every word. He said something like this, "Boys and girls, all over the world children are wondering if they have been bad or good and whether or not Santa is going to bring them a gift. But Santa wants you to know, boys and girls, that Santa loves you just the way you are!" After a moment of stunned silence, the children broke out in leaping joy as if a tremendous burden had been lifted from their shoulders. An equally, if not more, amazing process occurred simultaneously among the large crowd of adults present. As Santa expressed his words of acceptance, both relief and an uplifting of spirits was palpable, as if a load of emotional weight was erased, at least for a few moments.

The impact of being accepted in a therapeutic relationship works in much the same way. In this atmosphere of acceptance, the client is freed from the burden of feeling "bad" or guilty for problems stemming from being judged as unacceptable. The client becomes free to explore and clarify those things that he or she has had to expend energy hiding in the past.

Collaboration

Working collaboratively permits the client to be invested in every aspect of therapy and is important to its success. There is a Native American prayer that says, "Tell me and I might not remember, show me and I might forget, involve me and I will understand." The work must have meaning for the client if he or she is to benefit from it. If the therapist or counselor selects the topic and prescribes the remedial steps without including the client's wishes and perspectives, whatever the client does will be to please the clinician rather than the client. Just like the old principle that says people are more likely to support what they have had a hand in creating, collaboration in therapy means that the client is involved in every step of the process. Picture the image of a client who walks behind a therapist versus a client and therapist who walk side by side; another image is putting a hand across to a client rather than a hand down. No matter how good the therapist's idea, it is not likely to help the client unless it also has meaning for the client. Clients often regard the therapist as the expert who will provide answers and direction. In subtle ways, if we are not careful we will assume the expert role and in the process will create a dependency role for the client. If we do not create a collaborative relationship, we also run the risk that the client will attribute successful changes primarily to the therapist rather than to a greater mastery of his or her life problems. Consider the images in Figure 4.1 as you ponder the importance of collaboration.

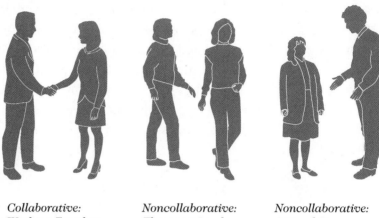

	Collaborative:	*Noncollaborative:*	*Noncollaborative:*
Figure 4.1	*Working Together*	*Therapist Leads*	*A Hand Down*

Which of these images represents the kind of relationship you would like to develop with your clients?

Courage

In a therapeutic relationship, helpers must have the courage both to assist the client with difficult issues and to deal with difficult issues themselves. How can a therapist who is afraid to examine his or her difficulties or who is unwilling to recognize them when they emerge help clients with their difficulties? By the same token, how can a client have confidence in someone who seems afraid to help the client look at what is troubling, painful, or confusing? Therapists have to learn to avoid applying Band-Aids to clients' wounds before cleansing the injuries. Sometimes, unresolved issues in the therapist's life prevent him or her from hearing the client. For example, while observing one counseling session, it became clear that the therapist was ducking the client's anger. It appeared that either the counselor did not know how to address the client's anger or that he was afraid of it. The client had made several statements expressing his anger about some serious matters without any acknowledgment or exploration by the counselor. After the session, while getting feedback from his supervisor regarding the need to address the client's anger, the perplexed counselor said, "Anger? . . . what anger? What are you talking about? My client is not angry." The therapist's response indicated the problem was not only not knowing how to address anger, but not being able to hear and see it. It became clear to the supervisor that the counselor had so distanced himself from his own anger he was unable to perceive it in his client. Although this example may seem amazing at first glance, this phenomenon is more common than you might realize.

In another case the therapist had been seeing a client for a number of weeks and realized that the final session was but three weeks away. The therapist planned to make note of this with her client before the end of the next session. After the session, she expressed her frustration as she realized that she had forgotten to address the upcoming termination; she planned to discuss termination with her client at the next session. Again, she somehow forgot. In supervision, the therapist could not believe that she had once again forgotten to discuss this important issue. She realized that she had one session left and termination had not yet been discussed. Carefully planning, the counselor decided to bring up termination as the first topic of the session to make the best use of the time remaining. Forty minutes into the session, the therapist came to a bewildering realization that only 10 minutes were left and she still had not discussed termination with her client! In the final 10 minutes, a hurried and awkward process of termination took place. The therapist came out of the session banging herself on the forehead for handling termination so poorly. While exploring her behavior in supervision, she began to realize that she had a number of losses with which she had not come to terms and that in general she did not know how to say good-bye. These dramatic examples illustrate how therapists' important unresolved events and feelings can manifest themselves in the therapy process. In both of these cases, the therapists realized that in order to move forward in their training, they needed the courage to examine and resolve their own hidden pain.

Another example of the need for courage to meet and know oneself can be found in the case of a woman in training for an advanced degree in counseling. She struggled with feedback, she struggled with what she should be doing with her clients, she struggled with the purpose of counseling. The process was a difficult one for her. At one point in her training, she went in to her supervisor's office and said she realized what the problem was. She handed her supervisor an envelope that contained a mirror with the following words written on the mirror's face, "Thanks for holding the mirror so that I could see myself, and therefore, meet myself!"

Another facet of courage is being willing to handle what the client is wanting and needing to discuss. Sometimes clients need to explore some profoundly devastating experiences such as incest, parental rejection, suicidal depression, brutalizing by a spouse, or the aftereffects of rape. Such experiences can be tremendously difficult for clients to explore and resolve. It has been said that counselors and psychotherapists need to be virtually "unshakable," meaning that we cannot be overwrought or blown away by the client's presenting problems. If we were it might indicate that we are not able to handle the very things the client is afraid of handling. Early in her training one therapist had a client who only hinted at or talked around some profoundly painful issues. The client clearly needed the therapist's assistance to more directly face the problems and feelings that had been plaguing her for years, yet the therapist was extremely reluctant to acknowledge or address the client's difficulty. When challenged in supervision to be more responsive to the client's presenting material, she exclaimed, "What right do we have to be talking about a client's pain? That is so personal!" Clearly, this therapist was not able to help the client because of her own discomforts or fears.

Healthy Therapeutic Distance

Maintaining a healthy distance between client and therapist is important for a variety of reasons. Such a distance prevents overidentifying with your clients' feelings and struggles. Healthy distance enables you to be objective and to avoid being drawn into the clients' morass of feelings. For example, you may find yourself taking responsibility for the client's feelings, rather than letting him or her take responsibility for them. You may find yourself forgetting that it is your client who is sad and lonely, not you. You may find yourself wanting to save your client from himself or herself. You, as a sensitive human being, are bound to have strong reactions and feelings at various times when working with clients, and learning to work with your feelings is crucial. Ruminating about their clients or their sessions is a common problem for beginning counselors and psychotherapists. They worry about what they should have said or done. They worry about what they should do to fix a session that did not go well. One psychotherapist called his supervisor to say, "I could not stop worrying about what I should have done to help my client in yesterday's session. So, I went to the library and looked up cases similar to his, and now I think I know what to do. I was thinking of calling my client today to tell him what I found out." This situation did not involve an emergency of any sort, it was simply a case of the therapist not having a healthy degree of therapeutic distance and feeling responsible for the client's feelings. Learning to not worry is an important part of your training. Some experts recommend giving yourself a few minutes to ruminate (15 minutes or so) and then learning to let it go (Egan, 1994). Rumination will quickly wear you out and will render you much less effective in your work with clients. Chapter 5 provides a larger discussion of the issue of therapeutic distance.

Limits and Boundaries

The therapist's ability to establish clear, reliable limits and boundaries is related to healthy therapeutic distance. Even things such as starting and stopping the session at the agreed upon times lets the client know that you mean what you say and that you can be counted on to be consistent and reliable. Consider a situation in which your client is 30 minutes late. If the client is working hard in the remaining 20 minutes, do you let the session go 30 minutes longer to complete a full session? While it may be tempting to extend the session, as a general guideline it is important to stick to the agreed upon time frame. What if the client was late a second or third time and said, "Sorry I'm late but some things came up and delayed me a bit, and you have not minded in the past that I have been late, so I did not think you would mind this time." What messages do we give clients if we are unclear with our limits? Also, because some clients have great difficulty setting their own limits and boundaries it becomes all the more important that we as counselors and psychotherapists are clear with ours.

To take this idea further, consider a case in which the client wants your home phone number so that he or she can reach you if necessary. Are you going to give it? What do your instincts tell you to do? To go further still, what if a client says that he or she is impressed with you and wants to be your friend after the counseling relationship is finished? Just thinking about such situations should help underscore the need for clear and stable boundaries. Although these situations can be discussed in terms of the ethical problems involved, understanding their therapeutic impact can help you better conceptualize their importance.

Another example to consider is the topic of touch in a therapeutic relationship. Expert advice runs the gamut from "do not touch clients" to "always exchange a hug at the end of a session." If you decide that sometimes a hug may be appropriate and sometimes it may not, then what factors make the difference? One factor is the importance of having a diagnostic appreciation of the client and therefore considering what the hug may mean to him or her. Another factor to consider is the therapist's motive for hugging. Is it done for the therapist's or the client's benefit? These are just a few of the issues to consider when looking at the topic of limits and boundaries. The importance of clear and stable boundaries to the success of the therapeutic relationship cannot be stressed enough.

A Therapeutic Atmosphere

In a therapeutic relationship, we need to create an atmosphere in which clients feel challenged rather than threatened (Combs, 1989; Combs & Gonzalez, 1994). That is, clients will handle their problems better if they feel they can deal with them reasonably well, and effective helpers are able to create such an environment. One problem with a threatening environment is that the client's perception typically narrows. Threat also causes people to defend their behaviors rather than feeling free to explore and understand them.

We now know that when faced with threat, the human brain literally downshifts (Caine & Caine, 1991). And if the threat is great enough, the brain's downward shifting can reach a level that is sometimes termed the reptilian brain—that is, the fight-or-flight response may be engaged and our higher cortical functions may be less available to us. Obviously, we don't want to create these conditions in a relationship that is supposed to be welcoming and nonthreatening. However, people do tend to respond well when faced with a certain degree of challenge. Part of the therapist's job is to challenge the client to face his or her dilemmas and to search for meanings and solutions to them. This needs to be done in a supportive, caring atmosphere, one that makes it more rather than less possible to face that which is scary or difficult.

Therapist Impact on Therapy

Clearly, certain characteristics, attitudes, or beliefs held by the therapist may have an impact on therapy. Specifically, beliefs in the following four areas have been found to notably impact the helping process: (1) frame of reference (internal or external), (2) perception of others, (3) perception of self, and (4) perception of purpose (see Table 4.2).

Frame of Reference

Good helpers recognize the importance of the client's internal world and know that it is difficult to help anyone if you do not appreciate

55

that person's phenomenology. Good helpers are concerned with how things seem to the person seeking help. On the other hand, poor helpers are more concerned with external factors such as details, pressures, and how things seem to themselves (Combs & Gonzalez, 1994). A breakdown in communication or in the relationship is likely if the helper fails in this particular regard. Consider a therapist who says, "I feel really good about where my client is. She is doing the things that I suggested and the things that I feel should be done if she is going to get better." What is missing here is what the client thinks and feels about the situation.

Perception of Others

Becoming a counselor or psychotherapist requires a close examination of your beliefs about the nature of human beings. Sometimes, you may not have a keen awareness of such beliefs because they have been formed in subtle ways since you were young. Becoming a therapist, however, mandates that you realize what beliefs you hold about what constitutes basic human needs, how people develop, how people change, how pathology develops, and so forth. Research on effective helpers supports the notion that they see people as able, dependable, and worthy and that poor or ineffective helpers regard others as unable, undependable, and unworthy (Combs & Gonzalez, 1994). Combs (1989) further noted that if you don't think people are able, you don't dare let them.

Perception of Self

Obviously, your self-concept affects your skill as a therapist. Poor or ineffective helpers see themselves as unwanted, unacceptable, and not good enough, while effective helpers see themselves as wanted and liked and as people with dignity and integrity. Because many clients suffer from poor self-concepts it is antithetical to a healing or curative environment to have therapists or counselors with negative feelings about themselves.

Table 4.2 *Differences Between Effective and Ineffective Helpers*

Effective Helpers	Ineffective Helpers
Frame of Reference	Frame of Reference
People	Things
Open to Experience	Closed to Experience
Internal	External
Perception of Others	Perception of Others
Able	Unable
Worthy	Unworthy
Dependable	Undependable
Trusting	Suspicious
Perception of Self	Perception of Self
Identified	Unidentified
Able	Unable
Positive	Negative
Perception of Purpose	Perception of Purpose
Freeing	Controlling
Revealing	Concealing
Larger	Smaller

NOTE: Adapted from *Helping Relationships: Basic Concepts for the Helping Professions*, by A. W. Combs & D. M. Gonzalez. Copyright © 1994 Allyn & Bacon. Reprinted by permission. For an expanded description of 14 studies that looked at good and poor helpers in a variety of helping professions see Combs & Gonzalez (1994) or Combs (1969).

Perception of Purpose

Effective helpers are concerned with freeing clients' perceptions, broadening their perspectives, and increasing their horizons, while ineffective helpers seem more concerned with controlling, maneuvering, and directing their clients. Like the counselors who do not respect their clients' capacities, ineffective helpers find themselves saying things such as "If I could just convince my client to do such and such" or "If I could get my client to . . . ." These approaches, in effect, limit rather than expand a client's perceptions.

Multicultural Considerations

As America becomes more and more diverse, the need to be more diverse as a counselor also naturally increases. The likelihood is much greater that you will have clients from various racial, cultural, and ethnic backgrounds. It is one thing to be empathic, authentic, and respectful toward people from your own familiar background, but it is quite another to have those same qualities with someone whose worldviews, values, and cultural practices are unfamiliar to or opposite from yours. In order to create and maintain a therapeutic relationship with people from the many possible backgrounds, you must overcome the barriers to communication. Sometimes those in the helping professions like to think of themselves as being without prejudice. Although that is a nice thought, it is, in actuality, like saying you have no history. Everyone has some degree of prejudice, some more than others. If you wish to work in the helping professions, however, we contend that you should make a commitment to treat all people in a fair, equitable, and respectful manner. To that end, counselors need to engage in a variety of activities to enhance their effectiveness with people from all cultural backgrounds.

Conscious and unconscious prejudices are at work in all of us. Here are some steps you can take to overcome possible prejudices and thus become more effective with people from a variety of backgrounds and cultures:

1. Educate yourself about other cultures (religion, values, foods, attitudes toward mental health, recreation, etc.), including course work, reading, and workshops.
2. Educate yourself about gender, sexual, and other lifestyle differences.

3. Educate yourself about your own cultural, gender, and lifestyle background to understand its central values and its overall impact on your worldview.

4. Stop seeing others as imperfect versions of yourself.

5. Explore your self-awareness. Actively search to discover your prejudices. Find ways to deal with them so that others are not negatively affected by your biases.

6. Value diversity rather than fear it.

7. Have contact with persons from various backgrounds.

8. Understand the values of the dominant culture, including sociopolitical forces.

Summary

In sum, the purpose and nature of a therapeutic relationship is unique. If therapists and counselors successfully create and maintain a collaborative relationship, clients will have the opportunity to make significant changes in their lives. In actuality, the complexity of a therapeutic relationship makes it difficult to explain in writing.

Following are some evaluation forms designed to assist you in your development (see Forms 4.1 and 4.2). It is important to actively seek feedback from others so that you know what to improve upon and where you are in your development as a counselor or psychotherapist. It is natural to feel a bit defensive when being evaluated; however, if you can set your defensive feelings aside long enough to receive feedback, the potential benefit is great. Take the feedback, consider it, and discover how you might integrate the suggestions into your training rather than expending energy trying to explain why the comments are not true. You are in training to gain the skills necessary to be an effective therapist, a goal you cannot achieve without a significant amount of feedback from supervisors and peers.

Form 4.1
Evaluation

| | MINIMAL | WEAK | MODERATE | GOOD | EXCEPTIONAL |

Empathic Ability

1   2   3   4   5   6   7   8   9   10

Comment:

Degree of Authenticity

1   2   3   4   5   6   7   8   9   10

Comment:

Respect for Clients

1   2   3   4   5   6   7   8   9   10

Comment:

Openness to Experience

1   2   3   4   5   6   7   8   9   10

Comment:

Openness to Feedback (to both hear and integrate)

1   2   3   4   5   6   7   8   9   10

Comment:

Ability to Be Collaborative

1   2   3   4   5   6   7   8   9   10

Comment:

Courage

1   2   3   4   5   6   7   8   9   10

Comment:

Ability to Maintain Optimal Therapeutic Distance

1   2   3   4   5   6   7   8   9   10

Comment:

Ability to Create a Challenging, yet Nonthreatening Environment

1   2   3   4   5   6   7   8   9   10

Comment:

MINIMAL		WEAK		MODERATE		GOOD		EXCEPTIONAL	

Confrontation Skills

1	2	3	4	5	6	7	8	9	10

Comment:

Ability to Work with Clients of Diverse Backgrounds

1	2	3	4	5	6	7	8	9	10

Comment:

Form 4.2
Therapist Beliefs

Ineffective Helping Likely	Effective Helping Likely

Frame of Reference

EXTERNAL								INTERNAL	
1	2	3	4	5	6	7	8	9	10

Comment:

Perception of Others

NEGATIVE VIEW OF OTHERS						POSITIVE VIEW OF OTHERS			
1	2	3	4	5	6	7	8	9	10

Comment:

Perception of Self

NEGATIVE SELF-CONCEPT						POSITIVE SELF-CONCEPT			
1	2	3	4	5	6	7	8	9	10

Comment:

Perception of Purpose

PURPOSE IS CONTROLLING						PURPOSE IS FREEING			
1	2	3	4	5	6	7	8	9	10

Comment:

References and for Further Reading

Caine, R. N., & Caine, G. (1991). *Making connections: Teaching and the human brain*. Alexandria, VA: Association for Supervision and Curriculum Development.

Clarkson, P. (1995). *The therapeutic relationship: In psychoanalysis, counselling psychology and psychotherapy*. London: Whurr.

Combs, A. W. (1969). *Florida studies in the helping professions* (Social Science Monograph No. 37). Gainesville: University of Florida Press.

Combs, A. W. (1989). *A theory of therapy: Guidelines for counseling practice*. Newbury Park, CA: Sage Publications.

Combs, A. W., & Gonzalez, D. M. (1994). *Helping relationships: Basic concepts for the helping professions* (4th ed.). Boston: Allyn & Bacon.

DeMarinis, V. M. (1993). *Critical caring: A feminist model for pastoral psychology*. Louisville, KY: Westminster/John Knox Press.

Egan, G. (1994). *The skilled helper* (5th ed.). Pacific Grove, CA: Brooks/Cole.

Fox, R. (1993). *Elements of the helping process: A guide for clinicians*. New York: Haworth Press.

Kottler, J. A., Sexton, T. L., & Whiston, S. C. (1994). *The heart of healing: Relationships in therapy*. San Francisco: Jossey-Bass.

Lueger, R. J., & Sheikh, A. A. (1989). The four forces of psychotherapy. In A. A. Sheikh & K. S. Sheikh (Eds.), *Eastern and Western approaches to healing: Ancient wisdom and modern knowledge* (pp. 197–236). New York: Wiley.

Patterson, C. H. (1985). *The therapeutic relationship: Foundations for an eclectic psychotherapy*. Pacific Grove, CA: Brooks/Cole.

Patterson, C. H., & Hidore, S. C. (1997). *Successful psychotherapy: A caring, loving relationship*. Northvale, NJ: Jason Aronson.

Teyber, E. (1996). *Interpersonal process in psychotherapy: A relational approach* (3rd ed.). Pacific Grove, CA: Brooks/Cole.

Walborn, F. S. (1996). *Process variables: Four common elements of counseling and psychotherapy*. Pacific Grove, CA: Brooks/Cole.

Welch, I. D. (1998). *The path of psychotherapy: Matters of the heart*. Pacific Grove, CA: Brooks/Cole.

5
✑

The Nature of the Therapeutic Alliance

I take the far view
things look small.
I take the near view
things look big.
I take the inner view
things look personal.
I take the large view
I touch wisdom.

David Welch wrote this poem on a mountaintop in Wyoming. Wyoming is a land with few people and with horizons so distant you can see the curve of the earth. Quiet, unspoiled nature calls out and perspective seems, for a moment, an easily obtainable goal. It is difficult, however, to maintain the large view for long. We get caught up in the flow of ordinary life and the daily routine and forget the large view, instead moving among the far, near, and inner views. Yet, the helping professions demand that we maintain the large view.

The Client

The concept we are speaking of is therapeutic distance and is here labeled *Detached Concern*. It is a matter of perspective. The large view requires maintaining balance between one's own psychological or emotional integrity and demonstrating caring and concern for the client. The imbalance of the far, near, and inner views leads to dangers for both clients and helping professionals.

Let us take a moment to examine the concepts of detachment and concern and to look at their relative importance as a way to understand the dangers in the far, near, and inner views. This is a word game that holds the possibility of meaning. What if we write these words in the lowercase—detached concern (dc)? This is the far view. It makes things small. It is the view of minimalism where clients' issues, problems, and dilemmas are seen as insignificant and are perceived with disinterest. This is the view with the least understanding. The observer cannot see the sources of disquiet in the other person when viewing from a distance. The observer may react with amazement at what seems to be bizarre behavior. The observer may react with disdain at what seems to be outrageous behavior. The observer may react with loathing at what seems to be abhorrent behavior. In every case, the observer has imposed an external judgment based on assumptions without the benefit of understanding. Viewed from a distance, the presently felt meanings that drive behavior cannot be discerned. If one takes the far view, things do indeed look small. The danger is that those far from the events and circumstances of pain feel too little compassion to be of any help. This view is of little use in the helping professions.

In the near view the concept might be written this way—Detached concern (Dc). It is the view of aloofness. Observers in this view fear that the concerns of others may overwhelm and touch their own sensitivities. They emphasize their detachment and refuse to permit themselves compassion or care. In the helping professions such persons might perform their duties carelessly or even callously or may find ways to limit their direct contact with clients. Others may adopt strategies that lessen any real need for empathic responding and instead use preplanned, prepackaged, and/or commercially marketed treatments that demand little of their personal concern. The dangers for clients are both financial and emotional—financial because money is being paid for treatments with only an accidental chance of success, and emotional because the issue, problem, or dilemma in their lives has remained unclassified and not understood, and no real action has been undertaken to better prepare them to cope. This is an antiseptic view of helping in which the professional has risked little, given little, and been of help only by accident.

Some helping professionals become too involved with clients. This is the inner view and it is the view of detached Concern (dC). In the inner view psychotherapists have identified with clients and have lost their sense of separation and distance. They have lost their perspective and in so doing have lost their ability to be of help. Seeing the world, events, circumstances, situations, and others from the same perspective as clients, the counselor has no additional clarifying viewpoint to offer. Such psychotherapists have simply become verifying forces in the lives of clients. The danger for clients is that they remain just as they are without any possibility of authentic change. The most easily recognized danger for psychotherapists who become sympathetic and identified with clients is romantic or sexual involvement. Once psychotherapists have crossed that boundary, then it is obvious to even the most casual observer that any sense of clear perspective has been lost and the possibility of psychotherapeutic assistance has been forfeited. It also is possible to become identified not only with clients but with particular client concerns. Psychotherapists who deal with victims face this danger. Those who specialize in working with victims of domestic violence, child abuse, and sexual abuse must take special care not to identify with their clients to such an extent that they prevent their clients from moving away from their victimization.

These dramatic examples of identification overshadow other less serious, but still problematic, concerns. Psychotherapists may become so involved in the misfortunes of clients that they feel compelled to lend money, provide shelter, give clothing, or provide meals. Each of these is an act of charity. Each is compassionate. Each is a sign of caring. And, in the interaction between psychotherapists and clients, each is wrong. This is sticky business, of course. Psychotherapists may *help* clients identify sources of money, shelter, clothing, or food. In this sense, psychotherapists may help people to help themselves. But that line, however faintly drawn, cannot be crossed. There is a difference between being a philanthropist and being a psychotherapist, and that difference lies precisely in understanding the relative importance of detachment and concern. Psychotherapists provide a special relationship—the relationship of empathy, respect, and nonjudgmentalism. If this relationship is altered into friendship, romance, sex, or caretaking, then the perspective necessary for the large view has been sacrificed and the clients have lost the opportunity they were promised when they entered the psychotherapeutic relationship.

The large view provides for the optimum level of involvement with clients. It is the view of Detached Concern (DC). In the scales of psychotherapy one must balance concern with distance. Psychotherapists must recognize their separateness and remain authentic individuals. They must compassionately understand the urgencies, tensions, and forces that clients bring to their lives and that culminate in their need for psychotherapeutic help. The absence of or overemphasis on either detachment or concern distorts the psychotherapeutic process. The old saw says, "Sometimes we get so close we can't see the forest for the trees." If we are too distant we can't see the tree for the forest. If we are inside the tree, then we have lost all perspective and become absorbed in the very same dynamics that are poisoning the tree. Forgive us for this shaky analogy: In order to understand, we must be close enough to understand that the soil surrounding the tree might be toxic, that there is not a root system sufficient to maintain stability, that there isn't enough sunlight, that other trees smother the opportunities for growth and steal nourishment, and that there is no water. In order to help we must be separate enough so that we are not pulled into the psychological lives of clients to such an extent that we are as incapacitated as they are.

Throughout this book, we will allude to the necessary conditions of effective psychotherapy—empathy, authenticity, and respect. Both therapeutic distance and concern require all three. Therapeutic distance requires empathy because it is in understanding that one recognizes dangers to identification and overinvolvement. Distance requires authenticity because it provides for perspective that is therapeutically genuine, undistorted, and undemanding. Distance requires respect because it allows clients to discover, remember, and/or create responses to their life situation for which they can claim full credit.

Concern requires empathy, authenticity, and respect as well. Empathy ensures that the concern is not misplaced. It is the necessary path toward clarification and effective action in psychotherapy. Authenticity is necessary to genuine concern because it makes psychotherapists trustworthy. If they are real, then their concern is real and clients may trust their growing sense of self-worth. Genuine therapeutic concern allows clients to struggle through to their own solutions or strategies and their own sense of personal strength.

The Profession and Society

Clients are not the only force in psychotherapy for which psychotherapists are asked to keep perspective. Some expectations involve the discipline or the profession itself. There are legal and ethical concerns. There is also the undefined but widely held view that the profession to which we belong deserves a degree of respect and honor. It should not be dishonored through inattention or design.

If we take the far view, then the danger is in seeing the procedures and duties outlined in legal and ethical codes as too distant to be effective guiding principles. Psychotherapists who undervalue standards of practice and instead substitute their own individually arrived at values and standards may make mistakes that call the profession into disrepute. To routinely substitute personal values over the agreed upon standards discounts the consensual understandings that have been reached around many troubling issues in psychotherapy and is an act of arrogance.

The near view leads to submission. Some psychotherapists approach decisions too timidly and fear making any determination that is not ethically clear. The difficulty with this position is that often our ethical codes are not at all clear about many things. Here is one example. Regardless of the psychotherapist's discipline (i.e., social work, counseling, psychology), codes of ethics usually advise against dual relationships. It is not recommended to enter into a psychotherapeutic relationship with a business acquaintance, friend, or relative. This is sound advice. However, one of us once met a psychotherapist from Alaska. He said that he was the only psychotherapist for a huge geographical area of the state and that some clients even flew into his town for their therapy sessions. He knew every person in his community and some were clients. Now, what should he have done? Should he have refused to provide mental health services to the local grocer, mechanic, or banker because he had commercial or financial dealings with him or her? What do the codes of ethics say in this regard? Although the situation is unclear, most psychotherapists would come down on the side of providing services, because overall the welfare of clients often supersedes specific recommendations of ethical codes. Psychotherapists have to make judgment calls (more often than not with the help of advice from other professionals) to temper the ethical codes. Taking the near view can make the ethical codes loom so big and decisions so mechanical that you simply become a subservient automaton reading rules to clients who need help.

The danger with the inner view is that ethics and laws become issues of morality. Morality is a personal judgment of what is right and wrong. Codes of ethics, of course, are not judgments of right and wrong but suggestions agreed upon by members of a profession to help guide professional behavior. Laws are highly structured rules governing specific acts of behavior. Here is an example of the difference among the three. Take a situation involving dual relationships. Legally no law would preclude a psychotherapist from treating a relative. Ethically this is usually advised against. Morally there is little guidance for a question this specific. Religion provides another example. Legally nothing prevents a psychotherapist from encouraging a client to adopt a particular spiritual perspective. Ethically such behavior would be frowned upon. Morally it might be expected that all believers try to convince nonbelievers. If psychotherapists take the inner view and make law, ethics, and other forms of recommended standards of practice personal, then the danger is that they will become moralistic, proselytizing zealots who believe that the rules are always more important than personal judgment.

The large view is that the profession and its standards of practice should be respected. If some standard of practice, ethical recommendation, or even some law has to be questioned, then it should be justifiable in ways other practitioners can understand and support. In the earlier example of the isolated psychotherapist, it is not difficult to understand a decision to see as clients members of the community with whom the therapist has business dealings. It would be difficult, if not impossible, to avoid social contact with them altogether. Few would question a decision by a psychotherapist in a small town to accept clients known to him or her. The large view permits psychotherapists to make judgments, defend those judgments, and act in the best interests of their clients when faced with a vague ethical situation.

The Therapist

> This above all: to thine own self be true,
> And it must follow, as the night the day,
> Thou canst not then be false to any man.
> *Hamlet*
> —William Shakespeare

We all know this advice. We learned it in high school. Some might say we memorized it. We are uncertain because sometimes the word *memorized* means to "learn by heart." We wonder how many of us "learned by heart" to take care of ourselves? It is more likely, is it not, that we learned it by "rote"—a memorizing process often without full comprehension (*American Heritage Dictionary*). The far view would distance us too far from ourselves. Too invested in client concerns, we might fail to take proper care of ourselves. The near view might see our contributions as being of too much significance and prevent us from recognizing that the power for change lies within clients and not with us or our techniques. The inner view has a danger of self-absorption. Narcissistic psychotherapists truly seem a contradiction in terms, yet they do exist, reminding us of the importance of balance in our profession. The large view says that it is reasonable, fair, honest, and true to balance our concern for clients with concern for our physical and mental health. It is a view that permits us to be of service to others.

Summary

Keeping perspective is a fundamental element of effective counseling. Whether considering the client, the profession, society, or ourselves, it is important to balance the needs of each. In this exacting balance our help can be decisive, directed, focused, and accurate. In the far view we are in jeopardy of undervaluing the needs or concerns of one element of the scales of psychotherapy. In the near view we may attend too closely to the needs of one at the expense of the others. In the inner view the danger of absorption can cloud judgment to such an extent that no one is well served. The perspective needed to be an effective helper rests in the large view. In the large view lies the wit to balance the needs of the client, the profession, society, and ourselves. This is the perspective of balance. This is the view of wisdom.

References and for Further Reading

Bordin, E. S. (1994). Theory and research on the therapeutic working alliance: New directions. In A. O. Horvath & L. S. Greenberg (Eds.), *The working alliance: Theory, research, and practice* (pp. 13–37). New York: Wiley.

DiGiuseppe, R. (1995). Developing the therapeutic alliance with angry clients. In H. Kassinove (Ed.), *Anger disorders: Definitions, diagnosis, and treatment* (pp. 131–149). Washington, DC: Taylor & Francis.

Dryden, W. (1989). The therapeutic alliance as an integrating framework. In W. Dryden (Ed.), *Key issues for counselling in action* (pp. 1–15). London: Sage Publications.

Godenne, G. D. (1995). Forming a therapeutic alliance with teenagers. In R. C. Marohn & S. C. Feinstein (Eds.), *Adolescent psychiatry: Developmental and clinical studies* (Vol. 20. Annals of the American Society for Adolescent Psychiatry). Hillsdale, NJ: Analytic Press.

Henry, W. P., & Strupp, H. H. (1994). The therapeutic alliance as interpersonal process. In A. O. Horvath & L. S. Greenberg (Eds.), *The working alliance: Theory, research, and practice* (pp. 51–84). New York: Wiley.

Horvath, A. O., & Greenberg, L. S. (Eds.). (1994). *The working alliance: Theory, research, and practice.* New York: Wiley.

Inderbitzin, L. B. (1990). The treatment alliance. In S. T. Levy & P. T. Ninan (Eds.), *Schizophrenia: Treatment of acute psychotic episodes* (pp. 139–159). Washington, DC: American Psychiatric Press.

Klein, R. (1995). Establishing a therapeutic alliance. In J. F. Masterson & R. Klein (Eds.), *Disorders of the self: New therapeutic horizons*. New York: Brunner/Mazel.

Meissner, W. W. (1996). *The therapeutic alliance*. New Haven, CT: Yale University Press.

Raue, P. T., & Goldfried, M. R. (1994). The therapeutic alliance in cognitive-behavior therapy. In A. O. Horvath & L. S. Greenberg (Eds.), *The working alliance: Theory, research, and practice* (pp. 131–152). New York: Wiley.

Rush, A. J. (1989). The therapeutic alliance in short-term cognitive-behavior therapy. In W. Dryden & P. Trower (Eds.), *Cognitive psychotherapy: Stasis and change* (pp. 59–72). New York: Springer.

Watson, J. C., & Greenberg, L. S. (1994). The alliance in experiential therapy: Enacting the relationship conditions. In A. O. Horvath & L. S. Greenberg (Eds.), *The working alliance: Theory, research, and practice* (pp. 153–172). New York: Wiley.

The Foundation of Counseling and Psychotherapy

This section provides therapists in training with a useful model of the counseling process. We will examine the importance of theory and the role it plays in guiding successful therapeutic practice. Operating without a coherent, consistent theory is a serious liability and we intend to illustrate those dangers. Inevitably, a therapist who operates without a theory will be faced with a situation in which he or she will not know how to proceed. Chapter 6 demonstrates that a theory offers the therapist a guide on how to proceed in most situations, no matter how complex.

The United States is becoming an increasingly diverse nation. As counselors and psychotherapists one of our professional duties is to become aware of the forces that influence human behavior. Surely, it is no stretch to recognize that the bosom of the family and the cradle of culture nurtures each of us and contributes to our view of the world, of what is right and wrong, normal and abnormal, wholesome and destructive. As counselors and psychotherapists we must seek to understand not only the individual client but the cultures, gender viewpoints, and lifestyle orientations that impact our makeup as persons. This section provides a look at how culture, gender, and lifestyle influence the foundation of counseling and psychotherapy.

How change actually occurs has been a subject of fascination and debate for many in the helping professions. We provide a model that gives one explanation as to how change occurs. Because it is our belief that clients would not be seeking help if they did not want change, it seems important to examine the sometimes elusive process of change in order to become more skilled at making it a real possibility. Finally, this section includes an examination of some of the ethical considerations that therapists are faced with in the practice of psychotherapy. Ethical dilemmas are common in this field and educating yourself about the guidelines will allow you to provide helpful and professional service to your clients while avoiding any ethical problems in the process.

6

〜

The Role of Theory in Counseling and Psychotherapy

*P*sychotherapy is not a trial-and-error process. "Therapists must understand very specifically what they are trying to do in therapy—where they are going and why—in order to be consistently helpful to clients. Without a conceptual framework as a guide, decisions about intervention strategies and case management are too arbitrary to be trustworthy" (Teyber, 1997, p. 4). Combs (1989) provides similar but more personally directed advice: "To assure that counselor behavior is truly responsible and effective requires a comprehensive, accurate, and internally consistent personal theory" (p. 62).

Theory as a Guide

That brings us to the role of theory in psychotherapy. In the realm of science there is a hierarchy of certainty. It is a ladder of conviction that reassures its members that some ideas are more trustworthy than others. The bottom rung of the ladder is a guess, hunch, or intuition that something may be so. Hunches are turned into hypotheses, which are stated in such a way that they can be disproven. If after sufficient testing hypotheses are not disproven, then they may be systematized into theories. The final step on the ladder of science is identified as a law. A law is a proposition, the outcome of which is unvarying—no matter the circumstances the predictive value of the law remains constant. It is true no matter what. An example is the law of gravity.

In human behavior, there are no laws, but there are a number of theories. It is important to know that a theory in this ladder of certainty occupies a high place in scientific thought. A theory of personality or counseling is not a mere whim, guess, or hunch. A common mistake is thinking that only statistical, experimental research is acceptable. That is not true. In medicine, for example, an acceptable strategy is labeled *clinical trials*. It is a multiple case study method that is considered effective in the study of a new drug. Many approaches have been used to test theories. Freud used a case study method. Rogers used statistical, experimental design. Erikson used naturalistic observation. Major theories of personality and counseling represent tested and systematized ideas that have stood the test of research and of time. This said, let us look at the role of theory in psychotherapy.

From time to time we hear someone ask beginning psychotherapists how they would handle a particular case. They might answer with, "I'll do anything that works," but there are two problems with this response. First, the implication is that they will try different approaches until they hit upon one that "works." Even a blind squirrel will find an acorn every now and then, but he or she is also going to be the skinniest squirrel in the woods. The point of this old axiom is that sometimes good things may happen by accident. Positive outcomes can come about through trial and error.

Another problem with this response is that we cannot rely on chance to ensure survival; people do not come to psychotherapy to be experimented upon. Clients expect, rightly so, a knowledgeable and competent practitioner. Effective psychotherapists are those who know beforehand that the methods they use are effective. Although the previous sentence seems improbable, it is true. It is true because the methods and practices have already been proven effective, and it is the methods and practices themselves for which psychotherapists are accountable. Clients, not their psychotherapists, are accountable for the outcomes of their therapy. Effective psychotherapists do not attempt any treatment with clients that is not already a proven effective and sound psychotherapeutic intervention. Psychotherapy is a purposeful activity, and these purposes come from personality and counseling theories. Without a comprehensive understanding of human behavior there is no guiding theory to inform psychotherapists that the therapy has "worked." For example, an art teacher who worked with young children was known for helping them create truly wonderful hand paintings. She was asked once how she was able to teach children how to create such beautiful works. She said, "I know when to tell them to stop." The children did not know about composition, design, balance, or symmetry, nor did they have a theory of art. The teacher did. In psychotherapy, aside from symptom relief, it is often the therapist who knows that the therapy is finished.

Personality Theories

Personality theories are meant to answer the specific question: Why do human beings behave the way we do? Some personality theories also address another question: When does human behavior develop; how does it come about? Thus, for psychotherapists personality theory answers two questions—why we do what we do and when that behavior developed. Perhaps in your study of psychotherapy you have read or been instructed that "why" is a question not often asked in a counseling session. "Ask why and get a lie." Trainers frequently use this little rhyme with beginning therapists to stop them from asking the "why" question. (We will return to the matter of question asking in Chapter 13.) There are at least two reasons for restricting therapists from asking why. First, it is an accusatory question that will likely put clients in a defensive frame of mind. They will usually answer with an expected and socially accepted reason for the behavior. Second, effective psychotherapists, those grounded in personality theory, know the answer before it is asked! Their personality theory has already answered the why question. Hence the purpose of such theories—to explain human behavior.

It is also important to understand the difference between "why" for psychotherapists and "why" for clients. Psychotherapists ask that

77

question to seek the underlying motivation for behavior. Clients, however, ask that question to seek an explanation acceptable enough to allow them to live their lives. Thus, it is crucial that clients actively participate in the exploration of "why," because they are the ones who must live with their explanations.

Competing Theories

A bewildering number of competing personality theories seem to provide apparently contradictory explanations of human behavior. Psychoanalytic theories point to the importance of an inner psychological world in constant conflict between the demands of psychic impulses and societal rules. Ego psychology, another form of psychoanalytic theory, emphasizes the importance of very early human relationships. One form of behaviorism maintains that behavior that is reinforced will likely be repeated. Cognitive theory stresses the role thoughts themselves play in influencing behavior. Humanistic theory accents the biological tendency toward organismic completeness or self-actualization and the development of a central organizing concept labeled the self. These theories postulate contradictory ideas regarding important questions such as the role of genetics versus environmental conditions and the role of biology versus the role of the mind. Other areas of conflict include whether behavior is a matter of choice or is determined by forces that lie outside the person. Personality theorists differ on whether motivation must be stimulated from outside persons or whether human beings have the capacity to resist strong outside pressures and through the force of personal will follow their own path. These are important questions that every psychotherapist must face.

Scientific Method

Two other questions also present themselves: Why are there so many apparently contradictory theories and which one is right? Freud, Skinner, Bandura, and Rogers cannot all be right. One must be right and the others wrong. If one is right and the others wrong, why are the wrong ones still around? Let's deal with the second question first. Which one is right? The answer might surprise you. No one knows! In order to understand this, it is important to know that a scientific theory has certain requirements, the most important of which is that it have explanatory power. A theory is a system of organized knowledge that is pertinent to a relatively wide range of circumstances. It is based on assumptions and is devised to analyze, predict, or explain—the subject in the case of personality theory is behavior.

Science has a peculiar way of investigating questions. It is not so much about what is absolutely true as it is about what is not wrong. Any question of science must be asked in such a way that it can be disproven. If it cannot be tested so that it can be proved false, then it is not considered a matter of science. This is one of the major differences between scientific inquiry and religious inquiry. The two great methods of addressing our major life questions begin from two very different assumptions. Science begins in doubt and religion begins in faith. Science is a process of disproving the false, whereas religion is a process of having faith in what cannot be proven. In this sense, all personality theories have demonstrated themselves capable of explaining human behavior and have not been proven wrong. Let us give you an example of an idea that was proven to be false.

The idea that certain behaviors and particular faculties might be localized in specific parts of the brain first appeared in the 1800s. Some people assumed that because faculties are localized in the brain that these areas would be enlarged and would influence the shape of the skull, hence the birth of phrenology—the study of human behavior based on interpreting the bumps on the head (Davies, 1955; Leahey & Leahey, 1983). It is possible to speculate any number of reasons for human behavior. What separates speculation from scientific theory is that speculation leads to hypotheses, hypotheses are tested, and if they are not disproven they may be systematized into a theory.

The major personality theories have suffered the indignities of scientific inquiry. They survive because they have demonstrated their ability to explain and, to some extent, predict human behavior. They explain the origins of behavior. They explain why people do what they do. So many of them exist because there can be a number of reasonable explanations for any human act. While it is possible that the number and location of bumps on our heads does not lead to any reliable prediction or explanation of human behavior, it is equally possible to understand that early events in our lives may account for current behavior. It seems reasonable and demonstrable that "as the twig inclines, so grows the tree" or that "the child is the father of the man." It seems equally possible that we tend to repeat behaviors for which we are rewarded and that some people won't even attempt some act because they don't feel personally worthy. Each of these ideas is explanatory, each has been tested and, at minimum, not proven false. Thus, even though some theories are mutually exclusive and antagonistic toward one another, each has carved out a place for itself in scientific personality theory.

The Role of Genuineness

A particularly difficult question for many, especially for beginning psychotherapists, is which of these theories should be accepted and followed. It is not a question of which one is right but more a matter of which one is right for you. This is a personal matter that requires study and time. To some extent, it doesn't matter which theory a psychotherapist follows. What seems more important is the concept of genuineness, or the correspondence between one's personal beliefs and values and the personality theory one embraces. It seems evident that all of us act on assumptions regarding human behavior whether we are aware of those assumptions or not. Each of us will explain to ourselves the meaning of another person's behavior. Look at Activity 6.1.

Now that you have completed that activity, recognize that you have very briefly set out your immediate assumptions about why people behave the way they do. What you will discover is that these immediate impressions often correspond with one of the major families of personality theory. You as a psychotherapist must explore, examine, and study personality theories until you find the one that most closely fits

Activity 6.1
Assumptions About Human Behavior

Jim is a 19-year-old college sophomore who has had trouble in school since childhood. His grade point average is low and he has had several run-ins with his professors. He argues with them in class and thinks they are naive liberals who believe in big government. He argues that the government cannot be trusted, that you cannot rely on others to take care of you, and that we have to be self-reliant. Jim has few male friends and it seems he has the most trouble with his male professors. He makes friends with females easily but tends to be dependent on them. Jim will join clubs, especially political ones, but often clashes with the elected leaders and seems to resent it if he is not immediately recognized for his leadership qualities and elected to a high office.

How would you explain Jim's behavior? Take a moment and in a paragraph of about five lines explain why Jim acts the way he does.

your basic assumptions. What did you discover? Did you tend to explain Jim's behavior based on early relationships with his parents? Did you tend to look more at his relationships with his teachers and his history of reinforcement? Perhaps you thought more about his poor self-image. Each of these is, of course, a rough approximation of the basic assumption of a personality theory. Cormier and Hackney (1993) propose that our assumptions regarding human behavior "may be crystallized into four broad categories: theories that emphasize feelings and affective states; theories that emphasize thought and conceptual processes; theories that emphasize behavior and how it shapes our reality; and theories that emphasize relationships and how they interact to manifest and support feelings, thoughts, and behaviors" (p. 124).

A personality theory is for the psychotherapist. Clients, more often than not, have little interest in the theoretical orientation of the therapist. Psychotherapy is not meant to be a classroom where clients are lectured in the theoretical explanation of their behavior. The theory guides the therapist, it does not necessarily guide the client. That brings us to the importance and understanding of a counseling theory.

Counseling Theories

Personality theory addresses the question "why," whereas counseling theory addresses "how." Cormier and Hackney (1993) suggest that "counseling theories can serve a number of functions. They serve as a set of guidelines to explain how human beings learn, change, and develop; they also propose a model for normal human functioning (and ways in which human dysfunction may be manifested); and they suggest what should transpire in the counseling process and what the outcomes of counseling should be" (p. 4). Thus, counseling theory addresses the question of how—how to deal with the issues, problems, or dilemmas presented by clients. The model described in Chapter 2 is a counseling theory. A counseling theory provides psychotherapists with a plan of action, a structure, or a model within which to begin the therapy. We have said previously that psychotherapy is not a trial-and-error process, and a counseling theory provides a purposeful approach to clients' narratives. Counseling theories are, naturally, frequently associated with a personality theory, although it is possible to have a counseling theory without a personality theory. While all personality theories are based in science, not all counseling theories are scientifically based. For example, some counseling theories may have a religious origin. Whatever its origin, a counseling theory provides the psychotherapist with guidelines regarding how to proceed in therapy.

Clearly, all psychotherapy must begin in empathy and to attempt to help anyone without understanding is, at best, fishing without a hook. You might catch a fish, but it would have to be a terribly hungry one to bite a string and hold on long enough for you to get it out of the water. Counseling theory guides how to form an empathic relationship and how to manage clients' stories. Some psychotherapists believe, in accordance with the personality theory to which they adhere, that clients' early childhood experiences are important, and they would collect a detailed and elaborate history to better understand their clients' difficulties. Others would not place so much emphasis on history and instead would concentrate on clients' explanations for their behavior, listening for the cognitive reasoning underlying their reported behavior. Others might isolate symptoms quickly and move to treat these identifiable behaviors concretely and expeditiously. Still another might believe that the dream life of clients was significant and would instruct them to record their dreams. Some therapists might need to know and understand the family and/or present living arrangements of clients. The model proposed in Chapter 2 suggests that it is important to create a relationship characterized by empathy, genuineness, and respect in a structure of exploration, understanding, and resolution. Other counseling theories have different emphases.

Eclecticism

Let us take just a moment here to discuss the issue of eclecticism. Suppose you were a well-informed client who approached a psychotherapist to ask his or her theoretical orientation and the psychotherapist replied, "I am basically psychoanalytical, but I use cognitive behaviorism when it is appropriate." Well, this is just nonsense. Go back to Activity 6.1 and suppose my response was something like this: "I believe Jim is suffering from an obvious Oedipus complex and hasn't been properly reinforced for his acceptable behavior toward authority figures. He is in an existential crisis and is filled with despair. He has a poor self-concept and clearly hasn't come to terms with the shadow part of his personality." This is nothing more than jargon strung together reflecting a mindless mishmash of hot words from various theories. This form of eclecticism is unacceptable and perhaps even dangerous, if not for psychotherapists, then for their clients. It has been said when referring to personality theory that one should "stay close to home." However, we do not mean to imply that every psychotherapist must subscribe to a single theory of personality (i.e., Freudian, Rogerian, Adlerian, or Jungian). In another form of eclecticism compatible elements of different theories may be systematically combined into a coherent personal theory, and it is likely that such a combination would still fit into one of the major theoretical families (i.e., cognitive, behavioral, phenomenological, or psychoanalytical). It is more helpful when explaining human behavior to stick to a comprehensive theory than to jump from theory to theory depending upon the diagnosis. For example, it would be a hollow psychotherapist who said, "Well, I use humanistic theory for problems of the self. But, for depression I find that cognitive theory is best. If a client has some form of spiritual crisis I like existentialism and for anxiety I use behaviorism." This is a counselor who has mistaken methods for the process. Combs (1989) warns us that "what therapists do, or do not do, in the counseling process is not a mechanical matter of applying the right method to the right client at the right instant. Instead, the behavior of counselors depends upon the counselor's beliefs, values, goals, and understandings applied to the problem of helping the client in the most effective ways possible" (p. 62).

There is no point in bouncing from theory to theory to deal with different symptoms because a careful study of any one theory reveals theoretical explanations already in place. A psychotherapist who hops from theory to theory in explaining symptoms is intellectually lazy and has not thoroughly studied that particular theory.

Another form of eclecticism that has been labeled *technical eclecticism* (Lazarus & Beutler, 1993) has to do with using a variety of techniques or strategies in psychotherapy. While unsystematic eclecticism in personality theory is not helpful, using a variety of counseling strategies becomes a matter of practicality. Personality theories differ widely, but there is much overlap in what psychotherapists actually do. One of the reasons it is possible to make a statement like "all psychotherapy begins in empathy" (Welch, 1998, p. 6) is because in practice it is virtually impossible to be of help to someone unless we understand. Psychotherapists are, largely, compassionate people who want to be of help. It is no surprise then that in practice psychotherapists seek to understand what clients need help with. It follows that practitioners from one theory borrow from one another. Strategies or techniques may be understood from a variety of personality theories.

Let us give you one example. Frankl's logotherapy has a technique he calls *paradoxical intention*. Behaviorism has a strategy called *negative practice*. Gestalt practice has what is called *exaggeration*. In each of these techniques, clients are asked to do something that seems just the opposite of what they say they want. One example is fingernail biting. In negative practice clients would be asked to practice biting their fingernails! This method of dealing with human behaviors has even found its way into "commonsense" advice in what is called *reverse psychology*. In Joel Chandler Harris's Uncle Remus stories, Brer Rabbit pleads with Brer Bear and Brer Fox—"Whatever you do don't throw me in the briar patch. Please don't throw me in the briar patch." Brer Rabbit was, of course, "born and bred" in the briar patch and he tricked Brer Bear and Brer Fox into doing exactly what he hoped they would do. Throughout years of practice, psychotherapists from different theoretical orientations have discovered interventions that are effective in similar circumstances. "Practicing the problem" is one way to sensitize the self to a piece of behavior so that it may be brought under conscious control. Many theories can account for why this is so, and the fact that one theory may be credited with the discovery or creation of a strategy doesn't preclude others from using it. In this sense, a practitioner may be technically eclectic while remaining congruent within a personality theory.

Being Grounded

When psychotherapists are well grounded in a personality and counseling theory they are able to offer psychotherapy that is notable for several reasons. We have spent a good amount of time discussing the idea that psychotherapy is purposeful. Theoretically grounded psychotherapists are not stumbling blindly around in the lives of clients; their actions are systematic, orderly, and precise. While the world may appear in shambles to clients, this is not the case for the purposeful activity of psychotherapists. Consider for a moment a ship at sea. Storms come up and the craft is buffeted and assailed by the elements. Tossed and shaken by wind and water, it may seem to be mere debris at the mercy of a chaotic storm. Yet, more often than not, the ship weathers the storm and sails

85

comfortably to its final destination. Its survival is not a chance event. The ship survived because the sailors performed their duties purposefully and skillfully. Psychotherapy can be a stormy time, but it is precisely because the psychotherapist has purpose, knowledge, and skill that the turmoil can be navigated and weathered.

Another advantage theoretically well-grounded psychotherapists enjoy is a sense of confidence even in the face of the unknown. The great disadvantage of experience alone is that it does not teach one what to do outside one's experience. Teyber (1997) points out that "many therapists become exceedingly anxious in their early counseling work because they lack a coherent and practical conceptual framework. Uncertainty over how to conceptualize client problems and ambiguous guidelines for how to proceed in the therapy session heighten their insecurity and preoccupation with their counseling performance" (p. 4). One may learn to run one machine efficiently but be totally lost with another piece of equipment. A mechanical engineer, however, may know nothing at all about a new piece of machinery but will learn its secrets quickly because of an understanding of mechanics. Psychotherapists who are well grounded in theory can be faced with unusual and previously unexperienced human behavior and yet respond effectively and sensibly. Thus, they can be confident when they greet clients even though they have no idea what clients are going to bring to therapy.

It is in this way that psychotherapy can be spontaneous and creative. Theory does not provide practitioners with a map but with an understanding of climate, land forms, spatial patterns, soils, vegetation, and erosion. In this analogy, explorers/therapists may not fully know where they are, but they might be able to find water, tell direction, detect danger, and find food. They may respond creatively to necessity precisely because they have an understanding of principles in the absence of specifics.

We need to say a bit more about spontaneity and creativity because as we said before, clients do not come to therapy to be experimented upon. Clients are in a vulnerable state and therefore we cannot risk an intervention that does not have a high probability of success. But how can psychotherapy be spontaneous and creative without risk? There are two answers to this question. First, when psychotherapists experiment with a new intervention they themselves are the subjects, not the clients. Psychotherapists know that the new intervention should work because they read about it in a book or they had it recommended by a colleague, but they want to know if they can use the technique effectively themselves. Does it fit for them? It becomes a matter of congruence. Second, psychotherapists do invent interventions "on the spur of the moment." They creatively respond to a new situation with something they have never done before because they already know that the new intervention should work because they are guided by theory. It is not blind intervention.

Let us give you an example. In an episode of the popular television series (the original) *Star Trek*, members of the crew have been mysteriously spirited away from their spaceship to an unknown place and presented with challenges to test their skill. They are caught up in the experience when one of the crew, Mr. Spock, a highly cognitive and nonemotional character, conducts a simple experiment. It does not turn out the way it should. From this result, Mr. Spock concludes that the crew is experiencing an illusion. The crew questions his conclusion and doubts that their experiences are an illusion just because the experiment didn't work out. Mr. Spock replies, "That is precisely why I know this is an illusion. The experiment *should have* worked as I predicted. It did not, therefore the ordinary laws have been suspended. This is not real." Theory then becomes the sure ground from which to approach the unknown. It is not enough to "fly by the seat of your pants off the top of your head" (Martin, 1983, p. 222). Creativity and spontaneity are guided by a theoretical understanding of human behavior. This theoretical knowledge provides the courage to explore what is unfamiliar, foreign, and even bizarre.

Identifying and Developing a Personal Theory

As you move forward in your development as a counselor, it is important that you begin to identify and build a personally meaningful conceptual framework in your work with clients. Combs (1989) identifies this important task and states clearly that "what makes an effective therapist is the acquisition of a comprehensive, internally congruent system of beliefs—development of a personal theory. Information and experience provide the raw materials; but it is the personal exploration and discovery of meaning which puts it all together into a system capable of providing trustworthy guidelines for professional practice" (p. 159). This approach to counseling has been labeled the *self as instrument* approach by Combs and Gonzalez (1994) and leads to the conclusion that "how well helpers are able to use themselves as effective instruments is dependent on the quality of their belief systems" (p. 19). Study, time, and commitment are the necessary ingredients for developing this personal theory. Use the guidelines discussed in Activity 6.2 as a "map" as you begin this process.

Activity 6.2
Developing a Personal Theory

Phase 1: Exploration

STEP 1:   Explore your personal values and convictions about human beings and life in general. Do not be afraid to test your personal values and beliefs. Any value/belief worth having is one that can withstand close scrutiny.

STEP 2:   Explore the major theories of counseling and psychotherapy and subscribe to one theory that most closely resembles your own personal values and beliefs.

Phase 2: Examination
("Learning" the theory intellectually and experimentally)

STEP 3:   Examine the counseling theory extensively from primary source materials and seek to understand specifically what you agree/disagree with and why. If you discover that the theory does not truly approximate your values and beliefs, begin the process again at step 1.

STEP 4: Examine to what degree you are comfortable using the theory and discover to what extent the theory works for you in helping clients. At this step you may experience discomfort or lack of efficacy in using your counseling theory of choice. This may occur for one of two reasons. First, you may not fully understand the proper applications of the theory. If so, you will need to return to step 3. Second, the theory may not be a true approximation of your values and beliefs. In this case, you will need to return to step 1.

Phase 3: Integration

STEP 5: Once substantial intellectual and experiential knowledge of the counseling theory of choice is acquired, begin integrating selected aspects of other theories into your chosen theory. This integrative process can only begin, however, with a thorough understanding of other major counseling theories.

Aspects to be integrated fall into one of two categories. In integrating *techniques* from other counseling theories, it is important to be able to explain the integration from the framework of your theory of choice. The integration of *theoretical* aspects of other theories is a thorny issue. Theoretical constructs must be philosophically consistent with your theory in order to be validly integrated. Strive to be theoretically and philosophically consistent.

Phase 4: Personalization

STEP 6: The transformation to your own unique and personal theory of counseling is a natural result of all that has come before. The steps outlined above appear to be linear, but are actually more cyclical and representative of a dynamic process. As you continually work on the steps, your personal theory of counseling will continue to evolve. Step 6 is actually just the initiatory rite along the road to revising and clarifying your own personal theory of counseling.

From "Developing a Personal Theory of Counseling: A Brief Guide for Students," by R. E. Watts, Spring 1993, *TCA Journal, 21*, pp. 103–104. Special Issue: Counselor Educator's Theories of Counseling. Copyright © 1993 TCA Journal. Reprinted by permission.

References and for Further Reading

Combs, A. W. (1989). *A theory of therapy: Guidelines for counseling practice*. Newbury Park, CA: Sage Publications.

Combs, A. W., & Gonzalez, D. M. (1994). *Helping relationships: Basic concepts for the helping professions* (4th ed.). Boston: Allyn & Bacon.

Cormier, L. S., & Hackney, H. (1993). *The professional counselor: A process guide to helping* (2nd ed.). Boston: Allyn & Bacon.

Davies, J. D. (1955). *Phrenology: Fad and Science*. New Haven, CT: Yale University Press.

Lazarus, A. A. (1995, March). Different types of eclecticism and integration: Let's be aware of the dangers. *Journal of Psychotherapy Integration, 5*, 27–39.

Lazarus, A. A. (1996, Spring). The utility and futility of combining treatments in psychotherapy. *Clinical Psychology: Science and Practice, 3*, 59–68.

Lazarus, A. A., & Beutler, L. E. (1993, March–April). On technical eclecticism. *Journal of Counseling and Development, 71*, 381–385.

Lazarus, A. A., Beutler, L. E., & Norcross, J. C. (1992, Spring). The future of technical eclecticism. *Psychotherapy, 29*, 11–20. Special issue: The Future of Psychotherapy.

Leahey, T. H., & Leahey, G. E. (1983). *Psychology's occult doubles: Psychology and the problem of pseudoscience*. Chicago: Nelson-Hall.

Mahoney, M. J. (1993, March). Diversity and the dynamics of development in psychotherapy integration. *Journal of Psychotherapy Integration, 3*, 1–13.

Martin, D. K. (1983). *Counseling and therapy skills*. Pacific Grove, CA: Brooks/Cole.

Norcross, J. C. (1995, Summer). A roundtable on psychotherapy integrations: Common factors, technical eclecticism, and psychotherapy research. *Journal of Psychotherapy Practice and Research, 4*, 248–271.

Pinkster, H. (1994, Fall). The role of theory in teaching supportive psychotherapy. *American Journal of Psychotherapy, 48*, 530–542.

Teyber, E. (1997). *Interpersonal process in psychotherapy: A relational approach* (3rd ed.). Pacific Grove, CA: Brooks/Cole.

Watts, R. E. (1993, Spring). Developing a personal theory of counseling: A brief guide for students. *TCA Journal, 21*, 103–104. Special issue: Counselor Educator's Theories of Counseling.

Welch, I. D. (1998). *The path of psychotherapy: Matters of the heart.* Pacific Grove, CA: Brooks/Cole.

7

⨎

Cultural, Gender, and Lifestyle Issues in Counseling and Psychotherapy

*a*lthough we believe that empathy is the surest road to understanding another person, it has become increasingly important in our multidimensional society to understand the societal and cultural, gender, and lifestyle forces that contribute to the unique person who seeks us out for personal and emotional understanding. Developing a greater sensitivity to cultural, gender, and lifestyle issues can help counselors and psychotherapists respond more adequately and accurately to the initial contacts with clients from backgrounds other than our own. This is an enormous challenge in our increasingly diverse society.

Barriers to Understanding

Cultural, gender, and lifestyle differences can create enormous challenges to the empathy process. In one case, a traditional Hispanic woman was very concerned with her teenage son who was "out of control," hanging out with a gang and staying out at night. The woman sought help from a therapist who listened to her frantic pleas. The therapist handed the woman a book called *Codependent No More* and asked her to read it before returning for an appointment the following week. After the client read the book she became despondent and overwhelmed because she now felt like she had been a bad mother. Her culture was one of interdependence and affiliation where the family came first and the individual came second. The client sought out another therapist. Upon entering his office, she relayed the events of the past week. She clutched the book in her hand, feeling like a failure as a mother because so many of the practices advocated by the book were direct contradictions of her parenting techniques. She felt that somehow she must have learned to parent badly. The therapist, on a hunch, suggested that she throw the book in the trash. With a surprised, wide-eyed look, she paused, then threw the book in the trash and remarked, "You mean I don't have to believe what was written in the book?" She sighed with great relief. "You mean I may not be such a bad mother?" The first therapist had an empathic failure with the client because of a lack of cultural, gender, and lifestyle understanding. That therapist had a book that fit a set of the therapist's beliefs but had little to do with the client's world. Yet, the Hispanic woman felt like she had consulted an expert and in her respect for the expert had blamed herself for not behaving the way the book said she should. Furthermore, she felt like even more of a failure because she could not do what the book said and interpreted that as personal weakness rather than realizing the book simply did not fit for her.

This story is not an indictment of the book *Codependent No More*, but an illustration of a therapist who misapplied an understanding of how a parent should behave toward her children to a culture with a very different perspective, resulting in harm to the client. We are not implying it is necessary to be of the same cultural, gender, and lifestyle background in order to help clients, but this story does show the need to be educated not only about other cultures but about one's own cultural, gender, and lifestyle values and perspectives. Increasingly, it is an essential aspect of effective therapy to take cultural, gender, and lifestyle factors into consideration when trying to make sense of another's behavior (Castillo, 1997).

Multicultural Sensitivity

As we further hone our skills in dealing with different peoples, few would argue that it is important to be sensitive to our clients. In fact, people in our profession depend on being sensitive to other human beings. In terms of sensitivity toward ethnic minorities, there are ways of talking that show a person to be sensitive or insensitive, whatever the case may be. Perhaps the first thing to consider in discussing this matter is the definition of the term *sensitivity*. In this case, the term describes the capacity to "sense" what is salient, to "sense" what is an important issue, or, better said, to be sensitive to what a sensitive person should be sensitive to!

To illustrate, suppose a therapist who is working with a person from a minority group asks the insensitive question, "Have you ever experienced prejudice?" That question demonstrates that the questioner does not understand the nature of prejudice and does not understand that an individual who is a member of any "affected class"—whether that is people of color, people with "foreign" names, or people with foreign accents—has almost certainly experienced prejudice. The reader may object, saying that the question is merely meant to inquire about an important issue and that the person is showing concern by asking the question. However, by asking the question in that manner, the inquirer has created a real dilemma for the person being asked.

The feelings associated with experiencing prejudice often run deep, and, to a great extent, the question is therefore quite personal. Inherent in the experience is an attack on one's self-esteem, something that takes some effort to transcend. The dilemma in this case has a number of facets: (1) the person has been asked a very personal question, (2) the very personal question has been asked by someone who has shown no understanding of the nature of prejudice, and (3) the person has to decide whether or not to share experiences of prejudice with someone who is "insensitive," however innocent the insensitivity may be. The person may lie and say no, rather than share such a personal life experience, or the person may share despite the awkwardness created by the form of the question. One solution is quite simple. First, it is generally safe to assume that the person's life has been affected in some significant way by prejudice. Second, if the wish to know is sincere and appropriate, there are questions that are much more congruent with the reality of the situation, such as "How have you handled prejudice

93

in your life?" or "Would you feel comfortable sharing some of your experiences regarding prejudice?" There is no precise way that one must speak to be sensitive, but there is a guiding principle. The questioner should be aware of the sociopolitical forces and the fear and hatred in society and should know that people who are "different" in some way do feel the fangs of those forces and that the fangs do leave scars and that it is personal to show someone your scars. This slight change in wording can have a big effect. One effect is to raise the awareness of the questioner, and another effect is that it is sensitive to the person being asked.

Consider the example of an incident in a Hispanic college student's freshman year. Many students were excited to have their name appear in the university telephone directory; however, for the Hispanic student it meant the beginning of a continuous flow of racially motivated and harassing phone calls. The student's roommates were bewildered at the number of such calls aimed at him. They said they were beginning to understand that people victimized by prejudice undergo more overt prejudice than they could have ever imagined. This incident, which was one of many such episodes experienced by this individual, was not unlike the experiences of many people of color. So, you can imagine the impact of a therapist asking this student in a counseling session if he had ever encountered prejudice.

Gender Sensitivity

Saying that women and men are different and merely acknowledging the physical differences between them is an unperceptive and dull understanding of the forces that influence all of us. What is more telling, more informative, and more crucial is our inspection and introspection of the sources of the cognitive, emotional, social, economic, and status differences that still exist between the genders. From the earliest stages of life, both males and females are "shaped" to fit into the prevailing roles of what and how boys and girls "should" be. It is an enormous challenge for therapists to transcend their own deeply ingrained socializations regarding gender, yet if we do not do so, we run

94

the risk of inadvertently pigeonholing our clients in the cultural boxes marked "boys" and "girls," even when these identifiers may carry pathological meanings for them. The so-called battle of the sexes clearly has resulted in legitimate social struggles and personal pain for individuals and family groups as they seek to cope with new understandings and new social rules of behavior. As psychotherapists, it is important to resolve any such pain in order to be truly available to our clients regardless of gender. Strong "opinions" about what a client should do based on gender will most likely result in therapists unconsciously playing out their own personal and social issues even as they conceptualize the client's case.

Counselors and psychotherapists need to be as aware of the oppression of gender in our society as we are of cultural and ethnic discrimination. While gender discrimination affects both women and men, the feminist movement has taught us not only the economic price women pay, but the physical, social, emotional, and intrapsychic doubt that permeates our society and obstructs the healthy psychological development of both women and men. It might easily be said that the price of sexism is the limitation of dreams. This nagging doubt of our right to pursue our dreams, the need to second guess our hopes based on our gender is a cruel cultural lesson. We need to learn, study, and reflect on this crucial topic if we are to strip ourselves of cultural and ethnic insensitivity.

While both men and women are hindered in their development by gender stereotypes, the focus of oppression seems more directed at women than at men. As startling as that statement may seem, it has to do with a practical, even statistical, reality. It is much more likely that the clients we will see are women. They will bring with them not only their inner personal struggles, but a life circumstance, just as the struggles of ethnic minority clients are intensified by the behavioral and attitudinal forces of our society.

As counselors and psychotherapists, we must recognize that when we are dealing with gender discrimination the forces of psychopathology are not always intrapsychic. Welch (1998) has described the phenomenon of the level of difficulties in clients' lives as issues, problems, and dilemmas, whose source may stem from forces external to the individual. Some of our turmoil may indeed come from purely inner conflicts (intrapsychic). However, in our experience, we see so few of these situations that they occupy little of our psychotherapeutic time.

A major force in our lives is our relationships with others (interpersonal), which do occupy a good deal of counselors' and psychotherapists' time. Clearly, the cultural forces that influence our relationships with one another carry with them lessons that establish the roles, responsibilities, expectations, and worth of individuals in a relationship. Indeed, whether one conceives of a relationship as hierarchical, a partnership, a limited partnership, or something like a contractual arrangement has profound meanings for the interpersonal connections and alliance between the people involved. Counselors and psychotherapists need to be aware of these sensitivities as clients bring their concerns into therapy.

The third sphere of influence in our lives is our relationship with the groups and institutions of our society. This relationship has been labeled a number of ways (impersonal), but the intent of the labels is to capture the idea that we as individuals are deeply influenced by the formal and informal institutions of our society. Formal institutions include our schools, churches, and social and service organizations. Informal institutions include marriage, child-rearing patterns, the division of labor, and career opportunities thought proper. This is the realm in which feminist psychotherapy has had its greatest influence and created the greatest controversy. Feminist therapy and theory (Burman, 1990; Lott, 1994; Mirkin, 1994) suggest that the role of the counselor and psychotherapist is not only to explore, understand, and participate in the generation of effective action, but to act as an advocate for clients as they engage and confront institutional sexism in our society. This suggestion—that the source of the difficulty in the lives of women, especially, is not intrapsychic or merely interpersonal but cultural and societal—leads to a conviction that the solution to clients' disquiet is not introspection or greater self-awareness but a planned strategy of actively opposing the demeaning forces in their lives.

Regardless of how one conceptualizes matters of gender, a sensitivity to these concerns as they affect the profession of counseling and psychotherapy is another ingredient in the mix of extending our empathic reach as therapists. It is no exaggeration to suggest that as counselors, and as citizens, it is as important to recognize the oppressive effects of our society and our personal beliefs on women and men as it is to be sensitive to multicultural issues.

Lifestyle Sensitivity

A wide range of living arrangements exist in the United States. From time to time in the newspapers you find some advocate of "family values" describing a family as a unit in which the husband/father and the wife/mother in their first marriage live with their biological children in a home in which the mother is responsible for child-rearing and home care and the father works to support the family on a single income. For some, that image may evoke pleasant memories and a longing of how it used to be, but the difficulty with such a description today is that it fits so few American households. It leaves out single-parent families, remarried families, families with adopted children, couples without children, and same-sex couples, to name only a few.

This fairly straightforward demonstration of living arrangements found in the United States is meant to sensitize us to the wide variety of possible ways in which families may live together. It is a relatively painless way to introduce the topic of more delicate lifestyle decisions people in our society make as they struggle to find peace and emotional adjustment in the world. When we introduce the difficulties encountered by gay men and lesbians, then the issue becomes more powerful and more political.

Among the many issues that divide us is the gay and lesbian lifestyle. Gay men and lesbians remain targets for physical abuse, financial exploitation, and social ostracism. Much of the earlier argument about understanding the source of gender concerns applies equally well to the issues faced by gay men and lesbians even today. This continuing conflict of values and sexual orientation has been popularly labeled *homophobia*, a term meant to communicate an irrational fear of the homosexual orientation. D. Johnson, a psychotherapist in Boulder, Colorado, has studied this phenomenon and talks about "levels of acceptance" (personal communication, 1990). He views acceptance along a continuum from hatred to a lack of any issues with a homosexual orientation (no issue).

1. *Hatred–Hostility.* This irrational response to gay men and lesbians is the level at which violence is most likely to occur. A person functioning at this level would not be content to "live and let live." Instead, such a person might actively seek out gay men or lesbians to taunt and even physically assault them. Someone holding such a viewpoint would consider a homosexual orientation repugnant. If that person came from a religious background, then in all likelihood homosexuality would be branded a "sin." Religious responses to homosexuality might range from hatred to acceptance.

2. *Rejection.* At this level, parents might disown a gay son or lesbian daughter. They might feel such a violation of values that they would not be able to associate with their son or daughter and might even forbid mentioning his or her name in their presence. They would not be violent toward homosexuals nor would they actively seek to harm them, but they would go out of their way to avoid contact with a gay man or lesbian, including their own son or daughter.

3. *Avoidance–Fear.* At this level, the avoidance and fear is not directed so much at an individual but at the fear that somehow homosexuality might rub off and that it has something like a contagious quality to it. People at this level exhibit the fear of "latent homosexuality." People who avoid and fear gay men and lesbians mean them no harm; they simply do not want to associate with them and, again, would go out of their way to avoid contact.

4. *Tolerance.* This level suggests that there are people in the world who are willing to acknowledge that there are gay men and lesbians who can be tolerated. Such a person might not object to a gay or lesbian co-worker and would not complain particularly about it. They would not, however, be overly friendly and would not publicly defend the rights of homosexuals. Their position might well be, "If they don't bother me, then I won't bother them."

5. *Acceptance*. This is a difficult category because it holds many well-intentioned people who would actively defend gay men and lesbians. They would argue that gay men and lesbians ought to have the same legal protections as any citizen and that no person should be discriminated against because of their sexual orientation. They accept gay men and lesbians and might even become friendly and would accept an invitation to a gay or lesbian home. The difficulty comes about in the attitude they hold toward a sexual orientation. They might speak of it as a right but clearly believe that it is somehow not the right one. They might argue, for example, that "people have the right to be different." With this sentiment they exhibit an underlying feeling that there is something wrong with a homosexual orientation but that they are willing to live freely with the suspect decision of a gay man or lesbian.

6. *No Issue*. At this level people might work with gay men or lesbians, accept invitations to their home, or go to social events all without a second thought. It simply doesn't enter their minds that the person who asked them to go to the theater or to a basketball game is asking them to go for any reason other than companionship. In other words, if a well-known heterosexual man asks another well-known straight man to go to a game, the response to the invitation is based on whether or not the invitee wants to go to the game and not on the sexual orientation of the person asking. In other words, the sexual orientation of the person being asked and the person asking doesn't enter into the matter at all. This is the level of no issue.

These levels have important implications for counselors and psychotherapists. First, they give us a gauge of our own attitudes toward this social conflict. Second, they provide a way of understanding clients as they present their therapists with sexual issues and problems in therapy. Third, they provide a way for gay and lesbian clients to view the behavior and reaction of their colleagues, friends, and family to their sexual orientation.

Dominant Cultural, Gender, and Lifestyle Values

Part of understanding other cultures and their worldviews involves understanding *one's own* cultural, gender, and lifestyle views and values—that is, what are the cultural, gender, and lifestyle values that dominate the thinking of the majority culture and how do these values differ from other cultures? Often, people in the majority group in our culture say, "We study the African American culture, the Hispanic culture, the Native American culture, etc.—what about the white culture? Don't we have a culture?" When people are within the culture, it can be difficult to be aware of what the culture is, because it is everywhere. By looking at other cultures we can develop a contrast to help us define our own culture. If we are going to be empathic in working with different cultures, it may be useful to examine some of the dominant cultural, gender, and lifestyle values that shape our expectations and world views. The dominant culture of the United States is a compilation of white European ideals and values (Axelson, 1999). Axelson noted the first five values or ideals that dominate mainstream America and we have added two more. Much of our thinking as individuals and consequently as therapists spring from these values.

1. In the dominant culture of the United States, *the value of the individual often overshadows the good of the group.* The individual's success is seen as something to be admired. Think of the CEO who works late, travels the country for important business meetings, is involved in important conference calls. He or she is seen as a success. Yet, what about his or her family? What if the business executive decided to miss an important meeting to tend to a child who was ill. Once might be okay, but twice or more? The executive would be putting his or her job on the line. The family and one's personal relationships are clearly in second place, and it is not a close call for who or what will be first. The rugged individual has long been admired in our culture. By contrast, cultures in Japan, China, and Mexico, to name just a few, consider the good of the family over the good of the individual.

2. Another dominant cultural and gender value is an *action-oriented approach to problem solving*. This value says do something! If there is a problem, somebody should take some action—and produce quick and easily observable results. While there are many occasions when this approach is helpful, it is not the only way. If we fall and break a leg or if our house is on fire, we hope that someone will take immediate action. If a person were being beaten, we hope that someone would call the police or do something to help. Other situations, however, might call for a different response. For example, sometimes the best thing a person can do is nothing. Look at the incredible power that passive resistance has had in the area of race relations. Consider also that Gandhi's nonviolent efforts helped to free 600 million people from powerful British control. The dominance of an action-oriented approach to problem solving in our culture may blind us to the existence of other possibilities, other ways of helping our clients solve problems. Consider the current popularity of short-term therapies. While economic forces are certainly a major factor driving short-term models of helping, such models are also to some degree an extension of our action-oriented approach to solving problems.

3. Another dominant cultural value is our *adherence to a rigid time schedule*. The advantage of such an approach is efficiency. It allows us to be at the same place at the same time. It allows us to run a factory, have a stock market, and know when to pick up our children from school in an efficient and productive manner. There is a trade-off, however. We are much less able to participate in the spontaneous happenings in our lives. Who has not heard themselves complaining about not having enough time to do something? Often we complain about not having time for things that would be meaningful or would make our life more fulfilling. Clients from a different cultural, gender, and lifestyle background may have a very different relationship with time.

4. Our *reliance on the scientific method* is another powerful value. A phenomenon must be observable and testable in order to be valid:

this value has been a boon to sciences such as medicine and physics. We want to be sure that before a vaccine is injected it has been rigorously tested and retested. Before sending men and women into space, we need to confirm that certain scientific principles have been followed. At the same time, most of us would agree that although some of the most important things in life are not easily testable by the scientific method, they are real and vital to us. Things such as feelings, intuition, hopes, and dreams are difficult to accurately measure, but their importance is unmistakable. Other cultures have phenomena that are not easily tested, yet are realities. Our worship of the scientific method may result in us discounting such cultures as being ignorant, superstitious, and ill-informed.

5. The *work ethic* has a powerful place in our culture. Lots of images come to mind at the mention of this term. "Keep your nose to the grindstone"; "idle minds are the devil's workshop"; "work hard now and you will be rewarded later." In practice, we have a rat race society that is overworked, with not enough time for family or for ourselves. We often do not even know our neighbors. Who among you would dare take a 30-minute nap at work, if you desperately needed to, even if you have a stellar work record. The notion of sleeping on the job is abhorrent to most of us. Even though it would be physiologically healthier for us to take a brief rest after lunch to aid in digestion and to renew ourselves for the rest of the workday, we just cannot do it. It goes against our value system. Instead, we take antacids as we vigorously plunge back into our job. The notion of the Mexican siesta gets misinterpreted as representing laziness rather than something healthy.

6. *Material wealth is often regarded as the standard of success.* The accumulation of material goods is seen and felt as the measure of success by many. If one does not have a luxurious home, a beautiful car (or two or three), elegant furniture, stylish clothing, discretionary income for travel, and art collections, one may feel like a failure, like he or she is just not making it. Lack of the material goods to "prove" that one is successful can diminish a person's self-worth. By contrast, think of the potlatch ceremonies that are held in Native American cultures to give away one's wealth, to share with others what one has accumulated. The more a person can give away, the better. Such ideas are alien in our materialistic society. It is worthwhile to give some consideration to what other measures people might use to gauge their success in life.

7. *Formal education must occur in a particular format.* Our methods of education are rooted in the delivery of information to a passive audience who is supposed to listen. The prevailing mind-set says that teachers are supposed to do something. So teachers give students books, math problems, and so forth and the students are somehow supposed to discern the information's applicability by themselves. While few would argue that formal education is critical in so many ways, we often couch our concept of education in a very narrow fashion. We did not value the education system of the Native Americans, for example. Our government, in reflecting the values of its citizens, set out to "educate" Native American children. The children were forbidden to speak native languages, to practice their religion, and so forth. The system that taught children how to live in harmony with nature, the system that had poignant rituals to help children make the transition from one stage of life to another was not seen as education, it was not valued and has been dismantled by sometimes well-meaning educators. It does not mean that we should discard our education system, but rather we should be aware of how that system is limited and needs to be enhanced by other ways of educating. Although this discussion may, at first glance, not seem to fit the rest of the chapter, it is included here because of the dramatic lack of empathy demonstrated in our culture's attempts to educate those from backgrounds other than our own.

While this list of dominant cultural values is not complete, it should give us some greater understanding of the beliefs that drive the thinking of mainstream America and therefore is likely to exert great influence on any therapist steeped in the American majority culture. We do not intend to say that these values are necessarily bad or good, but rather to understand that these are values, not truths. There are clients who have other values and worldviews as well. Developing a comprehensive appreciation of other cultural, gender, and lifestyle values and practices is necessary to form an empathic relationship. To do so requires a commitment and a concerted effort to educate oneself about others' values and worldviews and a willingness to examine and resolve one's own prejudices. We contend that multicultural understanding is not possible until prejudices are overcome. Prejudices taint our perceptions so that our interpretations of what we learn about others, whether we are talking about cultures, gender, or lifestyle, are not likely to be accurate. This, of course, requires courage from each of us.

References and for Further Reading

Alexander, C. J. (Ed.). (1996). *Gay and lesbian mental health: A sourcebook for practitioners*. New York: Harrington Park Press/Haworth Press.

Aponte, J. F., Rivers, R. Y., & Wohl, J. (Eds.). (1995). *Psychological interventions and cultural diversity*. Boston: Allyn & Bacon.

Axelson, J. A. (1985). *Counseling and development in a multicultural society*. Pacific Grove, CA: Brooks/Cole.

Burman, E. (Ed.). (1990). *Feminists and psychological practice*. London: Sage Publications.

Caldwell, S. A., Burnham, R. A., Jr., & Forstein, M. (Eds.). (1994). *Therapists on the front line: Psychotherapy with gay men in the age of AIDS*. Washington, DC: American Psychiatric Press.

Carter, R. T. (1995). *The influence of race and racial identity in psychotherapy: Toward a racially inclusive model*. New York: Wiley.

Castillo, R. J. (1997). *Culture and mental illness*. Pacific Grove, CA: Brooks/Cole.

Chin, J. L., De La Cancela, V., & Jenkins, Y. M. (1993). *Diversity in psychotherapy: The politics of race, ethnicity, and gender*. Westport, CT: Praeger/Greenwood Publishing Group.

Comas-Diaz, L., & Greene, B. (1994). *Women of color: Integrating ethnic and gender identities in psychotherapy*. New York: Guilford Press.

Davies, D., & Neal, C. (Eds.). (1996). *Pink therapy: A guide for counsellors and therapists working with lesbian, gay and bisexual clients*. Buckingham, England: Open University Press.

Dynes, W. R., & Donaldson, S. (Eds.). (1992). *Homosexuality and psychology, psychiatry, and counseling*. New York: Garland.

Exum, H. A., & Moore, Q. L. (1993). Transcultural counseling from African-American perspectives. In J. McFadden (Ed.), *Transcultural counseling: Bilateral and international perspectives* (pp. 193–212). Alexandria, VA: American Counseling Association.

Greene, B., & Boyd-Franklin, N. (1996). African American lesbian couples: Ethnocultural considerations in psychotherapy. In M. Hill & E. D. Rothblum (Eds.), *Couples therapy: Feminist perspectives* (pp. 49–60). New York: Harrington Park Press/Haworth Press.

Hill, M., & Rothblum, E. D. (Eds.). (1996). *Classism and feminist therapy: Counting costs*. New York: Harrington Park Press/Haworth Press.

Huat, T. B. (1994). Therapeutic paradox: Its use and function in therapy in a predominately Chinese society. In G. Davidson (Ed.), *Applying psychology: Lessons from Asia-Oceania* (pp. 61–81). Carlton, Australia: Australian Psychological Society.

Jones, R. L. (Ed.). (1991). *Black psychology*. Berkeley, CA: Cobb & Henry.

Koss-Chioino, J. D., & Vargas, L. A. (1992). Through the cultural looking glass: A model for understanding culturally responsive psychotherapies. In L. A. Vargas & J. D. Koss-Chioino (Eds.), *Working with culture: Psychotherapeutic interventions with ethnic minority children and adolescents* (pp. 1–22). San Francisco: Jossey-Bass.

Lott, B. (1994). *Women's lives: Themes and variations in gender learning* (2nd ed.). Pacific Grove, CA: Brooks/Cole.

Mirkin, M. P. (Ed.). (1994). *Women in context: Toward a feminist reconstruction of psychotherapy*. New York: Guilford Press.

Pedersen, P. B. (Ed.). (1996). *Counseling across cultures* (4th ed.). Thousand Oaks, CA: Sage Publications.

Pedersen, P. B., & Hernandez, D. (1993). *A student workbook for counseling across cultures*. Honolulu: University of Hawaii Press.

Philipson, I. J. (1993). *On the shoulders of women: The feminization of psychotherapy*. New York: Guilford Press.

Rabinowitz, F. E., & Cochran, S. V. (1994). *Man alive: A primer of men's issues*. Pacific Grove, CA: Brooks/Cole.

Serafica, F. C., Schwebel, A. I., & Russell, R. K. (Eds.). (1990). *Mental health of ethnic minorities*. New York: Praeger.

Silverstein, C. (Ed.). (1991). *Gays, lesbians, and their therapists: Studies in psychotherapy*. New York: W. W. Norton.

Sue, D. W. (1996). *A theory of multicultural counseling and therapy*. Pacific Grove, CA: Brooks/Cole.

Wehrly, B. (1996). *Pathways to multicultural counseling competence: A developmental journey*. Pacific Grove, CA: Brooks/Cole.

Welch, I. D. (1998). *The path of psychotherapy: Matters of the heart*. Pacific Grove, CA: Brooks/Cole.

Young, E. P., & Wiedemann, F. L. (1987). *Female authority: Empowering women through psychotherapy*. New York: Guilford Press.

8

The Process of Change in Counseling and Psychotherapy

*I*f the counselor is able to achieve the attitudinal and atmospheric climate we have described in the preceding chapters and the relationship develops the collaborative, trusting, and challenging nature we described, then what is hoped for, and even expected, is change for the client. Psychotherapy represents a step in the process of change. Sometimes it is torturously slow and tedious for both the client and the counselor. At other times it is dramatic and flows at the pace of white-water rapids.

What follows is our attempt at describing the process of change as we have seen it in our clinical experience. We do not intend to imply that this is the only possible way one could conceptualize the process, and, in fact, it has been described by a number of others in both theoretical and research terms (Beitman, 1987; McConnaughy, DiClemente, Prochaska, & Velicer, 1989; McConnaughy, Prochaska, & Velicer, 1983; Steenbarger, 1992; Strong & Claiborn, 1982; Tracey & Ray, 1984; Welch, 1998).

Admission

Change begins in the recognition that something isn't working in one's life. Combs and Gonzalez (1994) mention that change begins in acceptance. What they are signaling to us is that the process of change for clients begins before they enter psychotherapy. Clients have identi-fied within themselves a need to change. We have labeled that process *admission*. In order to begin the process of change, one has to admit (or accept) that something is so. The word *admit* means "to permit to enter, to let in." It means to concede a fact and nothing more. It does not mean to approve of the fact or to like it or agree with it. The motivation for change lies in discontent and what is being admitted is not that one likes the behavior or life situation but that one has some-thing that needs to be changed. It is an act of intrapersonal honesty that precedes any effective meeting with a counselor. Admission is made to the self. It does not involve other people in any direct sense.

Acknowledgment

108

To some extent, change must involve others. Most of the time in order for change to occur the facts have to be acknowledged to someone else, which is different from admitting to oneself that change is needed. Acknowledgment means recognizing that change is possible. Acknowl-edgment recognizes that one needs help, that others can and want to help, and that in order for them to be of help they have to know what is needed, which means they must be told. Oftentimes a network of already trusted friends and relatives is sufficient to support the changes needed in persons' lives. In such cases, there is little or no need for involving professional helpers. In counseling, the other person is the psychotherapist. But when such a network is insufficient or nonexis-tent, it is the psychotherapist who hears the client's story. Acknowl-edgment is a significant step in the change process and one that we believe is dependent on the counselor attitudes and relationship char-acteristics described in previous chapters. Just as in any process, acknowledgment might be reached in layers, degrees, or stages. Clients often come to counseling with a presenting problem. If the counselor proves to be empathic and respectful and is able to create a collabora-tive and trusting climate, then the presenting problem might give way to more intensely experienced issues, problems, or dilemmas.

Accommodation

Change requires change. This seemingly redundant statement lies at the core of many failed, deeply wished for, but not acted upon life changes. It is not enough to explore and understand. It is necessary to act. Change requires accommodation. Accommodation means the gradual process of giving up old ways and adopting new ones. Yet, as clearly as this change process can be stated and as deeply as it may be understood, the process is often stalled at the point of actual change. We believe that what stalls it here is threat. Psychological defenses are fierce opponents that do not willingly give up entrenched coping styles. If the relationship between counselor and client develops well, then in psychotherapy threat may be reduced, opening the way not only for exploration and understanding but for lasting change.

Accommodation means altering the self to the demands of change. In the collaborative relationship, the external world's demands may be identified, understood, and, to the degree necessary and possible, accommodated. At this point in the change process clients have done all that can be expected of them. They have admitted the need for change, they have acknowledged the facts and areas of change to others, and they have begun the process of accommodating their lives to realistic life demands.

They have, in truth, done all that can reasonably be asked of them. Psychotherapy frequently ends at this point. Clients have clarified and understood issues, explored options, and identified and pursued courses of action. While the psychotherapy may end, the process of change should continue.

Actualization

The word *adapt* implies modifying the surroundings, circumstances, situations, and/or context. One has changed the self, now the world must adapt to the person. Development does not, and should not, stop when psychotherapy ends. People advance. The word *advance* means "to move forward." Years ago, interestingly enough, it meant "to lift up." Tragedy may lead to strength. People do live through, overcome, and even transcend life circumstances—*ad astra per aspera* (to the stars through difficulties). In psychological theory such development is labeled *actualization*.

Summary

Change leads to a process of life involvement and possible fulfillment. This is the hoped for positive outcome of psychotherapy. Counselors who present themselves as empathic, authentic, and respectful, and who hold a belief system that encourages empowerment and change can create therapeutic climates characterized by words such as *collaborative, trusting,* and *challenging.* Clients who come to counseling and experience such a relationship are freed to walk the path of change that makes its way from an initial personal admission of the need to change to a life in which they are more likely to be able to cope on more equal terms.

References and for Further Reading

Almond, B., & Almond, R. (1996). *The therapeutic narrative; Fictional relationships and the process of change.* Westport, CT: Praeger/Greenwood Publishing Group.

Beitman, B. D. (1987). *The structure of individual psychotherapy.* New York: Guilford Press.

Combs, A. W., & Gonzalez, D. M. (1994). *Helping relationships: Basic concepts for the helping professions* (4th ed.). Boston: Allyn & Bacon.

Connor-Greene, P. A. (1993, Fall). The therapeutic context: Preconditions for change in psychotherapy. *Psychotherapy, 30,* 375–382.

Curtis, R. C., & Stricker, G. (Eds.) (1991). *How people change: Inside and outside therapy.* New York: Plenum Press. (Especially look over the chapter by M. R. Goldfried on transtheoretical ingredients in therapeutic change.)

Dryden, W. (1991). *Reason and therapeutic change.* London: Whurr.

Dryden, W., & Trower, P. (Eds.). (1989). *Cognitive psychotherapy: Stasis and change.* London: Springer.

Friedman, S. (Ed.). (1993). *The new language of change: Constructive collaboration in psychotherapy.* New York: Guilford Press.

Greenberg, L. S. (1993). Emotion and change processes in psychotherapy. In M. Lewis & J. M. Haviland (Eds.), (*Handbook of Emotions*) (pp. 499–508). New York: Guilford Press.

Greenberg, L. S., Rice, L. N., & Elliott, R. K. (1996). *Facilitating emotional change: The moment-by-moment process.* New York: Guilford Press.

Greenberg, L. S., & Safran, J. D. (1987). *Emotion in psychotherapy: Affect, cognition, and the process of change.* New York: Guilford Press.

Greenberg, L. S., & Safran, J. D. (1990). Emotional change processes in psychotherapy. In R. Plutchik & H. Kellerman (Eds.), *Emotion: Theory, research, and experience: Vol. 5. Emotion, psychopathology, and psychotherapy.* San Diego, CA: Academic Press.

Hanna, F. J., & Ritchie, M. H. (1995, April). Seeking the active ingredients of psychotherapeutic change: Within and outside the context of therapy. *Professional Psychology: Research and Practice, 26,* 176–183.

Johnson, D. R. (1991). The theory and technique of transformations in drama therapy. *The Arts in Psychotherapy, 18,* 285–300.

Kanfer, F. H., & Schefft, B. K. (1988). *Guiding the process of therapeutic change.* Champaign, IL: Research Press.

Mahoney, M. J. (1991). *Human change processes: The scientific foundations of psychotherapy.* New York: Basic Books.

McConnaughy, E. A., DiClemente, C. C., Prochaska, J. O., & Velicer, W. F. (1989). Stages of change in psychotherapy: A follow-up report. *Psychotherapy, 26,* 494–503.

McConnaughy, E. A., Prochaska, J. O., & Velicer, W. F. (1983). Stages of change in psychotherapy: Measurement and sample profiles. *Psychotherapy: Theory, Research, and Practice, 20,* 368–375.

Meth, R. L., Pasick, R. S., Gordon, B., & Allen, J. (1990). *Men in therapy: The challenge of change.* New York: Guilford Press.

Mishara, A. L. (1995, Spring). Narrative and psychotherapy: The phenomenology of healing. *American Journal of Psychotherapy, 49,* 180–195.

Safran, J. D. (Ed). (1991). *Emotion, psychotherapy, and change.* New York: Guilford Press.

Shainberg, D. (1993). *Healing in psychotherapy: The path and process of inner change* (2nd ed.). Langhorne, PA: Gordon and Breach Science Publishers.

Siegfried, J. (Ed.). (1995). *Therapeutic and everyday discourse as behavior change: Towards a micro-analysis in psychotherapy process research.* Norwood, NJ: Ablex.

Steenbarger, B. N. (1992). Toward science-practice integration in brief counseling and therapy. *The Counseling Psychologist, 20,* 403–450.

Strong, S. R., & Claiborn, C. D. (1982). *Change through integration.* New York: Wiley.

Suler, J. R. (1991, March). The t'ai chi images: A Taoist model of psychotherapeutic change. *Psychologia: An International Journal of Psychology in the Orient, 34,* 18–27.

Tracey, T. J., & Ray, B. P. (1984). The stages of successful time-limited counseling: An interactional examination. *Journal of Counseling Psychology, 31,* 13–27.

Waters, D. B., Lawrence, E. C. (1993). *Competence, courage, and change: An approach to family therapy.* New York: W. W. Norton.

Welch, I. D. (1998). *The path of psychotherapy: Matters of the heart.* Pacific Grove, CA: Brooks/Cole.

Zastrow, C. (1988, Spring). What really causes psychotherapy change? *Journal of Independent Social Work, 23,* 5–16.

111

9

The Ethics of Counseling and Psychotherapy

*E*thical guidelines exist for the practice of counseling and psychotherapy. All the major organizations governing the helping professions—the American Psychological Association (APA) (1992), the American Counseling Association (ACA) (1995), the American Association for Marriage and Family Therapy (AAMFT) (1991), the Association for Specialists in Group Work (ASGW) (1989), and the National Association of Social Workers (NASW) (1996)—have a formal set of guidelines that their professional members are expected to not only be familiar with but to understand in depth and to make every attempt to follow when conducting their professional behavior.

Ethical guidelines have evolved for a number of reasons. We are increasingly accountable for our professional conduct to consumers, to our professional organizations, to our licensure and grievance boards, and, if the case involves legal matters, to the court system. The helping professions exist for the promotion of human welfare and counselors and psychotherapists should always conduct themselves with that as an overriding principle.

Protection for the Consumer

Ethical guidelines exist for the protection of the consumer. Such guidelines make it more likely that a client will receive professional and effective mental health services. Practitioners have a responsibility to inform clients of their rights and responsibilities.

Protection for the Counselor

Ethical guidelines provide information and direction to counselors about a number of issues that are sometimes unclear or confusing. Theoretically, by following the guidelines the therapist is much less likely to be sued in today's litigious society or is at least less at risk for losing a lawsuit. And indeed, malpractice lawsuits are a very real part of the counseling profession today (Austin, Moline, & Williams, 1990). Also, following such guidelines makes for a more professional form of treatment and/or practice. Although the primary purpose of ethical guidelines is to protect the consumer, such guidelines are also intended to educate practitioners on how to conduct themselves in their work.

Disclosure Statement

Good and ethical practice dictates that counselors and psychotherapists provide a disclosure statement to clients that spells out key information, such as (1) the limits of confidentiality, (2) the inappropriateness of sexual contact between client and therapist, (3) the counselor's theoretical orientation or methods of practice, (4) client rights and responsibilities, and (5) fees and billing practices. This information needs to be in writing and needs to be discussed with the client, after which both client and therapist should sign the document as proof that the information was provided and discussed. Some agencies and practitioners provide this information to clients in the waiting room and only discuss it if the client has any questions. We recommend taking the time to discuss the disclosure statement with the client. We do not see this activity merely as business to be taken care of before getting started. It is an important part of the process not only because it provides the necessary information to the client, but because it reveals the integrity of one's practice and contributes to a trusting relationship.

Confidentiality

Counselors and psychotherapists are obligated both ethically and legally to protect the confidentiality of their clients. From the time the therapist and client begin meeting, the therapist is required to let the client know that everything discussed will be held in the strictest of confidence. Any exceptions to this rule should be disclosed to the client before any significant information is exchanged. If the counselor will be discussing the case with a supervisor, the client needs to know that. When a client reveals information that requires the counselor to breach confidentiality before the client knows the parameters, the situation becomes extremely awkward and places the counselor at risk for being accused of unethical behavior. Typical exceptions to confidentiality are:

1. The client is a danger to self or others. If the client is in imminent danger of committing suicide, for example, the counselor is compelled both legally and ethically to take action to protect the client from himself or herself. The same is true if it is apparent that the client is intending to hurt someone else. The counselor either must notify the proper authorities or make an attempt to inform those in danger of the threat. Sometimes issues around danger to self or others are not clear cut. For example, it is not that unusual for clients to need to talk about thoughts of suicide without having to worry that confidentiality will be breached. That is an important part of counseling. A key word here is *imminent*. If, in the counselor's judgment, the client or someone else is in imminent danger or if there is good reason to believe that danger exists, then action must be taken. As stipulated by the ethical guidelines, clients in such cases need to be informed that confidentiality must be breached and must be given clarification as to why such action

115

is necessary. Counselors continually work to maintain a strong therapeutic alliance with their clients and occasions when confidentiality must be broken create a major challenge to that alliance. With the counselor's skillful handling of this delicate matter, it is possible to keep the working relationship intact. If, however, the ethical need to breach confidentiality is poorly conducted, then the therapeutic relationship is likely to be damaged beyond repair.

The matter of being a danger to others has become more complicated in recent years with the emergence of HIV as a potentially life-threatening disease. The ACA, in its 1995 revisions of the *Code of Ethics and Standards of Practice*, justifies breaking confidentiality if an identifiable third party is at risk for contracting a disease through contact with the client. Of course, such action should only be taken if the counselor is certain that the client has not informed or is unwilling to inform the person at risk of the danger.

2. The therapist discovers the existence of child abuse (sexual or physical). In this case the abuse needs to be reported. This scenario is often one of the most uncomfortable for counselors to face. If the client is a child who reveals to the counselor that he or she is being or has been abused, the counselor needs to report the abuse, even though the client may not want it reported. Sometimes the client only wants to talk with a counselor and does not intend for the information to leave the room. Once the child knows that a report is going to be made, he or she can become quite frightened about what is going to happen. He or she may fear getting into big trouble. The counselor needs to be sensitive to the child's feelings and should help provide some security.

From a therapeutic standpoint, reporting an abuse case to the authorities severely challenges the working relationship. Depending on the nature of the abuse, the child may be removed from the home or a parent may be jailed. Again, part of developing your skills as a therapist is learning to preserve the relationship even though you had to do something that may result in a major intervention for the family. As painful as this whole process may be, the child must be protected. At the same time, you must often keep working with the person or family.

Usually, the therapist informs the client that confidentiality will be broken and reminds him or her of the reasons why. Some therapists call the authorities with the client present so that he or she is involved in each step of the process. The client may be angry, frustrated, or embarrassed, all of which are understandable feelings in such circumstances.

3. The client is gravely disabled. This may include a psychological state like psychosis. In such a condition the client is unable to protect or care for himself or herself and may need the counselor to see that he or she is safeguarded by notifying family members or urging hospitalization.

Hallway Conversation and Confidentiality

Make certain that any discussions about a case with a supervisor or colleague take place in a private location such as an office with a closed door. If a waiting area at a clinic is within earshot, reassure clients that cases are never discussed where someone else might hear. Sometimes when passing a colleague in the hallway it is tempting to consult regarding a particular case, yet one never knows who is around the corner and may overhear such conversations. Clients' thoughts, feelings, actions, and lives in general are very private business. Counselors must respect the enormity of the responsibility that goes with being taken into another's confidence and must develop habits that preserve such information as private.

Confidentiality of Minor Clients

Typically, a minor's parents hold the privilege of confidentiality. In other words, they have a right to know what is discussed between child and counselor. In the case of divorced or separated parents, the custodial parent holds the privilege of confidentiality. Therapists cannot disclose information to a noncustodial parent without permission of the custodial parent. Obviously, having to break the confidentiality of therapeutic work with a child can be disastrous to the success of the counseling process. Learning to work with parents in a way that keeps them informed of the nature of their child's work and progress and at the same time provides the child with some sense that he or she can speak with the counselor privately is an important skill. Many parents understand the need for a child's privacy and are willing to work with the therapist without having to have verbatim descriptions of what was said. Rather, presenting themes of the child's clinical work and ways the parents can help in the child's progress often result in a successful therapist-parent relationship for the welfare of the child. The bottom line, however, is that if parents demand to know more about the therapy, it is their right to do so.

Files

Counselors have an obligation to keep professional files (e.g., intake, progress notes, supervision notes) in a secure location. Having files in a briefcase in a car or even in a cabinet with no lock runs the risk of having the client's confidentiality violated. Also, some experts recommend that therapists write their case notes such that if the client were to read them, he or she would not be surprised or offended. Part of the ethical treatment of human beings is learning to keep notes that are respectful of clients' humanity rather than writing as if they are disembodied cases.

Social Settings and Confidentiality

At some point, you will have the awkward experience of bumping into a client on the street or in a social setting. If other people are around, it is important that you not say hello to the client first. Doing so puts the client in the uncomfortable position of being asked by his or her companions as to your identity and could be a potential breach of confidentiality. The client may or may not want anyone else to know that he or she is in therapy. If the client says hello first, the polite thing to do, of course, is to return the hello and proceed on your way. During the next session, it may be important to discuss any awkward feelings that arose during the encounter to make sure that the client understands your actions and to have a way of mutually managing any such future encounters. If the client is alone and begins a conversation, we recommend keeping it brief and avoiding any clinical work in such an uncontrolled setting. Keep such work in the therapy room. On the other end of the spectrum, one of us was spotted by a client at a restaurant. The client gleefully said hello from across the room and said in a voice loud enough for many to hear, "That's my psychologist!" The client was obviously not uncomfortable with other people knowing that he was in therapy, and it was his privilege to disclose or not disclose that information.

Dual Relationships

Ethical guidelines note the import of avoiding dual relationships that might compromise one's ability to maintain objectivity. The most obvious and perhaps most troubling form of a dual relationship is a sexual and/or romantic relationship between a counselor and a client. Even though the impropriety of this situation should be absolutely clear, a certain percentage of therapists have engaged in sexual and/or romantic relationships with their clients. Some research estimates that 10% of therapists have done so. Even if the therapeutic relationship has ended, starting a personal relationship with a former client is fraught with difficulties and is highly frowned upon by professional organizations. Some states have a guideline that the therapeutic relationship must have ended at least six months prior to the beginning of a personal relationship. Other states have a longer time requirement. Florida has passed a law specifying that therapists and clients will maintain therapist-client status in perpetuity, meaning that any romantic relationship between therapist and client would be a felonious violation of state law.

How and why would professional helpers engage in such relationships when the ethical guidelines explicitly describe such relationships as a violation of the ethics code? In the course of working with clients, therapists will meet many wonderful people. In good therapy, the quality of the communication can be rewarding and appealing; however, that is no reason to form a personal relationship with a client. Clients were not seeking a dating service when they called a mental health professional for assistance. In a number of states such relationships are illegal and carry stiff criminal sanctions for such behavior.

Sometimes clients want to form a friendship with the counselor once the therapy has ended. Even if you were to wait six months before participating in such a relationship, there are many reasons to avoid this. If you form a relationship after ending a therapeutic one, you can never be that person's therapist again. And, remember, many clients have a therapist that they go to see periodically for years. Also, having a new relationship with new experiences can result in undoing much of your work with the client; with new experiences between the former therapist and former client, the client may reinterpret some of the therapeutic work. One other problem is that such relationships are inherently inequitable. The client has revealed secrets and vulnerabilities to the therapist while the therapist was in the role of expert in handling this material. The likelihood of being able to create a relationship in which the former therapist does not wield more power than the former client is slim at best.

Another odd form of dual relationships exists when a therapist and client trade services for payment. One supervisee said he could not see any problem with trading services. He was raised by a psychologist who engaged in this practice all the time. His father provided therapy for the tax accountant and the tax accountant did his father's taxes. Another case involved a therapist who had a client come to her home to do her gardening because the client did not have enough money to pay her bill. Avoiding dual relationships is a simpler process in bigger cities. If a friend asks to see you for therapy, you can easily provide a list of referrals and an explanation of the awkwardness and inappropriateness of beginning a therapeutic relationship. In a small town, though, things are not so simple. For example, we know of one small town in which the mental health center consisted of one therapist. Most people in this town knew each other. Nearly every person who needed help from the therapist knew him in some capacity. There was no one else to whom he could refer them. The therapist had to learn to minimize dual relationships to the extent that it was possible, but in some cases it simply was not feasible.

Abandonment

Abandonment in ethical terms refers to a variety of behaviors. For example, if a counselor refers a client to someone else with no explanation for doing so, that constitutes a form of abandonment. The client should be told the reason, whether it is because the client needs to see someone with more experience with the particular presenting problem or because the counselor feels the clinical work is not progressing. Whatever the case, the client needs to be given some information. Consider what an odd experience it would be to be referred to another counselor with no real explanation. You would be forced to speculate, which can be an uncomfortable and even painful process.

When taking vacations, counselors need to assess their clients' needs and make certain adequate coverage is provided by another therapist or agency. Going on vacation and leaving clients with no contingency plan is a form of abandonment and is unethical.

Another potential form of abandonment involves terminating the counseling relationship. This needs to be done with forethought and with the welfare of the client in mind. The counselor needs to be clear that therapy is not being ended prematurely and that any needed referrals will be provided to the client. Otherwise, the counselor may be guilty of abandoning his or her client.

Bias

Counselors are expected to refer a potential client if they hold a clear bias against him or her. For example, if the therapist has strong negative feelings about homosexuality, such clients should be referred elsewhere so that they have a chance for quality, objective counseling. It would be unethical for a therapist to harbor a strong prejudice against a client, yet continue to provide counseling services to him or her.

Practicing Outside Your Knowledge Base

Practicing outside your knowledge base is unethical. For example, it is inappropriate for a therapist to treat a client with a drug addiction when he or she has no training in addictions. Good and ethical practice would require referring this client to someone with proper training. If you have some training but are still learning, it is important to seek supervision to assist with the case and to further your training by doing so. This enables you to maintain a high level of treatment for the client while continuing to develop your skill level.

Test Interpretation

The guidelines spell out the need for knowing the impact test results can have on a client's life. Counselors need to recognize the client's right to know the test results and to know the basis for any conclusions that are drawn. Skillfully recognizing the limitations of testing is an ethical obligation.

Fees

You need to clearly spell out fees and billing practices for your clientele. If the time should come when a client can no longer afford your services, do not just end the therapy. Refer that person to another therapist who can accommodate his or her financial situation. Like any consumer, clients need to know specific information about fees to avoid surprises and confusion.

Insurance Companies

Counselors and psychotherapists commonly deal with insurance companies. Clients rely on counselors to know how to manage the necessary paperwork and how to bill in an ethical manner. Insurance fraud, even if done accidentally, is not conducive to a healthy counseling relationship nor to the survival of the counselor's practice.

Suggestions

The guidelines seem clear enough, yet somehow a certain percentage of therapists find themselves violating their code of ethics. Read the ethical guidelines spelled out by the professional organization to which you belong. Also, become familiar with the mental health laws of your state. Many states require a legal and ethical test as a part of the licensure process.

Some suggestions to assist in maintaining an ethical practice follow.

Emotional Considerations

1. Make certain that your primary needs are not being met through relationships with clients. In other words, your life outside of your work needs to be rich. For example, if your emotional needs for closeness are not being met in your life outside of counseling, you increase the risk of involving yourself in unethical behavior.

2. Make it part of your ethics that your needs for affection, love, sex, and intimacy will not be met through your work as a therapist. Make it clear to yourself that it is not even an option to consider your therapeutic relationships as potential sources for these needs. This is just not a domain in which to engage people in sexual or romantic relationships.

3. In times of unusual stress when your vulnerabilities may be heightened—such as marital strain, illness or death in the family, or financial problems—seek supervision or some source of support to avoid making poor or questionable decisions.

4. Become aware of your countertransferences through the course of your training and in your ongoing practice. These can have a powerful influence on your behavior. Knowing yourself in this regard can help avoid being seduced by your own needs.

Practical Suggestions

1. Discuss your cases and practice in general with your supervisor.

2. Offer at least two or three resources when providing referrals. Doing so gives the client some actual choices and also avoids the appearance of any impropriety of feeding clients to colleagues in some kind of "kickback" scheme.

3. Keep up to date and professionally written case notes. Make sure diagnosis and treatment planning are logical and supported and are working in conjunction with each other.

4. Take a course in legal and ethical issues even if your training program does not require it.

5. Attend professional workshops on legal and ethical questions because the guidelines are periodically revised and new legal decisions that affect the practice of counseling are rendered each year.

6. Read the journals and publications of your primary professional organization. There you will find some of the latest information regarding legal and ethical matters.

7. Some states permit the practice of unlicensed psychotherapists. If your state does have licensure, become licensed. By doing so, you are much more likely to receive the necessary training, information, and ongoing professional development about legal and ethical considerations.

Summary

This chapter discussed some of the more common ethical considerations. The actual ethical guidelines deal with a number of other important scenarios such as advertising one's credentials and practice and doing research both with humans and animals. In counseling and psychotherapy, one is entrusted with the most precious of things—people and their feelings, meanings, and personal information. We suggest that even if formal ethical guidelines did not exist, we would hope that counselors and psychotherapists would know what constitutes integrity and ethical behavior and that they would strive to conduct themselves accordingly. To borrow a concept from Don Juan's teachings to Carlos

Casteneda, working to be *impeccable* is perhaps a fitting notion for people in the helping professions.

References and for Further Reading

American Association for Marriage and Family Therapy. (1991). *Code of ethics.* Washington, DC: Author.

American Counseling Association. (1995). *Code of ethics and standards of practice.* Alexandria, VA: Author.

American Psychological Association. (1992). Ethical principles of psychologists and code of conduct. *American Psychologist, 47,* 1597–1611.

American Psychological Association. (1993). Guidelines for providers of psychological services to ethnic, linguistic and culturally diverse populations. *American Psychologist, 48,* 45–48.

Association for Specialists in Group Work. (1989). *Ethical guidelines for group counselors.* Alexandria, VA: American Counseling Association.

Austin, K. M., Moline, M. E., & Williams, G. T. (1990). *Confronting malpractice: Legal and ethical dilemmas in psychotherapy.* Newbury Park, NJ: Sage Publications.

Childs, E. K. (1990). Therapy, feminist ethics, and the community of color with particular emphasis on the treatment of Black women. In H. Lerman & N. Porter (Eds.), *Feminist ethics in psychotherapy.* New York: Springer.

Corey, G., Corey, M., & Callanan, P. (1993). *Issues and ethics in the helping professions* (4th ed.). Pacific Grove, CA: Brooks/Cole.

Koocher, G. P., & Keith-Spiegel, P. C. (1990). *Children, ethics, and the law: Professional issues and cases.* Lincoln: University of Nebraska Press.

Lakin, M. (1991). *Coping with ethical dilemmas in psychotherapy.* New York: Pergamon Press.

Lerman, H., & Porter, N. (Eds.). (1990). *Feminist ethics in psychotherapy.* New York: Springer.

National Association of Social Workers. (1996). *Code of ethics.* Washington, DC: Author.

Pope, K. S., Sonne, J. L., & Holroyd, J. (1993). *Sexual feelings in psychotherapy: Explorations for therapists and therapists-in-training.* Washington, DC: American Psychological Association.

Pope, K. S., & Vasquez, M. J. T. (1991). *Ethics in psychotherapy and counseling: A practical guide for psychologists.* San Francisco: Jossey-Bass.

Schoener, G. R., Milgrom, J. H., Gonsiork, J. C., Luepker, E. T., & Conroe, R. M. (1990). *Psychotherapists' sexual involvement with clients: Intervention and prevention.* Minneapolis, MN: Walk-in Counseling Center.

Strean, H. S. (1993). *Therapists who have sex with their patients: Treatment and recovery.* New York: Brunner/Mazel.

Swenson, L. C. (1997). *Psychology and law for the helping professions* (2nd ed.). Pacific Grove, CA: Brooks/Cole.

Thompson, A. (1990). *Guide to ethical practice in psychotherapy.* New York: Wiley.

Walker, L. E. A. (1990). *Feminist ethics with victims of violence.* New York: Springer.

125

Section Three

The Skill of Counseling
and Psychotherapy

*R*eaders may have noticed that it has taken a while for a concrete discussion of skills to appear in this volume. This is not by chance. We believe that there is much preparation to be done before anyone should consider entering a room to help a client. Understanding the essence and foundation of psychotherapy is crucial to using any skills knowledgeably. It seems natural enough to want to know what to do. However, we hope that by this point readers have come to realize that becoming a successful psychotherapist is also a matter of considering how to be. This section stresses the importance of listening, a skill that comes to most of us usually only after repeated and diligent efforts to become a good listener. So many events or factors may interfere with our ability to listen and because listening is so important to the process of helping, we have devoted an entire chapter to that skill. Furthermore, because most traditional forms of psychotherapy depend on language, we have provided some ideas and methods for developing language skills relevant to psychotherapy. It is important for someone who decides to pursue training as a psychotherapist to have a vocabulary consistent with that choice. The possibilities for effective practice for someone who wanted to become an auto mechanic but only had one wrench and one screwdriver are limited. Similarly, a therapist with an inadequate affective vocabulary is also limited. It is not enough to know just a few words like *mad*, *sad*, *glad*, and *confused*. It is important to have a rich vocabulary to connect more fully with your clients' experiences. Also, because important communication occurs both verbally and nonverbally, we provide a look at nonverbal understanding and responding. We also offer a careful look at facilitative and nonfacilitative therapist behaviors. A description for each behavior is provided, along with the rationale for it being helpful or not helpful. Finally, we discuss some of the techniques utilized by psychotherapists along with guidelines for the use of such techniques.

10

Listening:
The Fundamental Skill

here is a difference between hearing and listening. Hearing is a matter of sensation. Listening involves purpose and perception. Some have accused counselors of manipulating and imposing values because of the topics that emerge in counseling sessions. Some parents have objected to school counseling programs, seeking to restrict the delicate subjects with which counselors and students sometimes deal.

How should counselors defend themselves against charges of directing, manipulating, and imposing values? How can counselors explain how the choice of topics or issues emerges in psychotherapy? How, out of the many things that clients might say, do psychotherapists select those topics and issues that are most important to clients? Some might suggest that the easiest method would be to ask clients and to act on what they say. This suggestion begs two questions. The first is the commonly understood phenomenon of the presenting problem—an initial, genuine concern of low vulnerability to test whether the counselor is trustworthy. The second is the recognition that clients often come to psychotherapy with only a vague, undifferentiated sense of personal discomfort. If asked directly the nature of the problem, a client might well reply, "I don't know. I'm not sure." In spite of such statements, it would be premature and improper to provide psychotherapy for "mental confusion."

Listening is a matter of purpose. The purpose is to clarify, understand, and move toward effective action. In the situation of "metal confusion," exploration and clarification are needed as a counselor and client move toward understanding and action. What then does a counselor listen for? What are the tools of exploration and clarification?

Here is a four-part listening model that teaches how to identify content and discern meaning. The first component of listening is style. Style involves the degree of attention given the speaker. The second component involves content identification. It is the attentive "listening for" particular information. The third element in effective listening is problem identification. This addresses the concern that what is being talked over in psychotherapy actually comes from clients and is not imposed by the psychotherapist. The last aspect of the listening model is the degree of emotional involvement. It provides a system for recognizing how emotionally significant an identified problem is for clients.

Style

Consider what goes on at a dinner party or in restaurant conversation. People talk and listen to one another, but the level of attention may be cursory, intermittent, or unconcerned. This might be referred to as polite listening. The listener might give the appearance of listening and might have some vague idea of what is being said but has scant understanding of its details or of its importance. A joke of polite listening might be the daily greeting we give each other without actually listening to what we say. Two people meet at the office and the first one greets the other, "Mornin', how ya doin'?" The second replies, "Oh, okay, I guess." The first says, "Okay. Good to hear it. Have a nice day." The intent in the greeting was not actually to find out how the other person is coping in life but just to make polite conversation. Any response is usually lost in the expectation that the other party will respond in kind. If they do not, polite listening will frequently fail to detect it.

The degree of attention in polite listening is most often self-serving. There are two categories of polite listening—genuine and false. In genuine polite listening the listener may be sincerely interested in what the speaker has to say. The expected outcome is that the listener will acquire information, insight, or some other tangible gain from his or her efforts. False polite listening gives the appearance of attending while the intent may be social, financial, political, or sexual gain. False polite listening is what may be observed in any singles bar in America.

Compassionate listening changes the focus. Rather than being self-serving, the purpose of compassionate listening is other serving. The purpose is to understand, so it follows that the degree of attention is high and active. In compassionate listening the listener is trying to understand both content and meaning and is attending not only to words but to inflection, tone, and the unspoken as well as the spoken word. The energy of the listener is focused not on himself or herself but on the speaker. Posture, eye contact, and demeanor are inviting and alert. As you can well imagine, the manner of responding is different in polite and compassionate listening. In the chapter on responding (Chapter 11), these differences are discussed in detail. The most important difference between polite and compassionate listening is the focus of attention. In polite listening, the focus is on the listener. The goal is self-serving and attention is driven by expected gain. In compassionate listening, the focus is on the speaker and is driven by an expectation of understanding and positive service.

Content Identification

People come to psychotherapy with a story to tell. Often their stories are complex, rambling, wandering, and confused. Sometimes counselors befuddled by clients' stories resort to questioning to sort through the maze of details. In Chapter 13, the perils of question asking are explored in more detail, but for now let it suffice to say that a better strategy for understanding is purposeful listening and empathic responding. Listening on purpose for specific content assists the listener in bringing order to apparent chaos.

There are two important principles in purposeful listening. First, people do not say what they say in the way they say it by accident. Their words, tone, inflection, rate, and flow all carry meaning. Second, if psychotherapists know what they are listening for, then the confused, wandering stories of clients can be better understood and clarified even for the storytellers. What should guide our listening at the content level?

The 5WH Principle

Journalists have long advised us as to what an effective news story should contain. The reader should know quickly who the principal actors are, where the action took place, when the drama occurred, what happened, why things happened as they did, and how they happened. These are the guidelines for content identification, also known as 5WH. Listening on purpose can bring order out of seeming chaos and clarity from confusion. Such guided listening helps the counselor better organize information into understandable chunks. We sometimes even advise counselors to take notes for themselves as clients tell their stories and to jot down who, what, when, where, why, and how as it emerges from clients or is elicited by therapists. Take a moment to read Activity 10.1 and identify the 5WH in this client's story. As you read through this case, take note of the information that is provided and, perhaps, what is missing. It is important for understanding to know what you don't know as well as what you do. The missing information can then be elicited.

Activity 10.1
Joan Doly, 23, Caucasian.
Education: HSG (High School Graduate)
+ 1 semester of college.
Occupation: Bank Teller.

CLIENT: Well, I'm, you know, having trouble . . . in dating and . . . well, not dating . . . but with men. And, I came from a good . . . middle-class, I guess . . . home and my parents brought me up properly, you know? . . . Anyway, lately I have been acting just the opposite of the way I was brought up. You know, not even living by my own values.

Well, I work at a bank and dress like a businesswoman, you know. Sensible dress and attractive but not sexy or anything. Well, I don't know why but on the weekends I dress entirely different. Really wild and, low cut, you know. . . .

My mother, the nun, would just freak, you know. Well, not only that but I go to these clubs or bars, you know, that aren't the best . . . well, like biker bars. And I get picked up . . . and then go to a motel or somewhere, sometimes even in the parking lot, you know, and have sex. Well, I do things and act like somebody I'm not. I am really ashamed . . . really humiliated, it's terrible . . . of myself afterward but then the next week I do the same thing again. What do you think is going on with me? I know my Mom and Dad would be so hurt if they knew what I was doing. It's almost like I'm throwing it in their faces.

It's not that I don't enjoy it. It's afterward that I'm ashamed. Well, and about enjoying it, you know. I don't seem to like sex when it is regular. Like I see guys at work . . . dressed up . . . you know, good-looking but I just don't seem attracted to them.

I can't imagine what would happen if people at work saw me. And my parents would go crazy. I don't really know, you know, . . . if they would even recognize me. (Cries.) I'm really afraid.

Answer the Following Questions.

Who (Who plays a part in this story?): _____

What (What is happening?): _____

When (When does it happen?): _____

Where (Where is the scene?): _____

Why (Why does this behavior happen?): _____

How (How does this behavior unfold?): _____

As you seek to answer these questions, consider what other information you would want to have. What do you know? What is missing? This story isn't particularly confusing. It is coherent but there is a good bit missing. Answering the 5WH questions should give you an idea of what more you need in order to proceed further with this client. You might give some thought to understanding this story without any guidelines for listening. It isn't so much that psychotherapists would ask these questions directly, although it wouldn't do any great harm. It is just that as clients tell their stories order and clarity can be gained from listening for this content information. As you will see later in this text, it is probably better to make a statement of understanding or clarification than to ask a question because of the undesirable effects of probing questions. Nevertheless, clarifying is helpful for both the therapist and the client.

Problem Identification

When clients tell their stories they may talk about a number of different things going on in their lives. They may make a list without any real understanding themselves of what is central and what is peripheral. It is not uncommon for clients to enter psychotherapy without a clear knowledge of what is troubling them. Also, what clients sometimes identify as problems are symptoms or solutions used to deal with unclarified problems or issues in their lives. For example, clients will consider their depression as *the* problem without recognizing that some aspect of their lives is the source of the depression.

Whether or not clients are fully aware of the problems they bring to therapy, listening for frequency and intensity can be helpful in problem identification. The idea that things slip out is, of course, as old as personality theory. The importance of these two principles of listening is more compelling than theory alone.

Theory and Practicality

These principles of listening have the advantage of being practical and theoretically sound. It seems reasonable that forces of discontent, even at low levels of awareness, would invade speech. Both theory and experience support the notion that clients are not always aware of the importance of what they say. Theoretically, defenses are not always successful and information is revealed. Practically, people talk about what is important to them.

Logic and Emotion

This issue of importance is a matter of both logic (cognitive domain) and of the emotions (affective domain). It seems reasonable that people would talk about what is important to them (logic), but again experience teaches that often people have trouble talking about what is important to them (e.g., because of defenses). If clients have difficulty talking about their troubles, it follows that they must be in some sort of conflict because they have come for psychotherapy. They want to talk but they feel blocked. In their internal struggle things slip out.

Levels of Awareness

People are not always fully aware of their own motivations. But, if they are, then it makes sense that they would be able to talk about their own awareness with their psychotherapist. If they are not fully aware, whether blocked by defenses or simply confused, then in their struggle to communicate their internal discomfort they might ramble and wander around and through the conflict. It follows that the areas they touch upon in even a vague way can be put in order of importance because of the frequency with which they are visited and the intensity with which they are expressed.

Whether considering theory or practicality, logic or emotions, or awareness or vagueness, frequency and intensity are trustworthy guides to identifying troublesome areas for the people who come to see us. Clients reveal their concerns by repetitiveness and emotional force. Go back to Activity 10.1. I don't know what you would conclude from a simple reading of this case. Read it now with the principle of frequency in mind. What is the issue? A first reading might lead us to believe that the client's sexual acting out is the problem. The principle

135

of frequency, however, suggests that may not be the case. It might well be a problem of her interpersonal relationship with her parents. What do you think?

While intensity is more difficult to read in this case, I invite you make a judgment, based on the principle of intensity, about which parent is more central to this client's concerns. Using intensity is it possible to identify the parent with whom she is having more issues? As a clue, look at the descriptions she provides of each parent. . . . Ah, interesting isn't it?!

Emotional Involvement

There are four verbal clues to emotional involvement. We use the mnemonic DAMS to help us remember the four elements—drama, affect, metaphor, and symbol. Whenever clients speak with drama, pay special attention. Whenever clients respond emotionally, listen intently. Whenever clients use metaphors, they have moved from the bland to the notable—use the metaphor. Whenever clients use symbolic language, it is a clue to their underlying feelings and motivations—work on solving the riddle.

Let's look at some of the language used in Activity 10.1. Look at the phrase, "My mother, the nun. . . ." Does that strike you as dramatic? It does us. It makes us wonder. That is the role of listening to the dramatic in speech. What messages are clients trying to communicate when they use dramatic language? What pressures create the need for more than ordinary language? I don't know. But such words signal to us that we need to explore that language and meaning with the client.

The client in Activity 10.1 used "ashamed," "humiliated," and "terrible" to describe her feelings about her behavior. These are not light words. They are powerful and revealing and call for understanding. They mean dishonored, disgraced, and appalled. What happened in this client story that moved her from saying she was "having trouble" to shame and humiliation? This potent language discloses the emotional depth of the issue for the client and should not be ignored or passed over.

The client in this case said, "throwing it in their faces." This is a metaphor. What are the ordinary, and even literal, meanings we would give to this phrase? What does "it" mean? Is she throwing her shame in their faces? Does she mean to deface her parents? These are all questions that come from the use of metaphor. When clients use metaphors, we invite you to enter their metaphors with them and explore them to see what meanings they reveal. You will be surprised and encouraged by what you find. One last thought to consider. In this particular metaphor, we will leave to you the task of pondering the similarity of the words *faces* and *feces*.

In discussing symbols, we want to introduce some caution about becoming overly interpretative. Symbols invite exploration more than they invite explanation. Explaining symbols to clients does approach the problem of imposition. There may well be universal symbols; we are uncertain about this. We do know that there are personal symbols and that clients may use a symbol in ways we may not imagine. A skull and crossbones may represent death to many, but it might represent power to others. White may mean purity to most, but it can equally be seen as bland and uninteresting to others. Exercise some caution in exploring symbols. Seek to solve the puzzle of symbolic language in the same spirit that you approach a puzzle—you might know that something is there, but until the pieces are assembled, you cannot clearly know what it is. In the case presented in Activity 10.1, is it possible to view the client's sexual behavior as symbolic? Further, of the many options available for acting out (for "throwing it in their faces"), what led to the selection of sexually acting out? These are questions that can be explored in therapy. Clients speak symbolically. Sometimes they know the meaning of their symbols and sometimes they do not.

Let us give you two examples of symbolic speaking in therapy. Sometimes, as in these cases, symbolic language appears in the description of dreams. The first example is a 14-year-old girl who talked about two dreams she had. In the first dream she reported putting her panties into the microwave oven. Is this a signal of sexual abuse or could it be a dream about budding sexuality (as in panties

137

heating up)? In the second, she had a dream about buying Barbie dolls. Is this a dream about sexuality (of wanting a baby) or a symbolic desire to return to some earlier time in childhood (wanting to be a baby)? These are important questions and the direction of the therapy may well depend upon their answers.

Another client, a young man in his twenties, dreamt of racing tricycles in a race for money and becoming mired down in mud. Racer 1 is trying desperately to finish the race but Racer 2 approaches him and says, "We can quit now and not finish the race." Racer 1 replies, "No, I want to finish because it wouldn't be a real race if I don't finish." We know that dream interpretation is a slippery enterprise and that there are many ways to view this dream. In the exchange between the client and the therapist what emerged was a deeply felt concern of personal inadequacy in relationships. Racer 1 represented his idealism and Racer 2 his practicality. Tricycles represent old or inadequate technology. He viewed himself as inadequate to the tasks of relationships and needed new skills. Whether this is the "true" meaning of this dream, we do not know. We do know that for this client it was the meaning that he found revealing. It set the direction for the therapy and for a satisfying outcome. That is the role symbols can play in psychotherapy.

Summary

This chapter has provided a model for listening—a way of increasing our sensitivity to the significant disclosures clients make in therapy and of separating the serious from the inconsequential or less important. This model teaches that compassionate listening is focused on the speaker and on the expectation of service, which is supportive and helpful. Listening for specific content (who, what, when, where, why, and how), listening for frequency and intensity, and listening for drama, affect, metaphor, and symbol are positive skills that enhance, embolden, and extend psychotherapy. Listening in psychotherapy is not a passive process. It is active, purposeful, and directed toward understanding, and ultimately it is an active process of helping clients cope more effectively with the issues, problems, and dilemmas of their lives.

References and for Further Reading

Chessick, R. D. (1989). *The technique and practice of listening in intensive psychotherapy*. Northvale, NJ: Jason Aronson.

Gendlin, E. T. (1996). *Focusing-oriented psychotherapy*. New York: Guilford Press.

Jackson, S. W. (1992, December). The listening healer in the history of psychological healing. *American Journal of Psychiatry, 149*, 1623–1632.

Leva, R. A. (Ed.). (1982). *Psychotherapy: The listening voice: Rogers and Erickson*. Muncie, IN: Accelerated Development.

Towse, E. (1995). Listening and accepting. In T. Wigram, B. Saperston, & R. West (Eds.), *The art and science of therapy: A handbook*. Langhorne, PA: Harwood Academic Publishers/Gordon and Breach Science Publishers.

Watts, F. N. (1996). Listening processes in psychotherapy and counseling. In *The Hatherleigh guide to psychotherapy. The Hatherleigh guides series* (pp. 17–31). New York: Hatherleigh Press.

11

❧

Developing a Language of Empathy

*W*ords. We have learned since birth that words carry our meanings. Even though they are often inadequate for the task, they convey our experience, communicate our wishes, and serve as the social glue that binds us to one another. Words, perhaps more than any other single tool, are the servants counselors use to understand and to articulate our understanding of clients' thoughts, feelings, confusions, and mysteries.

The Language of Empathy

As you have read in the previous chapter, empathy demands that counselors communicate their understandings to clients in such a way that clients acknowledge that they feel understood. The language of empathy requires that the counselor communicate on two levels. First, counselors must demonstrate that they understand the content of clients' stories. Counselors must understand the narrative—the situations, events, and people in the story. Counselors must also understand the sequence, the connections, and the themes apparent in clients' life stories. This is the content of the narrative.

There is more to fully understanding than grasping content. The second level of empathy is understanding meaning. Counselors must understand the significance of the story, its meaning in the life of clients, or, perhaps, as so many have phrased it, clients' feelings or emotions. For example, if a client says, "I seem to be at such loose ends since my wife left me," it would be inadequate to merely respond, "You don't know what to do with yourself since your wife left." While that identifies what the client said, it does not communicate any understanding of the meanings or feelings the client has about his wife leaving. A more adequate response might be, "You feel lonely and even lost since your wife left." This response seeks to understand the feelings of the client as he talks about his separation from his wife. It is the two-level response on the part of counselors that both acknowledges the meaning of clients and, more importantly, begins to provide them with increasing clarity of what may be only vaguely understood personal meanings.

The Reflection of Feelings

One of the most frequently heard terms in counseling may well be *the reflection of feelings*. As often as it is used, it is just as frequently misunderstood. So often this idea of "reflection" is presented as a caricature. Clients say, "I didn't get anything from counseling. The counselor just repeated what I said." Somehow, over the years, reflection of feelings has come to mean paraphrasing to many. Rogers (1986), often credited with the concept, sought to distance himself from it by arguing that the very idea of the reflection of feelings did not accurately portray his relationship with clients. He wrote a short article clarifying his interaction with clients. He maintained in this article that "reflection of feelings" is not an accurate description of what he attempted to do in his work with clients.

Although acknowledging partial responsibility for the use of the term in counseling, Rogers (1986) reports that over the years, "[I have] become very unhappy with it" (p. 375). A major reason for his unhappiness "is that reflection of feelings has often been taught as a technique and because of that has become/is seen as 'wooden' or mechanical" (pp. 375–376).

Rogers (1986) recognizes that

> I know that many of my responses in an interview . . . would seem to be "reflections of feelings." Inwardly, I object. I am definitely not trying to "reflect feeling.". . . Puzzling over this matter, I have come to a double insight. From my point of view as therapist, I am not trying to "reflect feelings." I am trying to determine whether my understanding of the client's inner world is correct—whether I am seeing it as he or she is experiencing it at this moment. Each response of mine contains the unspoken question, "Is this the way it is in you?" Am I catching just the color and texture and flavor of the personal meaning you are experiencing right now? If not, I wish to bring my perception in line with yours. . . . On the other hand, I know that from the client's point of view we are holding up a mirror of his or her current experiencing. The feelings and personal meanings seem sharper when seen through the eyes of another, when they are reflected. (pp. 375–376)

From the client's point of view, we are holding up a mirror of the client's experience. The difference lies in the intention of the therapist. The intention is to understand rather than to reflect.

"So I suggest that these therapist responses be labeled not 'Reflections of Feeling,' but 'Testing Understandings,' or 'Checking Perceptions.' Such terms would, I believe, be more accurate. They would be helpful in the training of therapists. They would supply a sound motivation in responding, a questioning desire rather than an intent to 'reflect'" (Rogers, 1986, p. 376).

Active Empathy

The language of empathy is not passive. It is not merely listening and "saying what the client said." Brendtro, Brokenleg, and Van Bockern

(1990) report a dramatic and angry reaction to perceived passivity in a letter from a distraught mother following the suicide of her son.

> I wish you could hear the tape that David made on the night he died. He said on the tape that he had trusted you to help him. He was angry that you didn't help him, that you simply repeated back to him what he had just said. Adolescents are smart. They don't want nondirective listening when they need concrete help. Once David discovered that you were just parroting his statements, he gave you the answers you were looking for. He also gave up on finding help. (pp. 65–66)

However misguided this mother's sense of responsibility and however misdirected her anger, the danger of merely passive listening is dramatically highlighted in her anguished letter. The language of empathy is active, participatory, and clarifying.

144

Learning the *Language of Empathy*

The language of empathy is the language of the heart. This metaphor is one counselors should keep in mind as they struggle to convey their understanding of clients to clients. The language of meaning is the language of emotion. The language of content is the language of the head— cognitive, intellectual language. Both are necessary, of course, but the language of meaning is essential in communicating understanding to clients. Here is a rule—an axiom:

> *If counselors accurately communicate emotional understanding, then clients will assume that content is understood. But, if counselors only communicate an understanding of content, then clients will not assume that their emotions are understood.*

Developing an Affective Vocabulary

Each of us, in all likelihood, has developed a sophisticated cognitive vocabulary. We are able to communicate ideas in clear, concrete, and even subtle meanings. Yet, when it comes to expressing our feelings we often stumble, search for words, and cling to clichés that barely and inadequately communicate our genuinely felt emotions.

As simplistic as it may seem, the language of the emotions can be expressed in four words! It is a little mnemonic that can readily be called to mind when a counselor searches for a word to express empathic understanding: mad, bad, sad, and glad. In Appendix 1, an extensive list of "feeling" words is provided as an expansion of these four fundamental words.

Skills and Activities

As counselors struggle to increase and improve their affective vocabulary two sorts of activities may be used. Namely, it is possible to increase one's empathic ability by practice—one of the great benefits of a supervised practicum experience in any counselor training program. The observation and feedback, especially if coupled with videotapes that can be reviewed and replayed, are considered the surest teacher in the development of counseling skills. A model that includes not only the observations and feedback of a counseling professional but of one's peers has proven to be effective for two primary reasons: first, the experienced clinician can provide feedback regarding promising counseling initiatives, common early mistakes, and suggestions for future directions in the counseling session; and second, but equally important, as peers observe they begin to see opportunities in which they might have approached the session differently and when offering feedback they begin to articulate their own deeper and growing understanding of the counseling process. Prior to the practicum experience, beginning counselors can practice building empathy skills and developing a more extensive affective vocabulary by using activities such as the ones that follow.

145

Activity 11.1
Making Lists

Given the simple descriptions of feelings (mad, sad, bad, and glad) complete this activity. Under each of the words force yourself (without benefit of a dictionary or thesaurus) to generate five different words that define or expand the meaning of the original word. For example, if we begin with "sad" five other words might be: <u>depressed</u>, <u>blue</u>, <u>downhearted</u>, <u>unhappy</u>, and <u>dejected</u>.

Do this for each of the following words.

MAD	BAD	SAD	GLAD
_____	_____	_____	_____
_____	_____	_____	_____
_____	_____	_____	_____
_____	_____	_____	_____
_____	_____	_____	_____

The follow-up to this activity is to take each of the words you have generated and do the same activity for each of these words. We are going to go out on a limb with you. We *guarantee* that counselors and psychotherapists who regularly do this activity will increase their affective vocabulary!

Activity 11.2
Empathy Train

With a group of peers, have one of the members role-play a client with a life problem. After a sentence or two, have the "client" stop and have each participant respond with an empathic statement or word. The client, for example, might say, "I just can't seem to get over being fired. It just wasn't fair."

> Counselor 1 might say, "You are feeling . . . violated." Then,
> Counselor 2 must also respond but cannot use what
> Counselor 1 has said.
> Counselor 2 might say, "You are feeling . . . dumped on."
> Counselor 3, "You are feeling . . . shocked."
> Counselor 4, "You feel . . . confused."
> Counselor 5, "You feel . . . numb."

Then, the "client" would select the response that seems closest to what he or she was attempting to communicate and the process would continue.

Three important lessons can be gained from this activity. First, it forces beginning counselors to broaden their empathic vocabulary. Second, it begins the process of training one's response to be spontaneous and quick. Third, it teaches that any number of responses might be appropriate in acknowledging clients' feelings. It frees the beginning counselor from struggling to be "right" and instead teaches that "rightness" is a matter of exploration and winnowing. Initially, if a counselor is in the affective ballpark, then that is "close enough" for clients and they will continue the process of exploration and personal discovery that leads to effective action.

Activity 11.3
Word Ladders

This activity is meant to help beginning counselors become more precise in their affective statements. Often, as we respond to clients, we might find ourselves using adjectives that minimize or maximize a feeling rather than finding a word that more accurately describes the client's feeling state. In responding to anger, for example, a counselor might say, "You are *very* mad" or "You are a *little* mad." As counselors and psychotherapists gain experience, they become more precise, refined, and thus, more accurate as they recognize and respond to clients' feelings. This activity can begin the process of responding more accurately to those feelings.

If we use the example of being mad, we know that there are different levels of intensity for this feeling. Instead of giving in to the temptation of merely saying "very mad" or "really mad," force yourself to find words you already know, but use somewhat infrequently, to complete this activity. Again consider the word mad—if we start with this feeling, what might be two words that are less intense than mad? What might be examples of words that communicate more intense angry feelings?

<u>furious</u> (examples of more intense anger)
<u>provoked</u>
Mad
<u>irritated</u>
<u>annoyed</u> (examples of less intense anger)

Do this activity for each of the four words below.

_____ _____ _____ _____

_____ _____ _____ _____

MAD   BAD   SAD   GLAD

_____ _____ _____ _____

_____ _____ _____ _____

Again, you will begin to develop a more refined and precise affective vocabulary when you force yourself to complete activities such as this one. For each of the words you generated under each category you can construct another word ladder.

In the example for mad, we used the word *irritated*. We could then force ourselves to build a word ladder for this word.

_____	<u>exasperated</u> (more intense)
_____	<u>disturbed</u>
Irritated	Irritated
_____	<u>irked</u>
_____	<u>bothered</u> (less intense)

Again, our *guarantee*: If you do this, your affective vocabulary will develop, grow, and become more exact and elegant.

Finally, it is possible that words and their meanings can take on an enjoyable aspect. A more pleasant way of increasing one's vocabulary, whether cognitive or affective, is to make words and their meanings something of a hobby. Use a thesaurus and/or a dictionary as a way to relax. Look up words for the sheer pleasure of discovering the subtle differences in word meaning. A thesaurus can allow you to discover the connection between words you might never have known. Last, for those of us (a growing number!) who use a computer word processing program, a simple click moves us into the thesaurus tool and a list of words is presented. It is an easy and playful way to spend a few minutes!

Activity 11.4
The Training Stem

As we said in Activity 11.3, clients will assume that content is understood if the counselor accurately relates the emotions the client has expressed. One of the early mistakes beginning counselors make is merely responding with content paraphrases. This leads, of course, to one of the frequently heard complaints about counseling and psychotherapy: "All the counselor did was repeat what I said." This activity trains us to respond with *both* content and feelings—a complete empathy statement. A complete empathy statement would look like this: "You feel _____ when _____." It includes the emotional meaning and the situation in which it occurred or the content.

A client might say, "I think I must be going crazy. I just can't seem to get away from my feelings of my parents failing me."

The counselor might respond, "You feel <u>confused and even out of control</u> when <u>you think you just can't let go of the past</u>. Another counselor might respond in this way, "You feel <u>haunted by the past</u> when <u>you think how present your parents are in your life even now</u>." Each of these responses identified possible feelings and communicates an understanding of the client's situation and narrative.

Complete the following stems for yourself as a way to practice a complete empathy statement. There are no "right" answers, of course, but force yourself to use affective words for the feelings statement and identify content or the situation as well:

"I am a huge failure. Jim broke up with me last night and I don't know if I will ever find a person to love me."

"You feel _____

when _____."

"Whenever I do anything I'm not satisfied. I am just so critical of myself."

"You feel _____

when _____."

"My dog died."

"You feel _____

when _____."

"A long time ago in a galaxy far, far away I battled the evil empire for the future of all free creatures. I owe more than I can ever repay to Obi-Wan Kenobi."

"You feel _____

when _____."

(Just kidding!)

NOTE: Some years ago, Carkhuff (1987) proposed a similar training stem. His suggestion was that the stem should be:

"You feel _____ because _____." Our recommenda-

tion of "You feel _____ when _____" is based on our exprience of working with beginning counselors. In our experience, the "you feel/because" stem has created some problems for inexperienced counselors. When they used the word *because* it typically led to an explanation or an interpretation of the client's behavior rather than a description of the circumstances in which the feelings occurred. The use of the word *when* rather than the word *because* has helped beginning counselors avoid this therapeutic mistake.

The activities that follow are ones that beginning counselors may use to increase and improve their empathic responding during sessions. These are activities derived directly from our experience and we have used them to correct and improve our counseling and psychotherapy skills.

Activity 11.5
Responding from Experience

When clients talk to us it is often difficult to know which emotion, of the many possible in any human experience, to identify as the most important. One way to do this is to use our own experience as a barometer for the feelings of the client. We are not saying to clients that our experience and theirs is, or must be, the same. We are checking to see if our understanding of their emotional experience is accurate. One way to do this is for the counselor to ask himself or herself an internal question. "How must a person feel to have said what he or she just said?" This question is asked of the counselor, not of the client. What the counselor says to the client is the answer the counselor gives to himself or herself. If a client says, "I am wondering if I will ever get any better," then the internal question the counselor asks is, "How must a person feel in order to raise such a question?" Just asking the question internally conjures up a number of possible answers. "Defeated," "questioning the value of counseling," or "seeking reassurance" all come quickly to mind. The counselor must then make a judgment and respond. The answer completes the stem "You feel _____."

Whenever a counselor is lost or confused in a counseling session, this is a good tool to use to find your way back to understanding the client. This tool may be used during a counseling session itself. In the process of pushing oneself to improve skills, the practice of strategies such as this one becomes more and more a part of one's normal, natural, and ordinary way of responding to clients.

Activity 11.6
The Forbidden Word

Often beginning counselors find themselves locked into particular words that they use over and over. This activity is similar to word ladders and making lists except that it is based in actual experience rather than in a process of preparing oneself to enter a counseling session. It is another activity that forces counselors to build a more complete and thorough affective vocabulary. In our experience of observing beginning counselors, three words appear over and over and we have taken to identifying them early in the counseling process and "forbidding" the counselor in training to use them. These words are *frustrated*, *upset*, and *angry*. It is surprising both to us and to the counselor that upset, frustration, and even anger arise when it is suggested that these words not be used! The outcome, as one would expect, is that the counselors in training quickly learn to use other words in place of these.

In the same vein, as beginning counselors review videotapes and as others observe them, it may become apparent that the counselor uses the same word over and over in responding to a client. For example, a counselor might be fond of saying, "I hear you saying . . . " frequently during sessions. Once you become aware of some verbal habit it is a good strategy to forbid yourself from using it at all, which forces you to come up with some acceptable replacement word or phrase. As we mentioned before, two ways to do this are making lists and building word ladders.

Activity 11.7
The Rule of Three

Another habit that even experienced counselors and psychotherapists may fall into is the use of the same word or phrase to describe a client's feelings within a single session. One might respond to the client again and again with the same expression. The client may be reporting his or her experience in relating with a dominating and demanding spouse and the counselor may repeatedly say, "You are feeling angry." The **rule of three** states that once a counselor or psychotherapist has used a descriptive word three times in a single session that he or she will not use that word again until the summary phase of the session. Thus, if the counselor has responded to the client by identifying the feelings apparent in the relationship between the client and the spouse as anger three times, then the counselor is forced to find another word or expression to help in the exploration and understanding of the client's relationship. There are two reasons for this, the first of which is straightforward. We do not want to fall into a rut. The second is that if a counselor has used a descriptive word or phrase three times, then it must not be adding or contributing anything new to the client's exploration and understanding. It merely serves to spin the session into repeating over and over again the same level of affective understanding. It is important not only to respond with different words, but to respond with more meaningful words as we interact with our clients. The goal is to become aware within the session that we are overusing a particular word and correct it within the session. One way to become aware of this, naturally, is to review recorded tapes of the session and to be observed by supervisors who bring it to our attention. Awareness permits us to employ a strategy such as the one above to correct a habit that can inhibit our effectiveness as a counselor or psychotherapist.

Summary

The potent language of psychotherapy is the language of empathy, or the language of the emotions. Because clients will assume that we understand content when we accurately respond to their emotions, it is important to develop a vocabulary of the emotions that matches our vocabulary of the intellect. Clients feel most understood when the counselor is able to demonstrate that he or she understands both content and meaning. This is not merely a matter of paraphrasing what the client has said or even of "reflecting" feelings. It is a matter of searching our own experience and testing with the client whether our understanding of our own experience accurately describes the feelings and meanings of the client. This demands an active involvement from the psychotherapist. The activities provided in this chapter are aids to help beginning counselors develop their empathic capacity to respond accurately and sensitively to clients.

References and for Further Reading

Andersen, T. (1996). *Language is not innocent.* New York: Wiley.

Brendtro, L. K., Brokenleg, M., & Van Bockern, S. (1990). *Reclaiming youth at risk: Our hope for the future.* Bloomington, IN: National Education Service.

Carkhuff, R. R. (1987). *The art of helping VI* (6th ed.). Amherst, MA: Human Resource Development Press.

Efran, J. S., Lukens, M. D., & Lukens, R. J. (1990). *Language, structure, and change: Frameworks of meaning in psychotherapy.* New York: W. W. Norton.

Friedman, S. (Ed.). (1993). *The new language of change: Constructive collaboration in psychotherapy.* New York: Guilford Press.

Havens, L. (1988). *Making contact: Uses of language in psychotherapy.* Cambridge, MA: Harvard University Press.

Havens, L. L. (1996). Explorations in the uses of language in psychotherapy. In J. E. Groves (Ed.), *Essential papers on short-term dynamic therapy. Essential papers in psychoanalysis* (pp. 286–299). New York: New York University Press.

Haynal, A. (1992). Language and affective communication in psychotherapy and psychoanalysis. In A. Z. Schwartzberg, A. H. Esman, S. C. Feinstein, & S. Lebovici (Eds.), *International annals of adolescent psychiatry, Vol. 2* (pp. 29–33). Chicago, IL: University of Chicago Press.

Kershaw, C. J. (1994). The healing power of the story. In S. R. Lankton & K. K. Erickson (Eds.), *The essence of a single-session success* (pp. 146–149). New York: Brunner/Mazel.

Kopp, R. R. (1995). *Metaphor therapy: Using client-generated metaphors in psychotherapy*. New York: Brunner/Mazel.

Nathanson, D. L. (Ed.). (1996). *Knowing feeling: Affect, script, and psychotherapy*. New York: W. W. Norton.

Rogers, C. R. (1986, November). Reflection of feelings. *Person-Centered Review, 1* (4), 375–377.

Siegelman, E. Y. (1990). *Metaphor and meaning in psychotherapy*. New York: Guilford Press.

Winton, W. M. (1990). Language and emotion. In H. Giles & W. P. Robinson (Eds.), *Handbook of language and social psychology*. New York: Wiley.

12

∾

Nonverbal Understanding and Responding

When words send one message and the body another, believe the body! This direct and powerful advice is one of the secrets of empathy. Words do carry meaning and convey our thoughts and feelings—in part. Some say, however, that the greater share is carried by gesture, intonation, expression, and posture.

Nonverbal Concerns for the Counselor

Videotape can be a blunt teacher. In a supervisory session, a counselor in training was complaining that the client seemed reluctant to disclose anything meaningful. The client resisted becoming closer in the counseling relationship in spite of the counselor's appeals. What the videotape revealed was the counselor's verbal encouragement, but it also showed the counselor's arm extended with the palm out in the international signal for "stop." The communication to the client was ambivalent at best. What is one to believe in the face of a signal that communicates stop while the words are encouraging one to speak?

For the counselor, careful attention to nonverbal concerns can serve the client in two ways. First, attending to one's own nonverbal signals with the same attention we give to our verbal utterances can move us to a greater congruence between our words and nonverbals. Just as we can seek to improve and strengthen our affective vocabulary (see Appendix 1) as counselors, we can use nonverbal signals in therapy to congruently send a clear message to clients and improve our own expression. Second, by becoming sensitive to and aware of clients' nonverbal messages we can more deeply understand their sometimes (often) conflicting thoughts and emotions. At least, in the act of clarifying what seems to be a conflict between the clients' words and a gesture, clients can become clearer on their own conflicts, which may lie just outside awareness.

Let us deal with the counselor's nonverbal communication first. What is the message that we want to send? Counselors and psychotherapists say that they are interested in the lives of clients. We want to listen attentively and respond with clarity and understanding. One of the foundations of effective psychotherapy is counselor congruence. Thus, we can seek to develop congruence between our verbal and nonverbal messages. There are a number of different aspects of nonverbal communication: posture, eye contact, facial expression, gestures, touch, vocal quality, nonverbal distractions, and the counseling environment itself.

Posture

Like many things in life, ineffective posture is a matter of extremes. In seeking to communicate feelings of calm and lack of anxiety, a counselor may lounge back in his or her chair affecting an attitude of nonchalance. From the client's point of view this may reflect an attitude of indifference. On the other hand, a counselor who sits bolt upright and unmoving may appear statuelike. There is no great secret to an attentive posture. Go into any restaurant and you can pick out the people who are interested in one another. They are the ones engaged in conversation who are leaning toward each other. An effective counseling posture is one in which the counselor leans slightly forward and attends to the client. A description of a counselor listening to a client might read like this. The counselor leans slightly forward facing the client, with hands lightly clasped in his or her lap and feet flat on the floor or

---

Table 12.1   *Nonverbal Communication of Counselor Attitudes*

Counseling Dimension	Nonverbal Behaviors Likely to Be Associated with Ineffectiveness	Nonverbal Behaviors Likely to Be Associated with Effectiveness
EMPATHY	frown resulting from lack of understanding	positive head nods; facial expression congruent with content of session
RESPECT	mumbling; patronizing tone of voice; engaging in doodling or paperwork; lack of eye contact	spends time with client; fully attentive
WARMTH	apathy; delay in responding; insincere effusiveness; fidgeting; signs of wanting to leave	physical contact; nonjudgmental empathy; attentiveness
GENUINENESS	low or evasive eye contact; excessive smiling	congruence between verbal and nonverbal behavior
CONCRETENESS	shrugs shoulders when client is vague instead of seeking clarification; vague gestures used as substitute for specific verbal meaning	drawing diagram to clarify an abstract point; clear enunciation
SELF-DISCLOSURE	bragging gestures; points to self; covers eyes or mouth while talking	gestures that keep references to self low key
IMMEDIACY	turning away or moving back when immediacy enters the session	tone of voice congruent with expressed mood of the client
CONFRONTATION	pointing finger or shaking fist at client; tone of voice that communicates blame or condemnation; loudness of voice to intimidate; unsure of self	natural tone of voice; confident

SOURCE: From *Human Relations Development: A Manual for Educators* (5th ed.), by G. M. Gazda, F. S. Asbury, F. J. Balzer, W. C. Childers, and R. P. Walters. Copyright © 1995 Allyn & Bacon. Reprinted by permission.

comfortably crossed. The counselor sits in such a way that he or she is able to respond quickly when it is important to do so. In many ways, a counselor's sitting posture is much like a tennis player waiting to receive a serve—alert, "up on the toes," and ready to respond.

Eye Contact

Eye contact is not so much a matter of looking the client in the eye as it is a matter of being in contact with the whole client all the time and taking in his or her nonverbal signals in just the way one listens to their words. Eye contact is one of the areas in which sensitivity to multicultural concerns is necessary. Ivey (1994) addresses some of these cross-cultural concerns in nonverbal communication:

> One of the critical issues in interviewing is the fact that the same skills may have different effects with different individual and cultural backgrounds. Eye contacts differ, for example. In our culture, middle-class patterns call for rather direct eye contact, but in some cultural groups, direct eye contact is considered rude and intrusive. Some groups find the rapid-fire questioning techniques of many North Americans offensive. Many Spanish-speaking groups have more varying vocal tone and sometimes a more rapid speech rate than do English-speaking people. It is also important to remember that the word culture can be defined in many ways. Religion, ethnic background (for example Irish-American and Black-American), sex, and lifestyle differences as well as the degree of a client's developmental or physical handicap also represent cultural, gender, and lifestyle differences. There is also a youth culture, a culture of those facing imminent death through AIDS or cancer, and a culture of the aging. In effect, any group that differs from the mainstream of society can be considered a subculture. All of us at times are thus part of many cultures that require a unique awareness of the group experience. (pp. 11–12)

What is most important in this discussion is not that every counselor must be aware of every cultural and subcultural attitude and opinion on behavior, but that he or she be sensitive to and aware of the effect that culture can have and when confronted with clients who come from backgrounds different from his or her own to invest the time necessary to become informed about the client's culture. This includes remaining open to the impact of any nonverbal signals that may be interfering with effective psychotherapy. Welch (1998) discusses two main considerations in the issue of cross-cultural counseling. One is the path of knowledge. This is a matter of information and study either in general or as it regards a specific client. The second is the path of empathy in which the driving purpose of the counselor is to understand and to check those understandings with the client. In this path, any mistaken understandings can be corrected and the counselor will move in the direction of greater cultural, gender, and lifestyle sensitivity as one moves in the direction of more profound individual understanding.

Given these multicultural considerations, effective eye contact remains somewhere between direct eye contact and frequently glancing away. Clearly, ineffective eye contact ignores the client, looks down or away, or frequently breaks contact. Equally ineffective is an intense stare boring directly into the client's eyes. Effective eye contact means looking at the client when listening or talking in a relaxed and spontaneous way that is congruent with what is happening in the session at the moment. It is a matter of focusing one's attention on the client, not so much in the way one would focus a microscope on a fine detail but the way one would focus a wide-angle lens—taking in the whole person and communicating the awareness that he or she is being listened to.

Facial Expression

There is a difference between a counselor's facial expression when listening and when talking. When counselors listen it is important that our facial expression not express much. In supervision, we have found this a somewhat difficult concept to communicate. Obviously, a counselor's facial expression should not be blank or vacant, but, on the other hand, it should not communicate any disagreement, puzzlement, agreement, or emotion. But that is not exactly true. There is an emotion that counselors want to communicate—concern. So it is a matter of learning to congruently express what is genuinely felt in the counseling encounter—attentiveness, interest, and facilitation. If you look up the words *face* and *facilitation* you will discover that they are attributed to the same French root word *facere*, which means "to make or to do." Certainly, the counselor's facial expression can facilitate or inhibit client anxiety and willingness to enter more vulnerable areas of concern. In the first meeting, a reassuring smile along with a verbal greeting contributes to the client's first impression and begins the process of building a trusting relationship.

The shift from listening to talking is one with which beginning counselors often struggle. Sitting in the attending posture, listening intently, and focusing on the client, it is as if cement has begun to set and movement is nearly impossible. Sometimes beginning counselors become like statues or mannequins where only the mouth moves when they talk. The transition from listening to talking is one in which facial expression can communicate understandings as well as words. It is another example of the struggle for congruence. What we say and what we express nonverbally need to correspond.

The face is an exquisite message board. With our face, we communicate to one another our sadness, our surprise, our pain, our joy, and our anger. Our face is often what gives us away in our efforts to deceive. We use words such as *mask* in our recognition of the important role our facial expressions play in communication.

Gestures

"Yes," "No," "Come here," "Go away," "Stop," "Tell me more," "I don't know," "Heartfelt," "You're crazy," or "Up yours!" Each of these messages, and literally uncounted others, all lie within the capability of human gestures. One need look no further than sign language to understand that a full range of communication exists even in the absence of a spoken word. Gestures can invite or squash clients' willingness to tell their story. They can affirm or give lie to our words. A nod of the head can signal, "Continue, I am with you." An unfortunate shake of the head can send a message of disapproval. And, just as the counselor at the beginning of this chapter was speaking his or her message of concern and openness, his or her gesture was saying, "Stop. I don't want to hear it." The opening sentence of this chapter is, "When words send one message and the body another, believe the body!" Clients may not be able to articulate this learning, but they act upon it. Often what we refer to as intuition is a low-level recognition of a gesture. Often we know without being fully aware of where our knowledge comes from. Yalom, in *Lying on the Couch: A Novel* (1996), relates the story of a group of poker players. One of the players is a constant loser who cannot figure out why until the other players inform him of his gestural clues which are labeled *tells*. These tells are giveaways of when he is bluffing and when he has good and bad cards. Regardless of what he says, the other players in the game have good clues about his holdings. He is, of course, at a distinct disadvantage because he is unaware of his own nonverbal behavior and has not learned to read the nonverbal behavior of others.

163

Just as in the transition from listening to speaking, beginning counselors sometimes have trouble using their bodies to communicate and often look like talking statues. Their hands are immobile for fear that they will inadvertently make some gesture that will offend or miscommunicate. Although their sensitivity is justified, the strategy is self-defeating because it prevents them from profiting from their mistakes (!) and it limits their effectiveness.

Gestures can and do perform an important function in psychotherapy. They often communicate a meaning that words have trouble reaching. A clenched fist can often communicate anger more directly than words. In another context, a clenched fist can communicate resolve. One clenched fist can communicate one level of resolve, whereas two clenched fists speak to a deeper conviction (one fist = resolve; two fists = I am deeply resolved). A counselor might touch his or her head and say, "You know it here," communicating his or her understanding that the client has an intellectual grasp and then touch his or her chest and say, "But do you know it here?" checking to see if the knowledge is emotional as well as intellectual. These gestures are clear, focused, communicative, and sharper than words to the same effect. A counselor who is aware and purposefully uses gestures in therapy can serve clients pointedly, directly, and potently. The effective use of gestures can reduce the actual amount of talk needed by a psychotherapist, thus enabling clients to have more time to tell their stories and use the counseling hour more efficiently and effectively. The time is focused on the client and not on counselor talk.

Touch

Some years ago Montague wrote an intriguing book entitled *Touching: The Significance of the Human Skin* (1986). Montague, an anthropologist, focused on the significance of touch in cultures throughout the world and upon its psychological importance in the development of healthy human beings. The United States is a rainbow of ethnicities in one metaphor and a smorgasbord of nationalities in another. This diverse country is one in which the range of values, beliefs, and opinions on any subject can boggle the mind and defeat nearly any widely pleasing resolution. When to touch, how to touch, where to touch, who to touch, and even the meaning of touching have all been the source of debate in our society. Obvious ethnic, subcultural, and individual differences exist in our understanding of touch. Montague, however, seeks to transcend all of these levels and to penetrate to the core issue of the necessity of touch for human survival.

Montague maintains that without touch humans would die. What gets lost in the arguments about when, where, who, and so forth is that the focus has changed from the importance of touch for human beings to "inappropriate" touch. In this shift of focus, the rules and guidelines we sometimes make become proscriptions against touch itself. Let us be clear here. Counselors who touch are more effective than counselors who don't. A large body of research supports this assertion and we have listed only a few examples here for your consideration (Cronise, 1993;

Halbrook & Duplechin, 1994; Horton, Clance, Sterk-Elifson, & Emshoff, 1995; Kertay & Reviere, 1993; Kupfermann & Smaldino, 1987; Suiter, 1984; Woodmansey, 1988). We invite you to research this topic for yourself so that you are clear on the importance of touch for psychotherapists. Although it is important, necessary, and wise to know clearly the difference between appropriate and inappropriate touch, that concern should not interfere with the appropriate use of touch in the counseling relationship. Just as a reassuring smile can accompany our verbal greeting, so can a friendly handshake. At the end of a session as the client is leaving is the time for a good-bye handshake or a touch on the shoulder. These are important gestures and ones that have the solid support of research.

We live in a time of hypersensitivity to the relationships between men and women and a time when the relationships between same-sex individuals are being renegotiated. What was once considered harmless interplay has taken on new and often confusing meanings. As we struggle to sort out these things, some have responded with caution, some, perhaps, with abandon. Whether counselors ought to hug a client is open to debate. Whether counselors ought to touch their clients in the socially accepted manner of our culture (e.g., handshakes or a supportive grasp or pat on the shoulder) is much clearer. Let us repeat: Counselors who touch are more effective than counselors who do not. What is more open to debate is the behavior of counselors and psychotherapists who never touch their clients.

Vocal Quality

If we stretch the point of nonverbal communication just a bit, we can include the idea of vocal quality. The issues of intonation, volume, pace, and diction all contribute to the effectiveness of a psychotherapy session. Years ago there was a cartoon character named Dopey the Dog. Dopey always spoke with a flat, slow, and unemotional tone of voice. No matter what he said, he said it in the same slow and flat way. If he said, "You know what? I'm sad," then we would probably believe him. If, however, he said, "You know what? I'm happy," it is unlikely we would believe him because the feeling of being happy and a slow, flat delivery do not go together, and that is, in our counselor way of talking, incongruent. If we want to communicate effectively, then our tone of voice and our words need to correspond. When we are excited the tone is higher pitched than when we are sad. This is exactly true for pace and volume as well. Effective speaking is speech that flows in pitch, tone, and key and each of these aspects can convey meaning. Our words will have greater power when we use them with a sensitivity to the nonverbal characteristics of spoken language.

Just as with intonation, volume can intensify importance. Someone once asked, "Why is it that anything we whisper seems to take on importance?" This recognition of the importance of volume should not be lost on us as therapists. We can use volume as one more tool to serve the needs of clients. We can also recognize in the volume of the client's spoken language some clue to a better understanding of meaning. Does a softly spoken story reveal inner insecurity or lack of confidence? Does a loud voice reveal merely bravado? Can we be misled by a firm and seemingly self-confident speaking voice into taking the concerns of the client too lightly? Does a whisper mean shame? Whatever one answers, the question of volume is one to which counselors and psychotherapists should attend.

Volume is a tool of therapy as well. Clients may be instructed to increase their volume as they address issues in their lives. Self-truths might need repetition and volume as one speaks to convince oneself of the importance of a new idea (e.g., "I am important. I do count. If not to others, at least to myself"). It is important to give some consideration to how we speak as counselors. One of the observations we have made as supervisors is that some counselors dramatically change their speaking voices when they enter the counseling room. Consider these questions. Why would someone do that? Does it signal problems with incongruence? Does it signal some attitude toward therapy that can ultimately interfere with the process? These are questions that counselors in training have to face. It is probably good advice not to change one's normal speaking voice too much when one does therapy. Aside from the natural changes that would occur when speaking about emotionally charged life situations and events, a counselor's voice should be normal, pleasant, calm, and appropriately loud.

Dopey the Dog always spoke slowly. So slow, in fact, that some members of the audience became anxious waiting for him to finish a sentence. Clients might feel the same way about a counselor whose pace is slow. At the opposite end of the spectrum is a counselor who talks so fast that his or her words seem to be a runaway train. Talking too slow and too fast are both vocal qualities that interfere with effective counseling. The rate at which one speaks is determined by the rate at which a client can understand. Keep in mind an old mnemonic: KISS—keep it short and simple. Pace is not much of a problem if we speak in short, declarative sentences rather than paragraphs. Clients don't come to psychotherapy for lectures. If we can keep that in mind, then pace is not such an issue. In any case, keep counselor interventions frequent and short.

Diction has to do with our choice of words, especially with regard to clarity, correctness, and effectiveness, but it also has to do with our pronunciation and enunciation. As counselors we have some obligation when we speak to clients to pronounce words pretty much the way most people do. The other consideration is that we enunciate clearly (i.e., don't mutter or mumble). What this all boils down to is that we say what we want to say clearly and recognizably. One of us is originally from the southern United States and it would be no exaggeration to say that he has a regionalism in his speech. Yet, he falls well within the range of acceptable pronunciation and clarity of speech. Some might even find it pleasant. Certainly, there is no need to "talk like the man on the 6 o'clock news," but there is some obligation to be able to speak and articulate in understandable and nondistracting ways.

167

Nonverbal Distractions

Often we are not aware of our own behavior. We may have mannerisms or repetitive behaviors that can be distracting to the client. For many beginning counselors, and perhaps for some experienced ones as well, hands can be a constant source of wayward behavior. Just like a naughty child, they might go wandering around all over the place without our knowledge or permission. Some counselors seem to adopt odd-looking configurations with their fingers and hands that defy explanation. Some seem to be playing a version of "Here is the church and here is the steeple. Open the doors and there are the people." Others place their fingers together and perform some version of "finger push-ups" or seem right on the edge of sending the "itsy-bitsy spider up the waterspout." Whatever is going on, the result can well be a distraction for the client. It is better to "get a hold of oneself" and lightly clasp the hands together in one's lap.

As if the hands weren't enough trouble, our eyes sometimes seem to have a mind of their own and might blink or even close, defying our commands to be still and open. Worse, perhaps, would be an involuntary tic that sends a ripple through our eyelid or cheek. These troubling nonverbal behaviors might require more effort to bring them under control than our hands, but one tool that is helpful in changing any nonverbal behavior is the use of video recording. When we record our sessions we are able to return to them and observe ourselves as others see us. This can be embarrassing, but the profit is great. It is direct and immediate feedback and we do not have to take the word of someone else about concrete, observable behavior. The evidence is before us. Once a behavior can be brought into awareness, it is easier to change.

Counselors need to guard against fiddling, tapping, foot swinging, twirling our hair, tapping our temples, spinning our fingers, or any number of self-comforting but anxiety-revealing behaviors that can distract and annoy clients (not to mention one's supervisors!).

Such behavior might also involve what might be labeled *verbal tics*. These behaviors include "okay," "that's right," "uh," "awh," and a variety of other sounds that we might not even know we are making until either one's supervisor or tape-recording catches them.

Finally, many counselors seem to have trouble giving up power symbols such as pencils, pens, client folders, note pads, name tags, or even lab coats in medical settings. Smoking, although perhaps not as much of a temptation as it once was, might still be an issue for some therapists as well as drinking coffee, tea, soda pop, or water. All can interfere with the proper focus of attention. Each of these can be a distraction that calls attention to the therapist at the expense of focus on the client.

Matters of the Environment

A counseling setting should be pleasant. It should be neat rather than disorderly. It should lean toward the casual rather than the formal. It should have warm colors rather than cold. It should appear cheerful rather than drab or dull. Although the chairs should be comfortable, they should not be enveloping and overly soft. The counselor should not sit in a "throne" chair that is remarkably different from the chair(s) of the client(s) and the counselor should not sit behind a desk (another symbol of power). Overall, the environment should convey equality rather than authority and friendliness rather than aloofness. A counseling office is not a business office in the traditional sense and the trappings of power, wealth, status, and authority are best left to the banks and corporate offices of the business world. This is a place where one's vulnerabilities will be brought into the open, and it needs to be a place where this can be done without having to focus one's thoughts on the office furnishings. A counseling office should be pleasant, comfortable, and unobtrusive.

As you consider these nonverbal behaviors, use Table 12.2 as a way of evaluating your own nonverbal behavior.

Recognizing and Responding to Clients' Nonverbal Behavior

While supervising, one of us observed a client who repeated an unusual nonverbal behavior. While talking the client would frequently extend his right arm with the palm up, slightly cupped. The behavior was called to the counselor's attention and it was suggested that the counselor respond to it in some way. The counselor was reluctant and did

Table 12.2 Nonverbal Behavior Checklist

POSTURE

        Attending—Slightly Forward   _____

        Appropriate Position—Facing Client, Other   _____

        Relaxed   _____

        Hands and Arms Relaxed   _____

        Legs—Spaced, Flat on Floor or Crossed and Relaxed   _____

        Eager and Ready to Respond   _____

        Slouched   _____

        Armored—Arms and Legs Crossed   _____

        Sitting Sideways   _____

        Too Close   _____

        Too Distant   _____

        Rigid, Statue   _____

EYE CONTACT

        Relaxed, Spontaneous, Appropriate   _____

        Looks at Client While Listening   _____

        Looks at Client While Talking   _____

        Observing Whole Person   _____

        Shifty-Eyed   _____

        Looking Down, Away   _____

EYE CONTACT (continued)

    Staring Intensely   _____

    Breaking Eye Contact Immediately   _____

    Defiantly Looking, Competitive   _____

    Staring Blankly   _____

FACIAL EXPRESSION

    Calm, Attentive, Interested While Listening   _____

    Appropriately Expressive While Talking   _____

    Appropriate Smiling   _____

    Expressions Match Client Mood   _____

    Wrinkled Forehead (Frown)   _____

    Biting Lip   _____

    Face Rigid   _____

    Inappropriate Smiling   _____

    Face Disapproving/Aghast   _____

    Overly Emotional   _____

    Inappropriate Facial Expression (Not Matching)   _____

    No Facial Expression (No Change)   _____

GESTURES

    Appropriate Gestures for Emphasis and Point   _____

    Nods Head Appropriately   _____

171

GESTURES (continued)

Symbolic Gestures, Additive   _____

Gestures to Explain, Demonstrate   _____

Inappropriate or Wrong Gesture   _____

Continuous Head Nodding   _____

Statue, No Gestures   _____

Wild or Exaggerated Gestures   _____

TOUCH

Greeting—Handshake, Other Touch   _____

Appropriate Touch   _____

Inappropriate Touch   _____

Sexual Touch   _____

Interrupting Crying or Weeping   _____

VOCAL QUALITY *Intonation*

Change of Inflection, Tone   _____

Strong, Confident Tone   _____

Pleasant   _____

Monotone, Flat   _____

Too Emotional   _____

VOCAL QUALITY *Volume*

    High   _____

    Appropriate and Varied   _____

    Low   _____

VOCAL QUALITY *Pace*

    Fast   _____

    Appropriate   _____

    Slow   _____

VOCAL QUALITY *Diction*

    Precise   _____

    Clear   _____

    Pronunciation   _____

    Jargon, Slang   _____

NONVERBAL DISTRACTIONS

    Fiddling, Twiddling   _____

    Smoking, Drinking, Chewing Gum   _____

    Tapping Finger, Leg   _____

    Hand, Finger to Head   _____

    Scratching, Rubbing   _____

    Unusual Hand Configuration (Steeple, etc.)   _____

173

NONVERBAL DISTRACTIONS (continued)

    Playing with Hair, Beard   _____

    Trembling   _____

ENVIRONMENT

    Lighting   _____

    Chair Arrangement   _____

    Appropriate Chairs   _____

    Neat, Clean   _____

    Casual   _____

    Warm   _____

    Cheerful   _____

    Desk or Other Barrier   _____

    "Throne" for Counselor   _____

    Lack of Needed Materials   _____

    Seating Inappropriate   _____

not see the importance of the client's gesture. After three sessions in which the client frequently repeated the behavior, the supervisor insisted that the counselor in training address it by intervening with a comment such as, "When you make that gesture, I wonder what you might be carrying in your hand." The counselor reluctantly agreed and when the client repeated the gesture and the counselor intervened in the planned way the client burst into tears and through his sobs said, "It is my parents' divorce." What a dramatic demonstration of the power of nonverbal interventions. The counselor immediately, as you might suspect, became convinced of the worth of noticing and responding to nonverbal client clues.

Of course, not all nonverbal behavior is so laden with meaning and force. Still, there is often meaning in nonverbals. It is wise to consider all nonverbal behavior as symbolic, because this attitude allows the counselor to remain open to any symbolic meanings that might be present in the behavior. Not all behavior, of course, is symbolic and some is literally what it appears to be. Sometimes people will have their arms and legs crossed because they are psychologically armored, but sometimes the room may be chilly and they are merely trying to stay warm.

The Source of Nonverbal Behavior

If it is true that many of us are unaware that our nonverbal behavior is communicating something other than our words, then what is the explanation for this phenomenon? Personality theory addresses such questions. This particular question has to do with consciousness and with its levels or continua. As we consider nonverbal behavior we recognize two types of unconscious functioning. One is labeled *vertical* and the other *horizontal*. The vertical unconscious has to do with defensive behavior and its subsequent symbolic representation into conscious awareness. The horizontal unconscious has to do with the fact that the human brain is divided into two hemispheres, which seem to have different dominant functions. The left hemisphere tends to communicate with verbal language and the right hemisphere is said to be virtually mute and communicates through more physical channels. The left hemisphere might recognize a person by name while the right hemisphere might recognize the same person by the spatial relationship in that person's face. We have all had the experience of recognizing a person but not being able to remember the person's name. We might respond to this by saying something like, "It's on the tip of my tongue." The right hemisphere might grow increasingly irritated because it knows perfectly well who the person is and is impatient for the left hemisphere to come up with the language to identify him or her. That

175

impatience might show itself in a number of nonverbal clues—blushing, flashing eyes, hand gestures, or shifting feet. Thus, the source of nonverbal communication might be either a symbolic representation seeking to get by a defense or the right hemisphere of the brain seeking to communicate in the best way it can. Whatever the source, such nonverbal communication is one more indication that the meanings are worth understanding as both the therapist and the client seek to clarify the issues, problems, and/or dilemmas of the client's life.

How to Understand Nonverbal Behavior

Table 12.3 provides the reader with a list of nonverbal clues and some possible meanings of those gestures. Such lists should be viewed with caution because it is our conviction that while many behaviors are symbolic, and perhaps even universal, as psychotherapists we must always recognize that any client behavior may have a unique and personal meaning. Given a psychotherapist's interpretation of some symbolic client behavior and the client's explanation of the same symbol, we would tend to accept the client's understanding. Thus, it is, in our opinion, always a wise choice to recognize the symbol and help the client to come to some personal understanding of the behavior and symbol. In fact, we argue against interpreting symbolic behavior for the client and even resist, to the degree that we are able, interpreting the client's behavior for ourselves. It is a safer and therapeutically more accurate procedure to have the client do any interpreting that is necessary. Personally understood meanings will have greater therapeutic power than any interpretation given by a therapist.

Given these cautions, we use four guidelines to help bring nonverbal behavior into the counseling room.

1. Recognize that nonverbal behavior is symbolic (cautiously allowing room for the idea that it may be literal behavior).
2. Listen and respond to nonverbal behavior just as you would to verbal language. Dealing with nonverbal behavior directly, however, requires a sound therapeutic relationship. Early in the relationship,

Table 12.3 Nonverbal Clues and Some Possible Meanings

In counseling clients, nonverbal behavior may carry many clues to vague feelings. The following nonverbal behaviors must be taken with caution because nonverbals may or may not be symbolic in origin.

Behavior	Possible Meaning
HEAD	Hands on top of head may mean holding something back, keeping the lid on. Hand or fingers to the head might mean the person is being "intellectual"—"coming from the head."
HAIR	Running fingers through hair may mean stringing things along.
EYES	Wiping fingers under eyes may mean a dry tear or crying without actual tears. A dominant person maintains eye contact more than a submissive one.
MOUTH	Fingers stroking mouth might show a need for support or nurturance. Hand in front of mouth might mean something is being hidden or, perhaps, that what is being said is unimportant.
NOSE	The nose may be an object of hostility (thumbing the nose) and may represent sexual issues.
CHEWING	Chewing may be a way of releasing anxiety, or it may be a sign of anger.
THROAT	Touching the throat may be a sign of choking off some feeling. A lump in the throat may represent a need to cry or shout or may mean something is stuck.
NECK	A stiff neck may be a moralistic sign or may represent control and inhibition, an attempt to keep feelings from moving.
SHOULDER	Sore or stiff shoulders may be carrying a burden. Stiff shoulders may mean inhibited anger.
ARMS	Tension in the arm may mean a need to embrace—a person, an idea, a value. Crossed arms may mean feelings are being held in. Crossed arms may mean hugging the self as in a need for comfort.
HANDS	Hands represent emotions—a source of much information about feelings. Sitting on hands or a hand between the legs may mean hidden feelings. Tapping or drumming fingers may mean impatience. Steeple may mean intellectualization, coming from the head. Interlocking fingers may mean intertwined ideas, a puzzle, or putting things together. Picking lint off clothing may mean something is picking at the person or it may be an attempt to get rid of something.
LEGS	One leg bouncing may mean the person wants to kick someone. Two legs bouncing may mean impatience or ambivalence. Rubbing thighs may signal sexual thoughts.

Table 12.3	*Nonverbal Clues and Some Possible Meanings* (continued)

Behavior	Possible Meaning
VOICE	A soft voice may show lack of confidence. Fluctuating volume—what is said softly is an area of insecurity. A whiny voice may be a need for nurturance, a need to know people care. A monotone voice may show difficulty making commitments; tries to keep everything on the same level. Laughing or smiling may be a need to cry, or, typically, anger. Talking fast may signal running from something.
POSTURE	Sitting up, forward may mean eager. Slumped may mean defeated, bored. Head away may mean moving away. Holding an object may mean distancing.

178

therefore, therapists should not call attention to nonverbal behavior but should respond to it in the same way one would verbal behavior. (A client might make a tossing motion with his or her hand. Rather than calling attention to the hand motion, early in the relationship, the counselor would make a verbal response such as, "You would just like to get this issue out of your life.")

3. When formulating a response to an observed nonverbal behavior, describe the action rather than interpret it. (Often the first word that comes to mind is the one to use. If a client brushes his hair back the literal description is "brushing." If he is talking about his relationship with his girlfriend, then tie the act to the content and one statement might be, "You feel like you are being 'brushed off' by her." It is this literal tying of the act to the content that can help the counselor understand the meaning of the nonverbal behavior.)

4. As the relationship develops, increasingly ask clients to describe their own behavior. For example, the counselor who asked the client what he was carrying in his hand is dealing directly with a nonverbal behavior and is asking the client to describe the act and give it symbolic meaning for himself. The counselor's role has been to facilitate the exploration and not to, in any way, interpret or give meaning to the act.

These four guidelines seem to us to be all that is needed in dealing with nonverbal behavior with clients. It is no different from dealing with verbal behavior. It takes a belief in the importance and value of recognizing nonverbals in the counseling session, honoring the quality of the relationship, listening and responding to nonverbals, and allowing the client to describe and give meaning to the symbols rather than interpreting them. These steps will bring the nonverbal behavior into the session while still permitting the client to be in the lead both in terms of content and pace.

Summary

Nonverbal behavior carries meaning for both the counselor and the client. We think it is important that counselors in training spend time understanding their own nonverbal communication and seeking to rid themselves of any interfering behaviors that might distract clients. We also think that counselors and psychotherapists should spend as much time mastering their understanding and response to nonverbal behavior as they do mastering their understanding and response to verbal language.

The source of nonverbal language seems to us to come from both defensive behavior and from the unique structure of the human brain with its two complementary hemispheres that process and communicate in relatively distinct ways. It seems wise to listen to both hemispheres if we are to genuinely understand the way in which the client sees his or her own inner conflicts, issues, and problems.

The process of understanding and responding to nonverbal behavior is a matter of recognizing its importance in communication, responding to it just as one would verbal language, and moving clients toward recognizing and understanding their own nonverbals and their symbolic meaning. The wise course seems to be to stick to describing the behavior and tying it to present content rather than risking interpreting a client's actions. This strategy can be communicated to clients as well, teaching them to describe and connect their actions and their world as they seek to understand themselves.

References and for Further Reading

Argyle, M. (1988). *Bodily communication* (2nd ed.). London: Methuen.

Bull, P. (1989). Non-verbal communication. In A. M. Colmen & J. G. Beaumont (Eds.), *Psychology survey, 7* (pp. 57–75). London: Routledge.

Cronise, J. G. (1993, August). The taboo of touch in psychotherapy. *Dissertation Abstracts International, 54*(2-B), 1090–1091.

Gazda, G. M., Asbury, F. S., Balzer, F. J., Childers, W. C., & Walters, R. P. (1984). *Human relations development* (3rd ed.). Boston: Allyn & Bacon.

Halbrook, B., & Duplechin, R. (1994). Rethinking touch in psychotherapy: Guidelines for practitioners. *Psychotherapy in Private Practice, 13*(3), 43–53.

Horton, J. A., Clance, P. R., Sterk-Elifson, C., & Emshoff, J. (1995, Fall). Touch in psychotherapy: A survey of patients' experiences. *Psychotherapy, 32*(3), 443–457.

Ivey, A. E. (1994). *Intentional interviewing and counseling* (3rd ed.). Pacific Grove, CA: Brooks/Cole.

Kertay, L., & Reviere, S. L. (1993, Spring). The use of touch in psychotherapy: Theoretical and ethical considerations. *Psychotherapy, 30*(1), 32–40.

Kupfermann, K., & Smaldino, C. (1987, Fall). The vitalizing and the revitalizing experience of reliability: The place of touch in psychotherapy. *Clinical Social Work Journal, 15*(3), 223–235.

Mahl, G. F. (1987). *Explorations in nonverbal and vocal behavior*. Hillsdale, NJ: Lawrence Erlbaum Associates.

Montague, A. (1986). *Touching: The significance of the human skin*. New York: Perennial Library.

Patterson, M. L. (1990). Functions of non-verbal behavior in social interaction. In H. Giles, & W. P. Robinson (Eds.), *Handbook of language and social psychology* (pp. 101–120). New York: Wiley.

Suiter, R. L. (1984, February). A comparison of male and female professionals' and non professionals' evaluations of the use of touch in psychotherapy. *Dissertation Abstracts International, 44*(8-A), 2422.

Wallbott, H. G., Ricci-Bitti, P., & Banninger-Huber, E. (1986). Nonverbal reactions to emotional experiences. In K. R. Scherer, H. G. Wallbott, & A. B. Summerfield (Eds.), *Experiencing emotion: A cross-cultural study. European Monographs in Social Psychology*. Cambridge, England: Cambridge University Press.

Welch, I. D. (1998). *The path of psychotherapy: Matters of the heart*. Pacific Grove, CA: Brooks/Cole.

Woodmansey, A. C. (1988, Fall). Are psychotherapists out of touch? *British Journal of Psychotherapy, 5*(1), 57–65.

Yalom, I. D. (1996) *Lying on the couch: A novel*. New York: Basic Books.

13

Facilitation
Versus Blocking

*C*ounseling and psychotherapy are profoundly individual processes more comfortable with guidelines than with rules. Instruction in the fundamentals and methods of counseling is made more difficult because of the processes' inexact nature. Personality theory is widely disparate in its explanations of human behavior. Even given the metatheoretical assumptions of empathy, authenticity, and respect, the precise procedures of counseling and psychotherapy remain open to individual interpretation. It is, therefore, somewhat risky to lay out a plan for counselor observation in which the aim is to offer counselors a guide aimed at increasing effective practice. In spite of the risks, this chapter attempts to provide counselors and psychotherapists with specific guidelines for developing effective skills. Form 13.1 is a counselor observation form with both attitudinal and concrete behavioral categories so that an observer, or the therapist himself or herself, can observe a counseling session and code the climate and behaviors of the counselor. This process provides the therapist with concrete feedback on his or her counseling process so that specific changes can be made to enhance the counseling endeavor.

Form 13.1
The Counselor Observation Form

Counselor Observation Form

Observer _____   Date & Time _____

Counselor _____   Client _____

Observations

Facilitating Dimensions		Blocking Dimensions	
Content Paraphrase (Content Understanding)	_____	Content "Parroting" (Mere Repeating)	_____
Affect/Feeling/Meaning (Emotional Understanding)	_____	Using Power	_____
Genuineness	_____	Moralizing/Being Judgmental	_____
Warmth/Respect	_____	Advice	_____
Concreteness	_____	Interrupting	_____
Appropriate Technique	_____	Lecturing (Logic)/Arguing	_____
Appropriate Confrontation	_____	Inappropriate Confrontation	_____
Immediacy	_____	Evaluative Praise/Approval	_____
Open-ended Statement/Question	_____	Closed Question	_____
Clarification (Question or Statement)	_____	Probing Question	_____
Appropriate Self-Disclosure	_____	Labeling	_____
Productive Silence	_____	Explaining/Interpreting	_____
Appropriate Physical Contact	_____	Unproductive Silence	_____
Attending Posture	_____	Inappropriate Physical Contact	_____
Nonverbal Facilitation	_____	Humoring/Withdrawing	_____
Appropriate Summary	_____	Nonverbal Blocking	_____
_____	_____	Sympathy	_____
_____	_____	Minimizing/Maximizing	_____
		_____	_____

Facilitating Dimensions

The categories that form the facilitating dimensions promise to aid the counselor or psychotherapist in the tasks of exploration, understanding, and action. These include not only the metatheoretical conditions of empathy, authenticity, and respect but other dimensions that have proven themselves effective in helping clients come to terms with their life problems. As one uses the counselor observation form two sorts of observations may be made. One is a general observation that a category (e.g., warmth/respect or genuineness) was present in the counseling session. Another is a tally of each specific event in the category (e.g., a tally might be made for each probing question asked by the counselor). This sort of concrete feedback is especially helpful for a counselor trying to improve his or her counseling who is making a similar therapeutic mistake again and again. The frequency count can help bring the behavior into the therapist's awareness as he or she seeks to change an unhelpful habit.

183

Empathy

We have noted again and again the central importance of empathy in psychotherapy. All psychotherapy begins in empathy (Welch, 1998). A counselor's empathic communication has two parts—content and feeling/meaning. Sometimes a counselor will tend to provide content statements without including the affective aspect of the client's narrative. The counselor observation form is divided into both content and meaning to help the observer provide specific feedback on the relationship between content and feelings. The aim is to move the counselor's talk toward meaningful communication. Empathy is not, as we have stated, mere paraphrase, sympathy, or identification, but is, rather, an understanding of the client's experience at both the cognitive and affective levels. This understanding is communicated by the therapist in such a way that the client acknowledges that he or she is understood. In scoring, the observer recognizes that the counselor responds with accuracy to all of the client's deeper as well as surface feelings. The counselor is "tuned in" to the client's wavelength. The counselor and the client might proceed together to explore previously unexplored areas of experience for the client. In summary, the counselor is responding with a full awareness of who the other person is and with a comprehensive and accurate empathic understanding of that individual's deepest feelings.

Genuineness

This category, put nakedly, means that the counselor is not a phony. The psychotherapist has no hidden agenda and is not trying to manipulate the client toward some unacknowledged goal. The psychotherapist is present in the here and now as an actual caring person interested in the client, honestly seeking to understand what the client is saying from the client's point of view. This is authenticity. Beginning counselors find genuineness difficult for a number of reasons. First, there is the problem of American culture, which is action oriented, not particularly contemplative, and impatient with others. It is not a culture that lends itself well to the reflective, thorough, and persistent pace of psychotherapy. Second, there is the problem of having to cope with not trusting one's cultural instincts while being taught that therapists must act upon their hunches, guesses, and inner stirrings. This early contradiction can create hesitancy and an impression of reserve or holding back that might be viewed as judgmental or uncertain. In scoring genuineness, the observer recognizes the counselor as spontaneous in interaction and open to experience of all types, both pleasant and hurtful; and in the event of hurtful responses the counselor's comments are employed constructively to open a further area of inquiry for both the counselor and the client. In summary, the counselor is clearly being real and employing genuine responses constructively.

Warmth/Respect

Warmth and respect are often twins. Like twins they are often indistinguishable from one another, and like twins they are individuals. Warmth is an attitude of friendliness, approachability, and interpersonal openness. Respect is an attitude that regards the client as having the potential to be the expert in his or her own life. An attitude of respect communicates that the content, pace, and degree of change lie with the client. Both warmth and respect are attitudinal conditions that manifest themselves in the nonjudgmental attitude essential to effective psychotherapy. In scoring, it is clear that the counselor cares deeply for the present situation and the potential of the client and communicates a commitment to enabling the client to actualize this potential. In summary, the counselor does everything possible to enable the client to act most constructively and to emerge from therapy with new coping strategies that enable the client to deal more functionally with his or her life problems.

Concreteness

While some clients may come to therapy with a clear idea of the symptoms that are causing problems for them, often they are vague and, perhaps, even unaware of the causes of their personally felt distress. Concreteness is a process of defining, honing, and hemming up the vague and undifferentiated aspects of the client's life into a more precise knowledge of what the problem is, why it is a problem, and how to deal effectively and efficiently with it. A legitimate and worthwhile outcome of effective psychotherapy is greater clarity about the causes of a client's issues, problems, and dilemmas. In the action phase of therapy, concreteness is a matter of pinning down the action that the client wants to take, defining a plan, and moving toward implementation. In scoring, a counselor who demonstrates concreteness clearly involves the client in discussion of specific feelings, situations, and events regardless of their emotional content. There is no avoiding difficult content or feelings. In summary, the counselor facilitates a direct expression of all personally relevant feelings and experiences in concrete and specific terms and helps the client move toward definite steps to help develop more functional coping skills.

Appropriate Technique

As the reader will see in a later chapter (Chapter 14), techniques have a useful and even dramatic place in the process of psychotherapy. An analogy might be the utensils we use to eat our breakfast or lunch—a knife, fork, and spoon. Can we eat soup with a knife? Possibly, but the process is going to be long and messy. Can we cut hamburger with a fork? Yes. How about a steak? Well, we can but with more difficulty and less effectiveness than if we use a knife. The point here is that if we have proper utensils, then we can be more effective and efficient in our tasks. It is no less so in psychotherapy. Techniques are often the tools we use to be of service to clients. It is important to note that the knife, fork, and spoon are not the meal itself. And, techniques are not meant to be the substance of psychotherapy, which might more accurately be found in the quality of the relationship established between the counselor and the client. Nevertheless, the use of techniques can add zest and stimulation to a psychotherapy session. This category is used to help the counselor see whether or not appropriate techniques are being introduced into the therapy. In scoring, and in feedback, both the underutilization and overuse of techniques may be identified.

Appropriate Confrontation

Confrontation is a double-edged sword for the counselor. It may provoke the client into a deeper self-exploration, greater clarity of expression, or a more decisive plan of action, or it may create anger, resentment, or defensiveness. Two factors predict which outcome is more likely—the quality of the relationship and the intensity of the confrontation.

Confrontation, in all likelihood, is not a good intervention early in a counseling relationship. In order to confront client behavior a relationship of trust and an attitude of respect has to be established. Welch (1998) discusses this issue in regard to tough and tender psychotherapy. It is with the defenses that one is tough. The client, who is in a vulnerable state, should feel the tenderness of psychotherapy. It is important to remember that one confronts defenses and pathology and not the person himself or herself. The relationship should be sound and stable. In fact, the better the relationship, the more intense the confrontation may be and still be successful.

More often than not, the confrontation should be mild, but consideration must be given to the intensity of any confrontation. A confrontation that is too weak has little chance of success, and one that is too strong will provoke defensiveness and has little chance of insight or change. The guidelines for useful confrontation in counseling are straightforward but crucial if a counselor is going to be able to help the client explore, understand, and move to action.

- We have already indicated the first step—establish a relationship of caring and trust. It may take a while to reach such a point and that is why confrontation is not recommended for use early in counseling.
- Next, introduce any confrontation with genuine empathy that communicates to the client an understanding of the client's problem and a foundation for the confrontational statement.
- Early confrontation should be general rather than specific. Talk about people, events, and situations in general rather than about the specific client and his or her life circumstances. Do not back the client into a corner. Build in escape routes. For example, use phrases such as "sometimes," "maybe," "some people," "now and then," "occasionally," or "it could be that." This nonaccusatory tone allows the client to do the personalizing and to more easily accept what is said.
- Do not make the confrontation punitive, vindictive, or insulting. The purpose of confrontation in counseling is to be therapeutic. This is a place where one's heart must be pure. It must be clear to the client and to the therapist that the purpose of the confrontation is to advance the therapy in some meaningful way.

Strengthening the Confrontation. Later in the counseling process, the need may arise for stronger confrontations, which require that the counselor shift the focus of the confrontation somewhat.

- Personalize the confrontation. Be clear that the counselor is talking directly about the client. Use the client's name and focus directly on the situation or event that the client has identified.

• Be concrete and specific. The counselor should be clear and precise in identifying what is being confronted. There should be no doubt about what the counselor is doing and why. The easiest way to do this, of course, is to tell the client directly that you are confronting his or her behavior and why. As with any counseling intervention, this should be done respectfully and with a communicated understanding of the client's point of view.

• Confront immediately. If the counselor wishes to make the confrontation powerful, then it is important to intervene as close to the person, events, or situations as possible. This proximity in time increases the intensity of the confrontation.

• Confront words and actions. Sometimes people don't know or don't realize what they have said. Bringing their words to their attention can have a therapeutic effect. It is also possible that clients can deny their words, but if actions are confronted, then it is more difficult to avoid the confrontation. This makes the confrontation more intense.

• Use the past to confront the present. Use the client's own words, actions, and behaviors from previous sessions to contradict what is being said or done in the present. In effect, the client is being confronted by the client in this situation and not by the therapist at all.

It is important to introduce a word of caution here. Counselors and psychotherapists must be careful that their opinions, attitudes, and values are not the sole basis for a confrontation. If that is the case, then the purpose of the confrontation is not therapy but indoctrination. It is also important to remember to confront the behavior and not the person and to not cross the line between the two. Regulating the intensity of the confrontation requires the counselor's skill and judgment.

In scoring this category, the observer must judge whether the intensity of confrontation is strong enough to have an effect but not so strong that it causes the client to feel inadequate, react defensively, or be unable to find some constructive action. This may require some feedback to the counselor about the certainty that his or her motives were therapeutic.

Immediacy

This concept has two meanings. The first has to do with the recognition and acknowledgment of obvious emotions in the counseling session. Sometimes we are so concerned with underlying feelings that we miss and/or forget to acknowledge the obvious and immediate feelings being expressed by the client. The second meaning has to do with issues or problems that occur in the therapy session that are not directly related to the client's issues but that are interfering with the therapy. In one example, a male client bid good-bye to his female therapist by saying, "See you next week, babe." The counselor reacted by saying, "Bill, come back for a minute. When you said 'babe' it sounded as if you were seeing me as an eligible female, someone you might date. I need to be clear with you and let you know that I don't think I can be of help to you if you see me that way. I am your therapist and not an eligible woman." The client responded appropriately, left, and the therapy continued the next week. The counselor's response was immediate and effective. If she had not responded with immediacy, then the counseling process could have been negatively affected. In scoring immediacy, the observer has to indicate not only the frequency of the interventions used but also what sort of immediacy is involved: Either the counselor in a direct and explicit manner relates the client's expressions as they relate to the present counseling relationship or the counselor starts an open and frank discussion of factors not directly related to the therapy which seem to be interfering with the therapy.

Open-Ended Statements/Questions

One way of encouraging clients to talk and explore their presently felt concerns is to provide them with an open-ended question or an unfinished statement. While probing, accusatory, or inquisitive questions tend not to be helpful in psychotherapy, open-ended questions used appropriately can help clients examine the issues and problems of their lives. An open-ended or unfinished statement might look like this: A client says, "I am confused about my relationship with Julie." The counselor might respond by saying, "The part that is confusing is . . ." This unfinished sentence allows the client not only to complete the sentence but to give some further thought to his relationship with Julie. An open-ended question about the same issue might ask, "When you think of those confusing thoughts, what are they?" Such a question has the possibility of helping the client clarify his or her thoughts and pinpoint his or her concerns without leading the client. In scoring, it is important to distinguish between probing questions, which are not helpful, and open-ended ones which are.

Clarification (Question or Statement)

Clients can be vague. Their language may be imprecise and their references, although internally meaningful, may elude the counselor. Occasionally, in spite of well-developed listening skills, a counselor simply may not get what the client means. That is when a clarifying statement or question is appropriate. The client may say, "My sister, mother, and aunt came into the room and she hit me." Who hit her is unknown and is of some importance so the counselor could simply ask, "Who hit you?" This is just a matter of clarifying a confusion. Another example of clarification might be a matter not only of clarifying something for the counselor but of clarifying it for the client too.

A client might say, "I was really puzzled about what to do, but I think I did the right thing." The counselor might clarify this by saying, "You discovered a value that was important enough to stand up for." Such a response might help the client understand the reason for his or her action and bring the value into sharper focus. The observer is again responsible for separating what might be a clarifying question from a probing one. In scoring, it is not particularly important to identify whether what is being tallied is a statement or a question because both serve the same purpose.

Appropriate Self-Disclosure

Self-disclosure is appropriate when it is the intention of the psychotherapist that the disclosure help the client explore, understand, or move toward action. In a word, self-disclosure is appropriate when it is meant to be therapeutic. There are guidelines for self-disclosure that may help counselors understand its role in psychotherapy. Self-disclosure is most effective:

- When it emerges from the immediate relationship. It is not a random or isolated act and is related in some way to the content and meaning of the client's narrative.
- When what is revealed is appropriate and relevant. Therapeutic self-disclosure is not mere storytelling but has some therapeutic value in that it helps the client's exploration or understanding.
- When it is appropriate in degree. Self-disclosure is most effective when it is provided in steps or increments and a client is not overwhelmed by it.
- When the counselor checks to see the effect of the disclosure on the client. The therapist must check to ensure that the disclosure has not only been received but that it had the intended effect.
- When the relationship is strong enough to support the disclosure. This is especially the case when the self-disclosure may reveal some episode or time in the counselor's life when he or she was vulnerable. It is important that the relationship be strong enough that the client will not lose confidence in the therapist and will be able to hear that the events disclosed did not overwhelm the counselor and that there is a lesson to be learned from the self-disclosure.
- When it is true.
- When it is brief and not an extended and complex story.
- When it is not a case of one-upmanship in which the counselor's life experience somehow overshadows the experience of the client (e.g., "You think that's bad. Wait until you hear what happened to me!").

191

In scoring, the observer looks to see if the counselor gives the impression of holding nothing back and of disclosing feelings and ideas fully and completely to the client. If some of the feelings are negative concerning the client, the counselor should employ them constructively as a basis for an open-ended inquiry. In summary, the counselor operates in a constructive fashion at the most intimate levels of self-disclosure.

Productive Silence

Silence can often be useful in counseling. This is especially true when a client is weeping. During these moments it is probably best not to interrupt the silence and to allow the client to weep until he or she begins to talk or makes eye contact, signaling that he or she is ready to begin again. We tend not to offer clients tissues while they are weeping for fear that it communicates a symbolic message of "dry your tears." Tissues should be within easy reach so that if a client wants one, it is there. As a general rule, we tend to wait 3 to 5 seconds before talking. Generally, when silence no longer seems productive an open-ended comment such as "Let me in on the thoughts that are going through your mind right now" will elicit a client response. The counselor must make a judgment about whether the silence is productive or not. Often, a therapist will find it necessary to "reflect the silence." This means that all silences are not alike and the counselor may make an empathic response that recognizes the particular nature of the silence. It may be a sad, angry, hostile, contemplative, or puzzled silence. The counselor's accurate response will help the client identify inner concerns and communicate them verbally once the counselor has provided an open-ended understanding of the silence. In scoring this category, the observer must judge whether the silence is productive and whether the counselor has used the opportunity for silent contemplation.

Appropriate Physical Contact

Counselors who touch are more effective than counselors who do not (Smith, Clance, & Imes, 1998). In spite of this, we live in hypersensitive times and counselors should pay attention to their clients and the manner in which touch is used in psychotherapy. Anthropologists might label the dominant cultural, gender, and lifestyle attitude in the United States toward touch as a modified, touch taboo society. We have ritualized touch procedures and identified acceptable areas of the body that are touchable in social, nonintimate situations. Typically, a handshake or a firm touch on the shoulder is recognized as a friendly gesture that is difficult to interpret as romantic or erotic. Conversely, a touch on the knee or thigh is easily read as inappropriate. Hugging a client at the end of a session is perfectly acceptable and if this is done with permission and a pure heart, then in all likelihood the message communicated is one of care and not one of "coming on."

In scoring, the observer should note the presence of touch and judge its appropriateness.

Attending Posture

Each of us knows the attending posture. When we are interested in what another person is saying we lean forward, make eye contact, and listen intently. Many beginning counselors seem to come to the first session with either stiff formality or affected nonchalance. In the first case, it is difficult to believe that a clerk who formally collects information is genuinely interested in one's personal life. In the second example, the counselor may come across as relaxed but indifferent. While the attending posture may become an object of ridicule, even among beginning counselors, it is a way of sitting that signals to clients that what they are saying is of interest and concern to the counselor. In scoring, the observer notes whether the posture appears attentive versus distant or overly relaxed.

193

Nonverbal Facilitation

Words convey some of our meaning. Our gestures, facial expressions, and body convey meanings as well. In a dramatic example, a psychotherapist was saying to a client "This is a safe place where you may feel free to say what you want" while extending his arm with the palm facing the client. He resembled a traffic cop stopping an oncoming lane of cars! One look at the videotape, however, revealed to him the meaning of his gesture, and nonverbal communication became much more a part of his understanding in therapy. Gestures can invite or can quell clients' sense of openness and trust in psychotherapy. Our training as psychotherapists has taught us to use clients' nonverbal gestures, expressions, and posture as clues to meaning. What is good for the goose is good for the gander, as the old saying has it. We cannot claim to recognize the importance of nonverbal clues in clients while simultaneously failing to recognize them in ourselves.

The attending posture is a nonverbal clue. It signals interest in the client's narrative. A frown can communicate disapproval. This is tricky business here because it runs into the matter of genuineness. Nevertheless, while listening to clients talk, a therapist's face ought not to give any clues that might alter the client's story; thus, a counselor should appear interested and attentive without showing any apparent reaction to what the client is saying. This is difficult in the beginning because we have spent our life doing just the opposite—using our face to communicate our reaction to what other people are saying. We are subtly guiding their communication as they are picking up our clues so that they don't say anything particularly offensive or controversial. In counseling, we have to train ourselves to not subtly guide the clients' communication so that what clients say has a greater chance of accurately reflecting their thoughts rather than trying to please the psychotherapist. This changes, of course, when the counselor is speaking. Sometimes, beginning counselors have learned to sit quietly listening so well that when they speak they appear to be statues talking. The full range of facial expressions, gestures, and body movements are open to the counselor so that our understanding of the client's meaning can be fully communicated. Gestures that are physically inviting the client to continue talking such as nods and hand gestures (e.g., a "come here" gesture) can be used making words sometimes unnecessary in the session permitting clients to continue with their experiential flow without interruption but recognizing that the counselor is with them. In scoring, the observer is looking for both the problem of nonverbal clues that

194

will guide the client and the ability to use nonverbal clues to help the client more openly tell his or her story.

Appropriate Summary

We believe that the summary of a counseling session is one of the most important stages of the counseling encounter. It is a time when the gains of the session can be recognized and acknowledged. Sometimes clients express surprise during the summary when they realize that they did make progress. It is significant especially when progress is slow and the mill is grinding exceedingly fine. Small steps may be missed in the flow of the session and the summary helps clients know that progress is being made. One of us sometimes tells students that they can lift a car single-handedly! After a dramatic pause to allow the students to ponder this amazing tour de force, he informs them that all they need is a car jack. Jacks operate on the principle that little gains, held in place, can bring about huge change. Psychotherapy can operate in this way and the summary can help achieve that end. It is important in the process of change to acknowledge gains, no matter how small. The summary is not a time to review content but a time to look back over the meanings that have emerged during that day's session.

The summary usually has two parts: clients are offered the chance to look back and review what has emerged for them and the psychotherapist has the chance to point out additional meanings that seem important. The observer notes whether the psychotherapist permits the client to provide a summary and might also note therapist participation in it. One last note: The summary can also teach a counselor to be aware of the time in a session so that a sufficient period is allowed at the end for a reasonable summary.

195

Blocking Dimensions

The truth is that in the counseling profession we know more completely and with more certainty what doesn't work than what does. Effectiveness in psychotherapy is very much an individual process. Effective psychotherapists are ones who are authentic. Authenticity requires that one know "who I am" and be able to be present in psychotherapy as that "self"—not pretending to be someone else, not acting in a role, but being one's self as naturally and as without guile as possible. Given that that is the case, there are many effective ways to communicate empathy and respect. Thus, effective counselors may look very different from one another. The attitudinal metatheoretical conditions of effective therapy we have discussed are obviously communicated in individual styles.

On the other hand, it appears that ineffective psychotherapists tend to be ineffective in highly similar ways. Their mistakes tend to be common and identifiable (Welch, 1998). The blocking dimensions are categories of commonly recognized therapeutic mistakes that counselors need to avoid even as they struggle to find their individual, effective style.

Content "Parroting" (Mere Repeating)

Perhaps the most common complaint we hear from clients is that "the counselor just repeated back to me what I said." Their exasperation is understandable. Clients come with the hope that what is eluding them might be uncovered or discovered in therapy. Merely repeating what clients said provides no deeper understanding or help than they are able to articulate for themselves. Empathy, of course, is different from repeating a client's own words. As we have said, gains are made in therapy when the therapist can understand meanings that may be only vaguely felt or understood by the client.

When clients use emotional words in recounting their experience, the counselor's task is made a bit more difficult. A client might talk about some past relationship by saying, "I feel so sad about not having Juan for a friend anymore." Because so many of us have been taught to recognize and identify feelings and because with this statement the client has already identified the feeling, we may feel at a loss. Many beginning counselors might say, "So you are feeling sad." Well, of course, the client feels sad—that is just what he or she said! In order to discover an empathic response to this statement, a therapist could ask himself or herself, "How might a person feel in order to say he or she feels sad?" One response might be "guilty." Rather than repeating what a client has said, an effective counselor would try to help the client explore where the feelings of sadness are coming from. Perhaps the client feels that he or she did not do enough to maintain the relationship with Juan. In any case, merely repeating what the client says is ineffective and counselors who force themselves to respond in some other way develop a greater repertoire of helpful responses for clients. In scoring, the observer indicates each example of "parroting."

Using Power

Clients do not come to psychotherapy to be lorded over by psychotherapists. Authoritarian orders to change their attitudes or behavior reduce clients to objects of the counselor's will. The goal of psychotherapy is to empower clients. Psychotherapists are forbidden to use "power against" their clients. Other forms of power can be effectively used in psychotherapy such as "power to," "power for," and "power with." An example of "power with" is an effective psychotherapist who collaborates with a client to build a more functional coping strategy in the face of unavoidable conflict. Or perhaps a therapist who has developed a relationship of trust might encourage a client to face some difficult aspect of life. We observed a counselor working with a client on a phobia. When it came time for the client to actually deal with the phobia after a process of small steps leading up to that moment, the client said, "I'll do it because I have faith in you." This is a powerful statement that should remind us of our responsibility to clients. It is also an example of the "power to" use authority and trust to be of help to clients.

"Power for" may be represented by the ways in which counselors write reports, make recommendations, help clients get appointments at some agency, or help them make contact with a psychiatrist. For a more lengthy description see Welch (1998) where each of the uses of power is discussed in more detail. In scoring, the observer must judge

197

whether the counselor's interactions appear to be using power against the client, which might include the symbolic use of mannerisms or the use of objects such as pens, folders, or clipboards as signs of the counselor's higher status.

Moralizing/Being Judgmental

As Albert Ellis would phrase it, the counselor is "shoulding" all over the client! Moralizing and being judgmental can take many forms, such as a verbal or nonverbal indication of disapproval for the client or his or her acts or thinly disguised appeals to adopt a value or to shame a client into some assumed, important action. Put as simply as we can, these verbal or nonverbal actions indicate through word or deed what should or ought to be done and what is right. They may involve guilt, shame, or persuasion. Whatever they involve, the observer's task is to note each instance and to bring it to the counselor's attention so that this ineffective behavior is stopped.

Advice

Effective psychotherapists have learned that "if telling worked, then there would be no need for psychotherapy." There are plenty of worthwhile philosophies of life that one could follow. The problem is not a lack of advice about how we should live our lives but a lack of personal meaning for the individual to whom it is given. A Chinese proverb says, "Give persons a fish and you feed them for a day. Teach them to fish and you feed them for life." Psychotherapy is a process of creating or discovering within oneself coping strategies that one may use to deal with the people, situations, and events of life. Advice, however well intentioned, ultimately teaches clients that they are not capable of handling their own lives and they learn that they must always turn to others for help even when they themselves possess the resources to effectively and efficiently cope with their problems. Although the process may be slower, the result is longer lasting when clients come to solutions and resolutions through their own efforts. Psychotherapists can help, but they should not take over the client's life. The observer should note each time any advice is given. This can lead to a discussion of what might have been a more effective counseling intervention.

Interrupting

There are at least two reasons for interrupting. One is necessary and therapeutic and the other is simply rude. If the counselor interrupts for a therapeutic reason it is not scored here. Therapeutic interruptions of a fast-talking, "runaway train" help clients to hear their own talking, which they may be missing as they rush from word to word and sentence to sentence. But a stylistic "talking over" of clients is not helpful and should be brought to the therapist's attention. Thus, in scoring note only when counselors are talking before the client finishes, not when they interrupt on purpose. That is the behavior that is important to extinguish.

Lecturing (Logic)/Arguing

Psychotherapy is not meant to be an adversarial relationship. Clients are not attending class nor did they come to be exhorted to live a better life. Occasionally, persuasion may be important in therapy but it should be used cautiously, purposively, and sparingly. Therapists should not be trying to talk clients into something or lecturing them. Sometimes counselors who simply take too long to get out what they want to say are seen as lecturing. The observer must be sensitive to the counselor's intentions (checked during feedback) and must determine whether the counselor is trying to influence the client.

Inappropriate Confrontation

One helpful rule for all psychotherapists, whether new or old, is to be tough on defenses and tender with persons. Effective confrontations are timed accurately, with the appropriate intensity and within an atmosphere of trust. Even with this advice, it is important to remember that people in therapy are vulnerable and that a confrontation of a client's "personness" stands little chance of successfully elaborating a situation, providing understanding, or moving the client toward action. On the other hand, defenses should be encountered with strength and resolve. Observers must gauge not only timing and strength but whether the counselor is trying in some way to sway the client, especially if a value is being confronted. The reader might also want to see Welch (1998) for a thorough discussion of the need for both tough and tender psychotherapy.

Evaluative Praise/Approval

While praise seems such a good thing, the difficulty is that praise often requires an evaluation or judgment of clients and their behavior. The danger is that praise can create dependency and become a subtle form of manipulation.

It is sometimes difficult to separate praise from encouragement and appreciation. It is perfectly appropriate to encourage clients and to appreciate their courage and commitment. The difference seems to lie in what might be labeled *evaluative praise*. This sort of praise seems to be saying to clients, "When you act in these ways, I am pleased"—and that is the danger. The implication is that if the client does not act in those ways then the counselor will be displeased and possibly disapproving. Such praise seems to focus on behavior or client acts.

Encouragement is different in that it seems to focus on the person. Encouragement might take the form of saying, "I know this is hard right now but I believe you can do it." The focus is on the client and not on the action. Another term some use for this is *appreciative praise*. What is appreciated are clients and not an evaluation of their acts. In scoring, the observer should have these distinctions in mind and record only those evaluative events of praise and approval.

Closed Questions/Probing Questions

We attended a workshop in which former clients were evaluating their experiences in psychotherapy. One of the participants said, "There is too much psychological archeology going on out there." He went on to elaborate that he felt probed, invaded, even violated by his therapist's investigatorial questioning. It seemed to him as if he were a criminal in the hands of a vigorous prosecuting attorney. If we use a physical model, probing questions take the form of poking, jabbing, and opening sores and old wounds before the client is prepared to acknowledge them. The most unhelpful question seems to be "why." Probably each of us has had the experience of being asked why we did something and in frustration have shouted back, "I don't know why. I just did it." Our parents didn't believe us when we said it and we might not believe it now when our children say it to us. But, if we could somehow recapture the moment when we said it, it might, in all likelihood, be true. It is one of the foundations of psychological theory that many of us act without a clear idea of why we do the things we do. Clients are often searching for meanings in their lives that they can live with, but through experience seasoned psychotherapists have learned that the underlying causes of life, the motivations that push or pull us, are not open to direct investigation.

Closed questions are ones that may be responded to with a simple "yes" or "no" answer and might look like a game of 20 questions. While closed questions might not suffer from the shortcomings of probing questions, they offer little help in exploring clients' vague and undifferentiated sources of psychological distress.

It requires trust, a degree of safety, and discernment to move consistently in the direction of genuine understanding. Empathic responding is a better guide to the levels of awareness in human beings. Questioning may be used to pinpoint or clarify some confusion in the therapy but its usefulness is limited when it communicates to the client that once the questions are answered the counselor will have the answers to the client's life problems. The observer should tally each probing question as a way of helping the counselor move questions to clarifying statements and to empathy.

Labeling

It is difficult to understand, no matter how frequently it is done, the usefulness of labeling in psychotherapy. While diagnosis can play an important role in deciding on a treatment plan, saying directly to a client that he or she is a "borderline personality" or that he or she shows all the symptoms of "neurosis" or "mental illness" or that his or her "inner child" is injured seems to us nothing more than bombarding clients with jargon. Whatever those terms may mean to psychotherapists, clients can be completely lost regarding their technical meanings and the danger of reading more into a therapist's statements than the therapist intended is real indeed. Labeling can also be a form of using power, of distancing the therapist from a genuine relationship, and it may signal a fear of authenticity on the part of the therapist. This is one of those behaviors that we would simply advise not to do. Labels, no matter the intention of the therapist, merely stereotype the client into a group and deny the client's individuality. The observer scores this category by indicating the number of times the therapist labels the client. One is too many.

Explaining/Interpreting

It is very tempting for beginning counselors to instruct the client in their theory of personality. Naive counselors might listen for a while, but the allure of explaining their insights will prove too great and they will launch into an interpretation of why clients have the problems they do. Although clients are interested in finding the causes of their behavior, they need to discover a personally meaningful explanation rather than hearing the therapist's explanation. Such acts can be seen as disrespectful and even dumb because clients have already heard a number of explanations of their behavior from their exasperated relatives and friends and well-intentioned others. In scoring, the observer should code each incident of interpretation and in feedback should point out other more effective strategies.

Unproductive Silence

Sometimes silence is helpful and sometimes it is not. We use a rule of waiting about 3 to 5 seconds and if it is apparent that the client is stuck, puzzling, or contemplating, then we encourage the client to express the puzzling or contemplations out loud so the counselor can be aware of them. Silences that go on too long hold the danger of becoming judgmental, awkward, and even embarrassing. The observer must use judgment and score this category when the silence seems unproductive; it then becomes a topic for discussion in feedback.

Inappropriate Physical Contact

Touch is coded (or checked) when it is obvious that the client has been touched in some inappropriate way by the therapist. The mark should be readily apparent because this is a serious mistake. Inappropriate touch takes two forms. The first form, which is the most serious, is touch that implies some romantic or erotic intention. The leg, knee, thigh, genitals, chest, and buttocks are all inappropriate areas to touch in the context of a professional counseling relationship. It is more difficult to observe when the touch is in an appropriate place but its nature and intention is not therapeutic. Appropriate touch is both in an appropriate place on the body and firm (e.g., a handshake or a hello or goodbye pat on the shoulder).

The second form of inappropriate touch is not sensual or romantic, it merely interrupts an emotional moment. This may happen even when the counselor intends to comfort or show support. Most of the time touch takes the emotions away and returns the client to an intellectual frame. Thus, we recommend that during moments of weeping therapists do not touch clients, at least not until the client has ceased weeping and has begun talking or has made eye contact with the therapist. Then it would be appropriate to grasp the client's hand or to give a supportive pat on the arm. Each incident of inappropriate touch should be recorded and discussed with the counselor so that it does not occur again.

203

Humoring/Withdrawing

People often break tension with a joke. Sometimes this behavior carries over into the counseling room and a therapist will make a joke or seem to purposefully not acknowledge a tender or painful emotion. Obviously, we do not serve our clients well if we withdraw from their emotional hurts. The observer should indicate each time the counselor tries to kid the client, ignores a problem, tries to make light of a situation, continually avoids an issue, or talks around some obvious concern.

Nonverbal Blocking

Counselors who lounge. Therapists who sit behind desks. Counselors who sit stiffly with their arms crossed. Therapists who do not make eye contact or seem to be "shifty-eyed" or nervous, agitated, or bored. All of these people display behavior that can confuse and put off clients. Hand gestures that put up a barrier between the client and the therapist (much like the "traffic cop" described earlier) interfere with the open flow of information between a client and a therapist. In scoring, the observer should make a note of each incidence of nonverbal blocking for discussion in feedback.

Sympathy

Psychotherapists are not stones or statues without feeling. We are often touched by the stories that clients tell and we feel for them. It is a matter of training and discipline and the sure knowledge that sympathy is not helpful that allows therapists to respond with empathy rather than with sympathy. Sympathy, no matter how appreciated, tends to stop a person right where he or she is in the process and does not provide that person with any of the clarification necessary to move on in his or her life. Sympathy is a helpful response from our friends and loved ones, but not from psychotherapists. Sympathy would be scored when the therapist clearly is identifying with the client. Comments such as, "Oh my, how terrible for you" or "Oh, that's awful" or "Why that rotten SOB!" or "Awwwh" are all sympathetic responses. Crying with a client more often than not is a sympathetic reaction, but sometimes it comes from feeling our own pain in response to the client's reminders of pain in our own lives. The danger of sympathy is that the goal may be to make the client feel better or to make ourselves feel better by having the client not show so much emotion. The observer should score each example of sympathy so that they may be discussed in feedback.

Minimizing/Maximizing

More often than not, minimizing and/or maximizing are due to the inadequacy of the counselor's affective vocabulary. Saying "very angry" reveals the lack of a more descriptive word or phrase that might more accurately describe the client's experience. If a person is angry, then that is his or her experience. The counselor runs a risk by adding a modifier that the client may not feel and by so doing may end up leading the client toward a level of feeling he or she does not have. It is important to be precise in psychotherapy. Subtlety, nuance, and shades of meaning can lead to understanding and effective action.

Summary

This chapter introduced a counselor observation form that can be used to provide the foundation for feedback as counselors seek to improve their skills. Most psychotherapy training programs would probably agree with our list of facilitative dimensions, although individual differences and emphases might alter some of the categories a bit. We believe there would be even greater agreement on the blocking dimensions. These behaviors have been proven in research and in clinical experience to be ineffective in the counseling relationship. We encourage you to use this observation form as you review your own taped sessions and as you observe others. It offers the possibility of clear, concrete, and valuable feedback that can lead to positive change for developing counselors.

References and for Further Reading

Carkhuff, R. B., & Berenson, B. G. (1967). *Beyond counseling and therapy* (2nd ed.). New York: Holt, Rinehart & Winston.

Gazda, G. M, Asbury, F. S., Balzer, F. J., Childers, W. C., & Walters, R. P. (1984). *Human relations development* (3rd ed.). Boston: Allyn & Bacon.

Jourard, S. M. (1968). *Disclosing man to himself*. New York: Van Nostrand.

Jourard, S. M. (1971). *The transparent self*. New York: Van Nostrand Rinehold.

Lewis, J. M. (1991). Thirty years of teaching psychotherapy skills. *International Journal of Group Psychotherapy, 41*, 419–432.

Peachey, J. B., et al. (1991). Therapeutic skills. In I. B. Glass (Ed.), *The international handbook of addiction behaviour* (pp. 207–273). London: Tavistock/Routledge.

Raskin, N. J., & Rogers, C. R. (1989). Person-centered therapy. In R. J. Corsini & D. Wedding (Eds.), *Current psychotherapies*. Itasca, IL: F. E. Peacock.

Smith, E. W. L., Clance, P. R., & Imes, S. (1988). *Touch in psychotherapy: Theory, research, and practice*. New York: Guilford Press.

Welch, I. D. (1998). *The path of psychotherapy: Matters of the heart*. Pacific Grove, CA: Brooks/Cole.

14

Techniques in Counseling and Psychotherapy

The word *techniques* carries a variety of meanings in psychotherapy. Here the word is used to mean specific intervention strategies utilized during the psychotherapy session for a definite purpose (see Appendix 2). Examples of techniques are interventions such as visualization (Ayres & Hopf, 1987; Nelson, 1987; Turkington, 1987), empty chair (Conoley, Conoley, McConnell, & Kimzey, 1983), and storytelling (Hunter, 1983; Stirtzinger, 1983). This section will provide a review of some of the advantages of using techniques for both the therapist and the client. Among the inherent dangers in writing about the use of techniques in psychotherapy is that more importance will be assigned to them than is appropriate. Our observations as clinical supervisors teach us that many inexperienced therapists move too quickly into problem solving without an adequate exploration and understanding of the clients' issues. Armed with specific techniques, inexperienced therapists may be too eager to "get on with it" without a clear understanding of the client's dilemmas (Williams, 1988). There is a danger of dealing only with the apparent and not the real or causal.

The Role of Techniques

Techniques, in and of themselves, do not heal. We agree with Highlen and Hill (1984) that the likelihood of successful therapy is found in more subtle and more difficult predictors. The essence of therapy lies in the ability of a therapist to establish a therapeutic relationship with a client (Highlen & Hill, 1984; Kiesler & Watkins, 1989; Patterson, 1984). The most important dimension of that relationship is the therapist's capacity to understand the client and to communicate that understanding to the client (Okun, 1997; Rogers, 1980). Without empathic understanding, any technique or attempt to problem solve is merely a "shot in the dark." Occasionally, one will hit the mark, but seldom will one win any prizes for marksmanship. The same is true of psychotherapy. One may prove to be of some help to another person through genuine concern and by accidental interventions without much preparation or training; however, one cannot count on such accidents for continued and consistent success. Thus, empathy forms the foundation for successful psychotherapeutic intervention.

The effective therapeutic relationship is characterized by empathy, but that is not the only important aspect (Carkhuff, 1987; Gazda, Asbury, Balzer, Childers, & Walters, 1984; Patterson, 1984). It must be a relationship in which the client comes to trust the therapist with those parts of his or her life that are frightening, embarrassing, and painful. Thus, the therapist's suspension of judgment is crucial for the early therapeutic relationship.

One other aspect of the therapeutic relationship merits comment. Some therapists communicate a sense of faith in their clients' ability to contribute solutions to their own realized dilemmas remarkably well. In a word, some therapists are especially respectful of their clients' capacity to explore, problem solve, and cope.

These are the characteristics—along with others (e.g., self-disclosure, confrontation, concreteness) used to describe the therapist-client relationship—that are predictive of successful therapy rather than techniques alone. A client's entry into therapy for the purpose of exam-

ining the fearful, embarrassing, and painful parts of life is the first prerequisite of successful therapy. The second prerequisite is a therapist
who is able to understand and communicate that understanding, suspend judgment, and convey a sense of personal respect for the client's
strengths. These two qualities set the stage for the successful outcome
of a therapeutic relationship (Garfield & Bergin, 1986; Gladding, 1988;
Rogers, 1957). Techniques can strengthen the therapeutic relationship,
but, it should be clear, techniques alone are poor predictors of successful therapeutic outcomes (Mahoney, 1986).

Pointing out the limitations of techniques does not imply that they
are unimportant. Our experience, both as therapists and as clinical
supervisors of novice therapists, is that techniques often provide useful
structure for the therapist and valuable insights for the client. Techniques present the therapist both with hazards and opportunities.

The hazards, which have been discussed above, are the assumption
that the mastery of techniques makes one a master psychotherapist
and the danger of premature, and therefore inaccurate, problem solving. The opportunities are discussed in the following section.

209

The Advantages of Techniques

Our experience has shown that techniques often provide structure for
the therapist and insight for the client. In other words, techniques are
effective when used properly.

Advantages for the Therapist

Energy. The introduction of a technique can make the session
more active and alive. Techniques can add sparkle and vigor to sessions
that seem to be dull, unhelpful, and boring.

Pace. Techniques can modulate the rate of a session. If the pace is
too rapid, introducing a technique can slow it down so that information
can be understood and even reflected upon. In this case, the therapist
may employ purposeful interruption as a technique.

Obstacles. Techniques can "facilitate the process." Sometimes understanding and insight come with pain and grueling slowness. Techniques can be used to provide "end runs" around "defenses."

Content. Techniques can be used to expand the material of therapy. The techniques themselves may call to memory ideas, episodes, and events that were previously vague and undifferentiated.

Clarification. When the therapy is vague, when the issues elude, when the etiology is just too slippery, techniques can serve to clarify the therapy, pin down the issues, and identify the origins of the pain in concrete and understandable ways. Introducing techniques specifically designed to attack a particular knot can untie a therapy session and move it toward effectiveness.

Advantages for the Client

Energy. Not unlike for the therapist, the use of techniques may enliven the session for the client. The client may be invigorated, energized, and stimulated by techniques that introduce action into the session.

Novelty. Techniques inject a degree of novelty into therapy. The week-in-week-out strategy of therapy can bog down and can give the appearance of a repetitive discussion of the same old issue session after session. Techniques can make the sessions new and can make the client come to eagerly anticipate the session

Participation. Techniques can help make the client an active participant in the therapy. They offer clients a variety of methods to better express themselves and their own insights into their issues.

Integration. Techniques offer the client the opportunity to integrate what has been gained in therapy. They can provide just the distance clients might need to see their lives in different perspectives.

Insights that might escape clients in talking therapy might present themselves for inspection during the use of a technique.

Section Summary

In this section we have explored the role of techniques in psychotherapy and have examined some of the dangers of using techniques in therapy without both a proper perspective and proper training. These dangers include practitioners who confuse mastery of techniques with mastery of psychotherapy—some of whom may confuse certification in a technique workshop with the ability to practice psychotherapy independently without preparation, training, and supervision.

Even though dangers exist, there are advantages in using techniques in psychotherapy. For the therapist, advantages include infusing energy into the session, being able to moderate pace, overcoming obstacles, generating content, and increasing clarification. Techniques can provide therapists with a strategy for keeping therapy active, focused, and clear.

Advantages for the clients include an energetic session, the concept of novelty, active participation, and the integration of therapeutic themes from the therapy. Techniques can also provide the opportunity for clients to actively participate in therapy, clearly understanding the gains that are being made.

211

Principles for Using Techniques

We have developed seven principles involving the use of techniques in psychotherapy. These principles serve to remind the psychotherapist of the place and usefulness of techniques. Each principle is presented as a declarative statement followed by a short discussion to clarify meaning.

Principle 1. Don't experiment with clients. Without being maudlin, and yet still making a point, people who enter therapy are too vulnerable to serve as subjects in a trial-and-error experiment. A therapist uses a technique in therapy because he or she already knows the technique is effective and useful in that particular situation. It is a tangible violation of clients to experiment in therapy with some strategy for which a general idea of the expected outcome is not already known. In a phrase, therapists do not "try something, just to see if it works." There must be some theoretical or experiential prior justification for the use of techniques in therapy.

Principle 2. Don't rely on techniques. Techniques are not the essence of therapy; they are supplements (perhaps even special enhancements) to the therapeutic relationship. The essence of therapy lies more in the relationship than in specific techniques. A danger for beginning therapists is to use strategic interventions too much in any given session. Just as passive listening can become boring and useless, too many techniques become gimmicky and trite. A rule of thumb we follow is to use no more than three techniques in any single session.

Principle 3. Don't overuse a technique. Just as too many techniques in a single session can reduce effectiveness, so can using the same technique too frequently. Of course, it is important to cement the gains one has made in the therapy session and the sensitive repetition of an effective technique can do that. However, if a single technique is used repetitively, then it may become routine and lose its ability to illuminate new information and/or insight. We suggest, allowing for professional judgment, that at least one session intervene before the use of a technique is repeated.

Principle 4. Don't abandon techniques. Beginning therapists often will attempt a technique, with encouragement and with good results, and in later sessions will not grasp the opportunity to use it again when it is appropriate. In order to effectively use techniques, the therapist has to be sensitive to those points in therapy when a technique may be introduced with effectiveness. Also remember not to abandon the technique too quickly during a particular session. Beginning therapists may attempt a technique, fear that it is not working, and stop prematurely. It is important to stay with a technique. To some extent, this demands a belief, on the part of the therapist, that the technique will work and will provide useful information and/or insights for the therapy.

Principle 5. Techniques rarely fail. When supervising beginning therapists, it is not uncommon to see a therapist who uses a technique in the therapy session only to report, "I tried what you said and it didn't work." What is missing in this situation is an understanding of the use of techniques. Whether or not a client is able to do what is asked in a technique is irrelevant when judging the success of a technique. In fact, no matter how the client responds, information is generated when a technique is introduced into the therapy session. If the client is able to respond in the predicted way, then the material produced in the response is discussed. If the client does not respond in the predicted way and instead touches upon some other aspect of his or her life, then that material may become the focus of therapy. If the client is unable to enter into the technique at all, then that is significant in and of itself and the inability to enter the technique may become a focus of therapy. In essence, no matter what occurs when a technique is introduced, the material produced can be used to further the therapy.

Principle 6. Use the techniques you are good at. Not all techniques "fit" or are useful for all therapists. While we are familiar with many techniques, we don't use all of them in therapy sessions. Some techniques don't match the individual style or personality of particular therapists. Each therapist must struggle to find those techniques with which he or she is comfortable and to use those.

Now, let's discuss a bit of a paradox. Principle 1 advises that therapists not experiment with clients. That remains true. Nevertheless, one must experiment with techniques for one's own use. How does one get out of this seeming dilemma? There are two areas to consider here. First, this dilemma underscores the importance of training programs. It

213

is understood by volunteer clients that that is where new methods, techniques, strategies, or approaches are attempted. Understanding the following attitude also clears up the dilemma: When a therapist introduces a technique into therapy, the client is not being experimented upon because the therapist already knows that this technique has been proven effective with other clients in similar situations based on reports in the literature or the advice of the supervisor who has assured the therapist that the technique is appropriate. The therapist is testing whether or not he or she can use the technique effectively and comfortably. This is an important distinction. The technique should work; it has already been tested and reported in the literature.

Let us explore one more aspect of this problem. What is the role of creativity and spontaneity in therapy? How does one know that a creative intervention is not simply experimenting with a client? The answer to the first question is that creativity and spontaneity are important to effective therapeutic intervention. The answer to the second question involves the importance of being well-versed in one's theoretical orientation. One way to approach learning which techniques are comfortable is to try them out for fit. Another approach is to intellectually test them against one's philosophy and theoretical orientation. Although many techniques can be justified by several theoretical orientations, some cannot. This test of fit is another consideration of comfortableness. So far as creativity and spontaneity are concerned, an "on-the-spot" intervention still may not be considered trial and error because theoretically it should work. On the basis of one's theory one may create spontaneous psychotherapeutic interventions.

Principle 7. Use what the client is good at. In approaching clients, some techniques will prove more effective than others. Some clients may be more visual than others. Some may use audio cues. Others might be reluctant to enter into fantasy. Some might respond more readily to storytelling. Some might react negatively to behavioral rehearsal. Others might thoroughly object to an empty chair, while some seem to relish imagery. The principle of effectiveness is to honor the tendencies of the client. It is important to be sensitive to concerns such as learning style, gender, and culture.

Each of these may prove an impediment or a pathway to greater effectiveness with a client. To some extent, it is important to recognize that while "techniques rarely fail," some still do work more effectively with particular clients.

Guidelines for the Selection of Techniques

In our experience, two guidelines for the selection of techniques have emerged. One deals with when to use a technique in therapy and the other deals with what techniques to use.

Guideline 1. Select a technique for a specific purpose. A nontechnical way of phrasing this would be don't go on "fishing expeditions" to try to "hook into" something "spicy and delicious." The technique should be selected because the therapist already knows the usefulness and predicted outcome in the particular situation. Although serendipitous results may occur, that is not the intention of the intervention.

Guideline 2. Select techniques that fit you as a therapist. Therapists should only use techniques that fit their theoretical orientation, personal values, and personal style. One of the touchstones of effective therapy is that the client views the therapist as an authentic person. If the therapist uses techniques that make him or her uncomfortable, uneasy, or phony, then that discomfort is certain to be communicated to the client. Using the information presented in Principle 6, find those techniques that fit your theoretical orientation, personal values, and personal style—those techniques stand a greater chance of successfully adding to the overall effectiveness of the therapy.

References and for Further Reading

Ayres, J., & Hopf, T. S. (1987, July). Visualization, systematic desensitization, and rational emotive therapy: A comparative evaluation. *Communication Education, 36*(3), 236–240.

Carkhuff, R. R. (1987). *The art of helping VI* (6th ed.). Amherst, MA: Human Resource Development Press.

Conoley, C. W., Conoley, J. C., McConnell, J. A., & Kimzey, C. E. (1983, Spring). The effect of the ABCs of Rational Emotive Therapy and the empty-chair technique of Gestalt Therapy on anger reduction. *Psychotherapy, 20*(1), 112–117.

Garfield, S. L., & Bergin, A. E. (1986). *Handbook of psychotherapy and behavior change* (3rd ed.). New York: Wiley.

Gazda, G. M., Asbury, F. S., Balzer, F. J., Childers, W. C., & Walters, R. P. (1984). *Human relations development* (3rd ed). Boston: Allyn & Bacon.

Gladding, S. T. (1988). *Counseling: A comprehensive profession.* Columbus, OH: Charles E. Merrill.

Highlen, P. S., & Hill, C. E. (1984). Factors affecting client change in individual counseling: Current status and theoretical speculations. In S. D. Brown & R. W. Lent (Eds.), *The handbook of counseling psychology.* New York: Wiley.

Hunter, J. (1983, Fall). Truth and effectiveness in revelatory stories. *Revision, 6*(2), 3–15.

Kiesler, D. J., & Watkins, L. M. (1989, Summer). Interpersonal complementarity and the therapeutic alliance: A study of relationship in psychotherapy. *Psychotherapy, 26*(2), 183–194.

Mahoney, M. J. (1986, April). The tyranny of technique. *Counseling and Values, 30* (2), 169–174.

Nelson, R. C. (1987, October). Graphics in counseling. *Elementary School Guidance and Counseling, 22*(1), 17–29.

Okun, B. F. (1997). *Effective helping: Interviewing and counseling techniques* (5th ed.). Pacific Grove, CA: Brooks/Cole.

Patterson, C. H. (1984, Winter). Empathy, warmth and genuineness in psychotherapy: A review of reviews. *Psychotherapy, 21*(4), 431–438.

Rogers, C. R. (1957). The necessary and sufficient conditions of therapeutic personality change. *Journal of Consulting Psychology, 21*(4), 95–103.

Rogers, C. R. (1980). *A way of being.* Boston: Houghton Mifflin.

Stirtzinger, R. M. (1983, November). Storytelling: A creative therapeutic technique. *Canadian Journal of Psychiatry, 28*(7), 561–565.

Turkington, C. (1987, August). Help for the worried well. *Psychology Today, 21*(8), 44–48.

Williams, A. J. (1988). Action methods in supervision. *Clinical Supervisor, 6*(2), 13–27.

The Practice of Counseling and Psychotherapy

When the time comes to actually start seeing clients, numerous questions and circumstances may arise. Because in our experience the information you may find yourself seeking is not commonly covered in textbooks, we have tried to provide you with what you will need to know to prepare for your meetings with clients. We discuss in detail preparing for the initial client contact, an important event for both therapist and client. An initial therapy session that does not go well is greatly disappointing to both parties and may result in the client going elsewhere or giving up on counseling altogether. Hence, we provide information and ideas that enhance the likelihood of a successful initial interview. We discuss in detail conducting an intake and developing a thoughtful and meaningful treatment plan. Having a treatment plan gives the therapy process some direction by clarifying goals and providing a context in which to measure progress. Finally, we examine the complicated and important tasks involved in the process of termination. Earlier in this book you read about a therapist who was unable, at the time, to facilitate the ending of psychotherapy. We hope that the discussion included in this section will assist you in developing the skills needed for effective and graceful therapeutic endings.

15

❧

The Nature of Requests

*I*n the everyday turn of events, it is normal and natural for human beings to make requests of one another. The outcome of these requests, the degree of satisfaction, and the continuation of other requests is dependent on two factors—recognition and response. One other factor that complicates this matter is disguise. Before we turn to the requests themselves, let us deal with recognition, response, and disguise.

Recognition

It goes without saying that in order to respond to any request, one must know what is being asked. At the expense of sounding overly simplistic, recognition may be viewed as accurate or inaccurate. Much comedy is based on the misunderstanding of requests. Picture a scene in a restaurant in which one patron turns to another and says, "Pass the salt, please." This is a clear request for action. The other patron says, "Fine, thanks." We are left with no clue as to what was in the mind of the second patron. Another more complex example might be when the first patron says, "Pass the salt, please" and the second says, "No, I think I'll use it. I like salt." Here the second patron has heard a dietary request from patron one and declined it! The point of these rather silly examples is that in order to respond in any satisfactory way one must accurately recognize the nature of a request.

Many failures of recognition have identifiable roots of misunderstanding. Many simple requests are inaccurately recognized because of language and cultural, gender, and lifestyle differences. Regionalisms, slang, and usage may confuse. "Wow, that man is hot!" may mean he is sexy. It may mean he is on the run from the law. "Cool" may be good but "cold" may be bad rather than very good. Consider the frustration you feel when you are unable to get another to recognize what you actually want from him or her. We have probably all heard stories of the experience of American travelers abroad. A simple request for information can lead to extreme frustration. "Where is the train station?" may be met with a blank look by a native of Belgium. "Where-is-the-Traiiin-Staaation?" "Where Is The Traiiiiin Staaaation?!" "WHERE IS THE TRAIN STATION?!!!" Somewhere in our past, I suppose, we have all learned that if someone doesn't understand a request the solution is to make the request louder!

Customs can create confusion. One of us was in Germany and went into a Gasthaus and ordered a beer. He said, "Bier, Bitte" and held up his index finger to signal one beer. The waiter came back with two beers. After considerable back and forth, he finally learned that Americans begin counting with the index finger and Europeans begin counting with the thumb. The thumb is one and the index finger is two. Apparently, a shortcut for some is to use the index finger alone as a signal for two or to simply see the index finger as signaling two. Anthropologists point out that gestures vary from one culture to another. A "thumbs up" in the United States signals "good job," while in another nation it is a disparaging and insulting gesture.

One last example to cement the point. Once, when one of us was in the military, he drove to another military base to go to a movie. When he got there he didn't know where the theater was, so he drove up to a group of GIs and, because it was the sixties, said, "Hey, man, where's the flick?" The guy bristled and said, "Where's the what?!" So he repeated, "Where's the flick?" The GI relaxed and laughed and said, "Oh, man, I thought you said 'Where's the fight?'!" Viewing the outsider with initial suspicion, these GIs were prepared for trouble and heard a threat in the request. The sources of inaccurate recognition are numerous—language, culture, custom, context, values, situations, and so on. A failure of recognition may be funny, cute, and harmless or it may be potentially dangerous. The difficulties it can create in counseling, some of which will be discussed below, are mostly reparable.

Response

Even when a request is accurately diagnosed, the nature of the response determines the satisfaction of the applicant. Responses may be grossly separated into two large categories—facilitative and nonfacilitative. A nonfacilitative response may stem from an inaccurate understanding of the request as discussed earlier. Nonfacilitative responses can usually be classified as denying, nonresponsive, inaccurate, argumentative, condemning. Denying means a negative response to the request. (While denial of a request may be seen as nonfacilitative, it is not necessarily unsatisfying for the person making the request. A person may ask for a ride and the respondent may not be able to provide it. One person asked, the other said no, and that was the end of it. The question has been answered and although the action wasn't achieved the request was accurately responded to.) Nonresponsive means ignoring, withdrawing, or not acknowledging that a request has been made, such as the famous "silent treatment" many have experienced. Such interaction probably has a history but for whatever reason nonresponsiveness is unsatisfying. Inaccurate responding is usually based upon misunderstanding. More often than not it is the most easily corrected. The exception is, of course, purposeful misunderstanding, which is not misunderstanding at all but understanding used for humor or some other form of more malicious refusal. Argumentative responding is trying to dissuade the person from the request. Condemning is a legal, ethical, or moral position in which the request is judged as wrong and the listener decides the applicant needs to be shown the right way.

Facilitative responding requires two elements. First, the request must be accurately understood. Second, the response must satisfy the petitioner. Please be aware that a satisfactory response does not necessarily mean that the request is met. It means that the request was accurately recognized and the response met the petitioner's satisfaction ("Jim, can you give me a ride home?" "Oh, sorry, Bob. I'm working late today." "Hey, no problem. I'll check with Juan.").

Each request requires a different sort of response. What is facilitative is the accurate recognition of the request and the degree to which the response matched what has been requested.

Disguise

Life would be much simpler if requests were straightforward. Unfortunately for listeners, that is often not the case. The problem of disguise does not automatically imply deception, however. Disguise, in fact, may come in two forms—active and passive. Deception enters the picture when the speaker has an active intention to deceive. A less complicated explanation of an active intent to deceive is called a lie. When people lie to us it is difficult to accurately respond because those in the helping professions appear to be no better at detecting deception than people untrained in human communication. Thus it follows that the active intent to deceive is troublesome for psychotherapy. These problems are not insurmountable but they do reveal a unique aspect of the counseling relationship. Many are aware of how much trust the client must place in the counselor, but fewer recognize the trust the counselor must place in the client. As counselors, we rely upon clients to faithfully report their experience *as they understand it.* Counselors are prepared—trained by curriculum and attitude—to deal with concepts such as resistance, fear, anxiety, reluctance, and/or simple lack of clarity. What we are unprepared for are clients who actively distort their experiences for purposes unknown to us.

A classic experiment reveals our inadequacy in detecting purposeful disguise. Rosenhan (1973) sent students into mental health facilities with life stories leading practitioners to believe the faux clients were hearing voices, among other symptoms. The students were diagnosed and it was suggested they be committed. Even in institutional/resident settings under steady observation, the deception was not uncovered. In fact, when the ploy was revealed many practitioners refused to believe they had been tricked. It is simply not easy to assume that clients actively would mislead a counselor into believing that they require counseling when they do not.

Let us then turn to what is much more understandable for the counseling profession—passive disguise. Let us say that a person needs a ride to the bank. A straightforward request would go as follows: "June, can you give me a ride to the bank?" Easy to understand and easy to respond to. What about this one? "Gee, it's almost 2:30 and I have to be at the bank by 3:00." Is this person asking for help? Is there any request? In fact, it may well be a passive request for assistance, but it requires interpretation and clarification by the listener. Another example: "Boy, this new job is hard. I have to memorize technical manuals, study for tests, and even demonstrate procedures before a panel of judges." What is expected of the listener? Does the speaker want help with memorizing or someone to watch while he or she practices? Again, the listener is placed in an awkward position of interpretation and clarification. Listening and responding are more difficult propositions when the intentions of the speaker are unknown. Let us now explore the nature of requests themselves.

223

Requests

Following Gazda, Asbury, Balzer, Childers, and Walters (1984), requests may be classified into four different types based upon what action is needed to satisfactorily meet the request. These are requests for action, requests for information, requests for understanding and involvement, and inappropriate requests.

Requests for Action

A request for action is a straightforward entreaty for a specific performance. A request for action asks the listener to do something. "Pass the salt, please" is a request for action. So is "Can you help me get this computer into my car?" The proper response for a request for action is "yes," "no," or a conditional response based upon more information, detail, or clarification. Conditional responses then lead to "yes" or "no." An example of a conditional response might be when one roommate asks, "Can you help me clean up the kitchen?" The second replies, "I can help for 30 minutes. Will that be enough?" The request is responded to with a conditional clarification. In counseling, there are few actual requests for action. This unusual circumstance will be discussed later when we touch upon requests for understanding and involvement.

Requests for Information

"Where is the library?" This is a clear and unfettered request for information. The expected responses include the requested information, "no," or a conditional response. A conditional response might ask for clarification. "Do you want the public library or the university library?" Based upon the clarification, then the expected response would be the requested information. In counseling, there may be reasonable requests for information and providing information may well be an important aspect of the counseling relationship. Requests for information lie at the heart of counseling interventions such as bibliotherapy and involvement in information and support groups.

Requests for Understanding and Involvement

Requests for understanding and involvement lie at the heart of counseling. These are the requests that demand a unique response. There are two facilitative responses to a request for understanding and involvement. The first is to decline and refer. Perhaps the listener, for whatever reason, does not or cannot accept any deeper involvement with the speaker. What makes declining involvement facilitative is the addition of referring the speaker to someone or someplace that can do more.

The second facilitative response is accepting deeper involvement. This is the request that leads to a counseling relationship with all its concomitant demands. A request for understanding and involvement requires a peculiar form of response; it requires empathy, not action and not information.

Let us return for a moment to the problem of disguise. When a client says to a counselor, "I am just confused. I know that I am lonely and just don't know what to do. What do you think I should do?" this becomes a problem of diagnosis. Many beginning counselors hear a request for information in this client and set out down a dead-end path of providing advice on how to deal with loneliness. In counseling, this client statement and request represent a disguised request for under- standing and involvement. Providing information is not a facilitative response because information is not what has been requested. This is what often leads beginning counselors to what clients see as evasion, when the counselor either awkwardly responds that he or she is not there to answer questions or tries ineptly to redirect the question back to the client. The beginning counselor knows that his or her supervisor has said that responding directly to client questions is often unhelpful but really doesn't understand why, so he or she hems and haws and seems evasive. The client, of course, is confused about why the coun- selor won't respond to the request.

What would happen if the counselor recognized that the request was not a request for information but rather a request for understand- ing? Follow this earlier example. "I am just confused. I know that I am lonely and just don't know what to do. What do you think I should do?" Rather than propose some action or give information, suppose the counselor responded in this manner. "You seem to be saying that you have tried so many things already and feel cut off from nearly every- body. Things are desperate and yet you still have some hope." Would that be satisfying to a client? We think so. It not only recognizes what the client said but understands what was not said as well. It recognizes, for example, that the person is hopeful enough to come to counseling looking for help and it recognizes that the person has already struggled with some solutions.

Because we are educators of counselors, we know already the response some will have to this. They might say, "Well, the client is going to say 'Yes, and what do you think I should do?'" The difficulty is in the continued recognition that this is not a request for action or information but a renewed request for understanding. A counselor's response might be, "And that's the desperation. You might be saying, 'For cripes sake, just tell me what to do. I've lost the confidence that I can figure any of this out.'"

When a client asks, "Do you know what I mean?" the response is not "yes" or "no." This is not a request for information. It is a request for understanding. The response needs to be phrased as, "I understand that you feel. . . . "

As we have seen in Chapter 2, action is a part of the model of psychotherapy, but it is action that grows from understanding and more often than not is generated by the client rather than by the counselor. Certainly, the highest level of proposed action comes from the collaboration of the counselor and the client.

Inappropriate Requests

We will limit our discussion here to inappropriate requests in a counseling relationship, those made of counselors by their clients. Most such inappropriate requests entail some involvement outside the counseling relationship, such as social, sexual, economic, political, or religious suggestions that exceed the boundaries of the counseling association. A client might, in all innocence, ask a counselor out for coffee on some day when a session isn't scheduled or after the session. Clients might invite counselors to dinner parties or family celebrations. In more dramatic situations, a client might invite a counselor to a political rally or a religious service. The danger in all of these situations is that the counselor somehow becomes co-opted and loses his or her perspective as an understanding third party in the life of the client. The proper response for any inappropriate request is to respectfully decline, although in some cases it may require a more elaborate discussion of how the request interferes with the counseling process. A discussion of these processes can be found in Chapter 13 under the factors that facilitate the counseling relationship and those that tend to block it.

Summary

This chapter has focused upon the nature of requests and those factors that clarify them or make them more confusing. Requests may be classified into four separate types—requests for action, information, understanding and involvement, and inappropriate requests. It is important that a request be accurately recognized because recognition leads to accurate responding. Recognition can be complicated by passive communication styles that lead to disguised requests rather than to straightforward questions. Counseling is a process that relies upon clients to present their experiences *as they understand them* and often counselors are unprepared for purposefully deceptive clients.

Each of the separate types of requests invites a particular form of response. The counseling relationship, with its attendant forms of empathic, nonjudgmental, and genuine responding, is particularly suited to requests for understanding and involvement.

Activity 15.1
Recognizing Requests

Look at the questions below. Identify which type of request it is by placing the appropriate number in front of each question.

    1 = request for information
    2 = request for action
    3 = request for understanding and involvement
    4 = inappropriate request

_____   1.   Where's the beef?

_____   2.   What am I going to do?

_____   3.   Do you know anything about child care classes?

(cont'd)

Activity 15.1 (cont'd)

_____ 4. Can you get me any information about child care classes?

_____ 5. Maybe after our session, we can go out for a cup of coffee.

_____ 6. What time is the session over today?

_____ 7. May I look at my test scores?

_____ 8. Why do I do these things?

_____ 9. Where can I get career testing?

_____ 10. Can you help me with my work schedule?

_____ 11. Did you hear about the counselor at the mental health center? Do you know anything about it?

_____ 12. Did we schedule next Wednesday?

_____ 13. I know this is weird but I get paid tomorrow. Can I borrow $5 until then?

_____ 14. Do you mind if I call you by a nickname I made up?

_____ 15. May I borrow this book on anxiety?

Some Possible Responses

1. (1). A famous TV commercial. In all likelihood a request for information, although it could be considered a disguised request for action. Just for fun.

2. (3). A clear request for understanding and involvement. This is the sort of question that counselors need to resist answering and instead seek to understand.

3. (3) or (1). Sometimes it is hard to tell if a request is simply what it appears to be. In this case, is this a request for information or is there some underlying need being expressed?

4. (1). This seems much more direct and straightforward. A seemingly clear request for information.

5. (4). As friendly and sociable as clients may be, it is inappropriate to socialize. Such a request may reveal that the client does not have a clear sense of purpose or of boundaries in counseling.

6. (1) or (3). On the surface this appears to be a request for information. It may bear exploration because it may reveal something more important, such as a fear that not enough time is left in the session to bring up some important issue.

7. (2) or (3). A request for action. It might also reveal some concern with the scores.

8. (3). A clear request for understanding and involvement. Counselors must resist "why" questions from clients and instead explore with them the source of the question.

9. (1) or (3). Again, what may appear to be a simple request for information may reveal some unstated fear.

10. (2) or (3). Like many requests, this may be a simple request for action or it may reveal something else. As you are learning, almost all requests require judgment on the part of the counselor.

11. (4). Counselors must resist the temptation to engage in gossip and rumoring.

12. (1). In all likelihood, a request for information.

13. (4). No matter how pressing the need may appear, counselors cannot engage in an activity like money lending. It will destroy the counseling relationship.

14. (4). Whatever the source of a request such as this one, it is inappropriate.

15. (2) or (3). This may be a request for a book but it may also reveal that a client is experiencing some distress and bears checking out.

Chapter 15

References and for Further Reading

Gazda, G. M., Asbury, F. S., Balzer, F. J., Childers, W. C., & Walters, R. P. (1984). *Human relations development* (3rd ed.). Boston: Allyn & Bacon.

Rosenhan, D. L. (1973). On being sane in insane places. *Science, 179*(4070), 365–369.

230

16

∾

The Initial Interview

When does psychotherapy begin? In our view the therapeutic relationship begins with the first contact. Most often this happens over the telephone, and the client's impressions of the counselor's caring, confidence, and competence may well be influenced by that first encounter. We believe that the first telephone contact, the paperwork, the explanation of confidentiality, and the intake interview are part and parcel of psychotherapy itself. Throughout this book we have emphasized the importance of the therapeutic relationship and we believe it is a therapeutic mistake to exclude any aspect of contact with a client from the relationship.

First Contact

Initial contact most often comes through a telephone call. Clients may be referred by friends, former clients, or other professionals but they seldom come to meet a counselor in person. They call. Occasionally, a client will "walk in," a subject we will discuss more later. Obviously we cannot cover every possible situation, but in general the following steps will be helpful for the initial contact with clients. Our telephone skills are important and can be reassuring and inviting or cool and indifferent.

We are psychotherapists, not indifferent and disinterested clerks who merely collect information.

Answering Machines, Answering Services, and Secretaries. It is important that a client's telephone call be answered. In our modern technological age, this can happen in a bewildering number of ways. However a client's initial call is answered, it is important to ensure that the method is warm, concise, and concrete. This first contact sets the tone of the relationship. If an answering machine or an answering service is used, the message should reassure the client that his or her telephone call will be answered promptly. If a secretary is answering the phone, then a specific time can be set for an appointment or a return telephone call. We even recommend that the telephone skills of a secretary not be left to chance and that he or she be trained in exactly what to say and how to say it when responding to clients' telephone calls. If an answering machine or service is used, it is worthwhile to call the number to get a feel for the manner in which the message is conveyed. If the response time is too long or if an operator is rude, then you may have to change the message, the response time, or even the service itself. Clients are vulnerable people who may be more sensitive than others to their initial treatment.

Respond Promptly. Clients are anxious people who have summoned up their courage to make a contact for help. Their anxiety can surely rise the longer they have to wait. It is important to respond in a timely manner to a client's initial contact.

Leave Messages. When we return a telephone call and miss the person, then we have to leave a message. It is important to protect the client's confidentiality even in this initial contact. Thus, when you leave a message do not identify yourself by title (Dr., psychotherapist, counselor, social worker), agency (mental health center, counseling practice), or purpose of the call (wanting an appointment for counseling). Leave your name (John Smith, Jane Smith) and telephone number and say, "I'm returning your call and you can reach me at [specific time] and my phone number is [number]. Sorry I missed you and I look forward to hearing from you." We leave a vague message because we don't know, for instance, whether the prospective client will be embarrassed or even endangered if some-one finds out that he or she is contacting a psychotherapist. For these reasons, and for the continuing reason of confidentiality, it is recommended that any message contain little other than one's name and telephone number.

Be Caring, Concise, and Concrete. When returning a client's telephone call be prepared to answer a variety of questions, including appoint-ment times, theoretical orientation, expected duration of therapy, directions to the office, confidentiality, expected outcome, and fees. Be prepared to listen to the client's presenting issue in case it requires a referral. Although it is important to get some idea of why the client wants to come, this is not the time for a lengthy session and the counselor should acknowledge the client's issues and say, "Let's make an appointment and we will talk at length about this."

Make a Firm Appointment. Have appointment times handy and be clear about what is available. If your schedule is open, then tell the client that. If appointment times are limited, then list the available times and let the client pick. If he or she has trouble selecting an appointment from the available times, then it may be necessary to refer to a colleague or move to the next week. It is simply a matter of being firm and friendly if you have limited available times.

First Meeting

While a telephone contact may tentatively form some impressions in the mind of a client, the first personal meeting continues relationship build-ing in earnest. It is a time to identify the client and to introduce oneself. If it is a waiting room environment and more than one client is waiting, it is usually appropriate to call out a first name (e.g., Carlos or Michelle)

233

Box 16.1
Walk-In Clients

Sometimes clients just walk in and want to meet with a counselor. If it is not a crisis, then this is a matter of listening for a moment and making an appointment. If it is a crisis, employ your crisis management skills, which are discussed in Appendix 4. Otherwise, let the client know when a good time would be to come back, provide him or her with any available literature or handouts, thank him or her for coming in, and make a firm appointment. If there is time, then provide a walk-in client with the same information that would be given to a client in the first telephone contact. If there is not, then just as a counselor would not have a lengthy telephone conversation with a prospective client, it is necessary to gently, but firmly schedule the walk-in client to another time.

and then to introduce oneself. Obviously, if one client is male and only one male is in the waiting room, then it is appropriate to ask, "Carlos?" and then introduce oneself. Counselors must decide how to introduce themselves. Some therapists prefer to use their professional title and might say, "Juan, good to see you. I'm Doctor Smith." Or, another might say, "Michelle, glad to meet you. I'm Ms. Smith. I spoke to you on the phone. Let's walk down the hall." Other therapists might believe that a more informal relationship is necessary and say, "Carlos, good to see you. I'm John Smith. Let's walk down this way." Or, "Michelle, I'm Jane. Glad to see you." This is strictly a matter of personal choice and neither way is superior. It is a reflection of style and comfort.

Transition from Waiting Room to Counseling Room

Walking from the waiting room to the counseling room is a time for "passing the time of the day" or chitchat. The counselor might make conversation by asking, "Did you have any trouble finding the office?" Or, by describing the facility and saying, "We are just going down the hall and around the corner to my office." Whatever conversation the counselor makes should be considered in the context of understanding that the relationship is forming. The client is anxious and the counselor is responsible to help the client transition through awkward moments in the most therapeutic way possible, so the walk down the hall should not be allowed to become tense, awkward, or embarrassing.

The Intake Session

The relationship will take its most significant development in the first session. The style, depth, and even outcome are set in motion and the path is often laid in this early and meaningful session. Some stylistic concerns must be decided before the client arrives, such as how demographic information and even the clinical history of the client will be taken. There are at least three different approaches to this question and each has its advantages and disadvantages.

Triage Method

Some counselors and agencies prefer to have clients interviewed by an intake counselor prior to an initial therapy session with a permanent counselor so that an appropriate and qualified counselor may be assigned to a particular client. In these situations, an intake counselor will interview the client and record the initial information. A counselor will then be assigned and the client will be contacted for a first counseling session. The advantage of this system is that it allows the assignment of a counselor familiar with and trained in the client's presenting issues. The disadvantage is that any clinical insights that might be gained in the collection of client information are lost to the permanent counselor as is any relationship building that might have occurred in the intake session.

Data Collection Method

Some therapists prefer that the client complete a data sheet of demographic information and a written statement describing the presenting problem prior to any first session. In these situations, the client might be instructed either to fill out an intake form in the waiting room, to take it home to complete, or to bring a completed form to the first session. The advantage of this system is that these clerical matters are handled quickly and efficiently without taking any therapy time. The disadvantage is again the loss of any clinical insights that might be gained in the collection of information as well as the lost opportunities for relationship building.

Counselor-Client Interaction Method

Many therapists prefer to collect all the demographic, background, history, and presenting issues directly and personally during an initial intake session. These counselors will elicit the information, record it on the forms, and keep the records themselves. The advantages of this method are that it permits the therapist to interact directly with the client, find any areas of commonality, further the relationship begun on the telephone and in the waiting room, use follow-up questions as they arise, and be there as the client presents his or her issues for any clinical insight that might be gained from the words, tones, inflections, and body language of the client. The disadvantage might be the necessary use of time. Nevertheless, in our opinion collecting that information ourselves is the preferred method for three reasons.

First, it goes to the heart of the purpose of the session. We have said again and again that you cannot overestimate the predictive power of the quality of the relationship to identify positive outcomes in psychotherapy. It seems crucial that every opportunity for building a therapeutic relationship be seized and enhanced by therapists as we seek to be of service to clients. Further, it seems reasonable that the continuity from telephone conversations, intake sessions, and further therapy will simply flow more easily if the same therapist is involved at each step of the process. The discontinuous nature of the triage method seems to us to be less efficient, in the long run, than the interactive method.

Second, the methods that treat information gathering as mere data collection miss a significant opportunity for relationship building. The forms used in the initial session can be used not only for collecting data but as vehicles for the relationship. An intake form is not simply a clerical duty, it is a "relationship-building device." Each of the forms used in therapy has this potential. The demographic forms that provide name, address, telephone number, and so forth also offer opportunities for connections between the counselor and the client. Perhaps the client lives in the same neighborhood as the therapist. The counselor and the client might have the same birth month. They might have parents with the same first names. These are, of course, small matters, yet as one builds a relationship with a client they are stepping stones to a deeper, more therapeutic relationship.

The third reason is that clients often do not know what to expect as they enter therapy. The "formalities" of paperwork can ease the transition from anxiety to greater comfort as the client begins to tell his or her story. It is not simply a matter of "jumping in" without preparation. The process of collecting data not only helps build the relationship, it also allows a gradual shift from the everyday world of the client to the world of therapy.

Recognizing the potential of data collection as a method of continuing the relationship, using forms as relationship-building devices, and using the initial session to ease the client into therapy all seem to be important considerations as one prepares to meet the client for the first session.

Transition to the Presenting Problem

After the demographics and other data have been gathered, it is necessary to transition from this phase of psychotherapy to one in which the client describes the reasons and purposes for deciding on psychotherapy. This transition also carries with it a symbolic as well as a practical shift. When the counselor indicates to the client that the paperwork is over, the data gathering complete, and the family history collected,

Box 16.2

Alternative Seating Arrangements in Therapy Sessions

As one might imagine, psychotherapists have engaged clients in a variety of settings and seating arrangements. Historically, there appear to be five dominant seating arrangements:

behind-the-client
face-to-face
side-by-side
perpendicular
desk

Over the years, we have explored different seating arrangements in the initial session. We have found each method to have advantages for particular reasons. While most therapists prefer and use a face-to-face arrangement, we have changed this seating arrangement in the first session. The side-by-side arrangement has the advantage of allowing the client to see all of the forms and to respond to them without the necessity of asking questions. It also presents a symbolic representation of joining and alignment. For some clients with initial suspicions, it sets a tone of openness and disclosure that can be reassuring.

Sitting behind a desk is not normal-ly a useful arrangement for psychotherapy because it creates a symbolic barrier to open communication between the client and the counselor. The desk itself, however, is useful and even necessary in the administration of psychological instruments, thus it does have a place in the counselor's office.

While we have not found the behind-the-client arrangement to be helpful in ordinary therapeutic circumstances, it has proven its usefulness for certain techniques. In role plays (such as the empty chair), visualizations, and guided fantasies a seating arrangement in which the therapist is slightly behind and out of the view of the client can be helpful because it takes the counselor out of the client's sight lines. This allows the client to focus on the task and not to be distracted by the counselor. This is also a helpful seating arrangement in any teaching in which some form of free association is used.

A perpendicular setup is most often used in hypnosis and other forms of relaxation. This permits the client to stretch out in a lounge chair, for example, and also allows the counselor to reach out to touch the client for purposes of instruction for any physical techniques used in these strategies.

Each seating arrangement is useful in particular instances. Clearly, most psychotherapists use an unrestricted, unencumbered arrangement in which comfortable but not cushy chairs are set up face-to-face. This has proven itself to be the most effective arrangement for the majority of psychotherapeutic situations and circumstances. The other arrangements can be adopted when necessary to increase the effectiveness of the therapeutic encounter.

then there is a shift away from history and data to more personal and affective reasons for seeking therapy. The counselor might move from a side-by-side arrangement to a face-to-face one and introduce a transitional invitation such as, "How can I be of help?" or "What are your goals, expectations, and wishes for therapy?" or "What can I do to be of service to you?" Each of these implies that the client can tell his or her story. The counselor now assumes an attentive and open listening posture as the client begins to unfold his or her issues, problems, and/or dilemmas. As the clients tell their stories, counselors begin to respond as they seek to understand the meaning of clients' narratives. This is the use of the model discussed previously in which the goal of therapy is exploration, meaning, and action. As the time for the first session nears its end, the therapist must allow sufficient time for the next stage of the session which is a summary.

239

Session Summary

In our opinion there is no more important phase of a therapy session than the summary. It is a time in which clarity can be achieved, gains can be acknowledged and cemented, and themes can be identified. It is a time when the client can identify what was helpful and what was not, when goals can be further identified and steps in the process of change can be recognized. The summary is routinely left to the client. As the client summarizes the session, the counselor listens and points out if something important has been left out or not given sufficient weight.

The invitation to a summary alerts the client that the session is near its end and the client can begin the process of coming out of the attitude of psychotherapy and transitioning back into the everyday world.

Closure

After the summary, the counselor has an opportunity to talk about the coming session, future directions, and any homework that might be appropriate for the client. It is a time to give these assignments, confirm the next appointment, and say good-bye with a handshake or a pat on the shoulder. Any paperwork or room maintenance should be left until after the client has left the room.

After Session

After the session, counselors might again "chat" with the client as they escort him or her to the hall and say good-bye once again. It is another transition time in which a shift is being made away from emotional material to ordinary workaday social exchanges.

Summary

In this chapter we have presented the format and justification for the structure of the initial session. The first telephone contact is the beginning of psychotherapy in our opinion. It is not something that lies outside the purposes and goals of psychotherapy, it is psychotherapy itself. This is also the case with data collection, filling out intake forms, and fee setting. Any attitude that sees such activities as separate from the therapy does not lend itself easily to the necessity of continuity and connection important to developing a sound, effective, and helpful therapeutic relationship.

The tasks of the initial session are centered in relationship building. While information must be gathered, this task can be completed in the process of building a therapeutic relationship and can flow directly into the transition to the presenting problem. Every session should also have a summary and a time for closure, which set up the next therapy session.

References and for Further Reading

Combs, A. W., & Gonzalez, D. M. (1994). *Helping relationships: Basic concepts for the helping professions*. Boston: Allyn & Bacon.

Gazda, G. M., Asbury, F. S., Balzer, F. J., Childers, W. C., & Walters, R. P. (1984). *Human relations development* (3rd ed.). Boston: Allyn & Bacon.

Hutchins, D. E., & Vaught, C. C. (1997). *Helping relationships and strategies* (3rd ed.). Pacific Grove, CA: Brooks/Cole.

Ivey, A. E. (1994). *Intentional interviewing and counseling* (3rd ed.). Pacific Grove, CA: Brooks/Cole.

Lauver, P., & Harvey, D. R. (1997). *The practical counselor: Elements of effective helping*. Pacific Grove, CA: Brooks/Cole.

Okun, B. F. (1997). *Effective helping: Interviewing and counseling techniques* (5th ed.). Pacific Grove, CA: Brooks/Cole.

Teyber, E. (1997). *Interpersonal process in psychotherapy: A relational approach* (3rd ed.). Pacific Grove, CA: Brooks/Cole.

17

Developing a Treatment Plan

*R*igid psychotherapy is an oxymoron. Yet, sometimes there are pressures from within the discipline itself to plan the course of psychotherapy to a precise number of sessions and a selected treatment during those sessions. Some say that if you don't know where you are going, then you won't know when you get there. Others say that if you don't know where you are going, then it is hard to plan a route to your destination. Therein lies some of the controversy surrounding the concept of treatment plans. Effective psychotherapy can hardly be accomplished if one does not insist upon flexibility. Thus, any notion of treatment planning must be flexible, adaptable, changeable, and tentative. And that's a FACT. Flexibility, adaptability, changeability, and tentativeness do not mean lack of purpose. Psychotherapy is a purposeful activity. It is not, however, a lockstep endeavor. Effective psychotherapy does not wander aimlessly through the client's life simply touching random events, situations, people, and crises, nor does it leap recklessly at any issue or problem presented by a client quickly providing a ready solution or plan of action.

Process and Outcome Plans

This is a controversy with a relatively straightforward solution. This text provides a model of counseling and psychotherapy that does in fact involve a stage or phase concept of the therapeutic process. This model teaches that all psychotherapy involves an element of time that takes both the counselor and the client through a process of exploration, understanding, and action. This is a purposive venture, not one in which issues and problems are examined without consideration and deliberation. It is, nevertheless, an enterprise with a plan, although initially that plan is not focused upon any specific outcome. It is a course of action that identifies the process and choice of modality. It may also give some estimate of time.

Process Plans

A process plan involves four important considerations. First, it identifies as clearly as possible the client's presenting symptoms, issues, and/or problems. Second, after the initial session, the counselor must decide which modality is best suited for the particular client and his or her presenting issues. Is this presenting problem a matter of individual psychotherapy? Or, is it better to involve the family or to introduce the client into an ongoing group whose members are coping with similar concerns? Third, the frequency of meeting should be determined. While it may be common for sessions to be scheduled on a weekly basis it is, nevertheless, a therapeutic judgment that must be made in consultation with the client. Fourth, it may be important to estimate the minimum time needed to effectively explore and understand the client's concerns. This is important both for the counselor and the client. It is possible to provide a suggested number of sessions for a client with the provision that at the end of a certain number of sessions (e.g., 6 or 12) a review and evaluation be done to see if the client is profiting from the therapy. It is best to complete this process plan—including presenting issues, modality, and estimated length of therapy—collaboratively with the client. We do not consider it helpful for a counselor or psychotherapist to develop a plan of therapy unilaterally. Psychotherapy is a collaborative process and this should include planning the path ahead for both counselor and client. Form 17.1 is a sample treatment plan that may be used for these initial considerations. As the therapy unfolds, another more concrete plan will be developed that identifies more specific outcome goals.

Outcome Plans

Two things can occur in counseling and psychotherapy that make an outcome plan helpful and necessary. First, it may quickly become apparent that the client's presenting issues and symptoms are not merely initial and immediate issues but central and substantive. Given that this is the case and that the meaning of these issues is understood, then a clear plan developing coping strategies for the core issues in the life of the client is helpful and necessary.

An outcome plan is concrete, collaborative, and complete. Once outcomes are jointly identified and understood, then specific and detailed strategies may be developed to help the client move in the direction of his or her goals. An outcome plan has several components to it. First, the goals must be clear. Words carry meaning and the language of the goal should be explored with the client to ensure that what is written is what is felt and intended and, therefore, may be honored. Second, effective goals are concrete, which means that they are stated in such a way that some action is possible. While psychotherapy is not merely a behavioral process, change requires action. Welch (1998) provides a description of the change process in psychotherapy which is helpful in this regard (also see Chapter 8). The development of the outcome goals should involve discussions of not only the goals themselves but what acts can be undertaken to accomplish the goals. Third, goals should have a timeline. An old saying tells us that "work expands to fill the time allotted for it." Establish realistic timelines in which the client can devote an effort to change and can have time to measure the results as a part of the plan. Fourth, the goals must be attainable and realistic. They must be designed so that success is possible. In order for lasting

245

Form 17.1
A Sample Treatment Plan

COMMUNITY COUNSELING SERVICES

1234 EMPATHY RD.

ANY TOWN, ANY STATE USA

TREATMENT PLAN 1

Date _____

Client_____   Counselor _____

....

Issue 1 _____   Client's understanding _____

Goal:

Issue 2 _____   Client's understanding _____

Goal:

Treatment plan—Method of treatment_____

_____

_____

Frequency_____   Estimated length of treatment_____

Options to be used in addition to counseling: 1. _____   2. _____

3. _____   4. _____   5. _____

Supervisor's comments and review:

_____   _____

(Counselor's Signature)   (Date)

_____   _____

(Supervisor's Signature)   (Date)

change to occur realistic goals require effort. This requires discussion and finding a balance between attainability and struggle may take some experimentation and testing.

Fifth, it is possible to have both short- and long-term goals. Change is not an all-or-nothing proposition. Plans may be made for long-term goals with intervening short-term ones. Steps may be designed in any goals that allow gradual change and a measure of progress. Sixth, goals should be built using the client's strengths. Another old saying with some wisdom is that we ought to "find out what we are good at and do that." This is a process of building. What was absent or flawed is being built, repaired, and replaced. This is life and life is development. The goals of psychotherapy may be seen in this light as well. Seventh, goals should be developed in such a way that events, changes, and outcomes can be recorded. There seems to be some magic in writing. Thoughts slip away. Ideas get lost. Feelings fade. Writing, however, brings focus and an important aspect of outcome goals in psychotherapy is the reflection and discussion that takes place in the session after the client has struggled to put a plan into action. The thoughts, feelings, and acts themselves may be recorded in a journal and referred to in the therapy sessions. Eighth, some process of formal evaluation should be built into the goal. The effectiveness of the action needs to be considered so that any modifications in the outcome plan can be made. Ninth, and finally, any plan must be adaptable. The client acts, an evaluation is made, and then, if necessary, the goal should be modified, changed, or even eliminated. Goals are written on paper, not in stone. If they don't work, then they can be altered or discarded. This, in itself, can be a valuable outcome of psychotherapy. Form 17.2 provides a sample outcome treatment plan.

247

Do's and Don'ts of Developing a Treatment Plan

1. Ensure that the goals of the treatment plan come from the client rather than from the therapist.
2. Develop several individual and clear goals rather than a complex and complicated single goal.

Form 17.2
Sample Outcome Treatment Plan

COMMUNITY COUNSELING SERVICES

1234 EMPATHY RD.

ANY TOWN, ANY STATE USA

TREATMENT PLAN 2

Date _____

Client _____ Counselor _____

1. Nature of the problem/crisis:

2. Goals:

3. Objectives (what the client will do):

4. Methods (what counselor/agency will provide):

3. Be as specific and concrete as possible.

4. Avoid jargon.

5. Be realistic. Set goals and develop a plan that is attainable for both the counselor and the client.

6. Keep the plan within the competence of the therapist or develop referral plans.

7. Make sure the treatment plan can be adapted if necessary when more information is obtained.

8. Evaluate both the plan and the overall therapy once the treatment plan is implemented.

9. After the plan has been accomplished ask, "Why should therapy continue?"

10. Prepare a termination statement for the files when therapy is finished. Evaluate the treatment plan and its success or shortcomings in the therapy for the client. Use this post-therapy assessment as a way to further develop your skills as a therapist.

Summary

Many agencies, mental health centers, and college and university counseling centers require that a treatment plan be included in the client's records. Some such institutions may have exaggerated the need for such plans and insist upon detailed outcome plans after the first session. Such guidelines corrupt the necessary and essential exploratory function of psychotherapy that differentiates the presenting issues, problems, and/or symptoms from the central, core, or substantive issues in the lives of clients. Nevertheless, this chapter has presented a method that can be used to develop both a process treatment plan and an outcome treatment plan while protecting the welfare of the client. Process plans identify the presenting issues and/or symptoms, suggest a counseling modality, determine frequency of sessions, and collaboratively determine a minimum number of sessions.

Outcome plans are more detailed and specific. They should include an element of evaluation so that plans can be modified or eliminated, if necessary. It is important that both long- and short-term goals be developed so that any changes will be gradual and so that a sense of accomplishment is possible for both the client and the counselor. Although clients enter counseling and psychotherapy with a sense of vulnerability, and perhaps feelings of personal defeat, change seems to occur best when the path follows already identified strengths. Outcome plans should use the strengths of the client in any plan of personal life change.

References and for Further Reading

Horowitz, M. J. (1997). *Formulation as a basis for planning psychotherapy treatment*. Washington, DC: American Psychiatric Press.

Howard, G. S., Nance, D. W., & Myers, P. (1987). *Adaptive counseling therapy: A systematic approach to selecting effective treatments*. San Francisco: Jossey-Bass.

Hutchins, D. E., & Vaught, C. C. (1997). *Helping relationships and strategies* (3rd ed.). Pacific Grove, CA: Brooks/Cole.

Ivey, A. E. (1994). *Intentional interviewing and counseling* (3rd ed.). Pacific Grove, CA: Brooks/Cole.

Jongsma, A. E., Jr., & Peterson, L. M. (1995). *The complete psychotherapy treatment planner*. New York: Wiley.

Lauver, P., & Harvey, D. R. (1997). *The practical counselor: Elements of effective helping*. Pacific Grove, CA: Brooks/Cole.

Makover, R. B. (1996). *Treatment planning for psychotherapists*. Washington, DC: American Psychiatric Press.

Okun, B. F. (1997). *Effective helping: Interviewing and counseling techniques* (5th ed.). Pacific Grove, CA: Brooks/Cole.

Teyber, E. (1997). *Interpersonal process in psychotherapy: A relational approach* (3rd ed.). Pacific Grove, CA: Brooks/Cole.

Welch, I. D. (1998). *The path of psychotherapy: Matters of the heart*. Pacific Grove, CA: Brooks/Cole.

18

*

Completing the
Counseling Relationship

*F*ew beginnings anticipate their ending quite so carefully as psychotherapy. Experienced counselors and psychotherapists know even in the midst of building the relationship that its end promises greater success than its continuation. New counselors may struggle conceptualizing a process that seeks its own end, yet psychotherapy, perhaps more than any other enterprise, is a process devoted to its own dissolution.

Even as we begin this chapter let us introduce a caution. The termination session is not something different from psychotherapy, it is psychotherapy. This seeming play on words is important. A little story drawn from the world of teaching might help explain. A teacher comes to class and Bobby passes a note down the row to Carolyn Sue. The teacher intercepts it and gives it back to Bobby and says quietly, "Bobby, take care of this after class." Aaron and Ben are playfully punching one another in the back row and the teacher continues talking but stands close. Aaron and Ben, aware of her presence, stop punching one another. Jennifer and Juanita are whispering in the back of the room and the teacher ignores them. After class the teacher is in the teachers' planning room and another teacher asks, "Did you have any discipline problems in class today?" The teacher replies, "No, I didn't." The second teacher says, "Didn't Bobby pass a note to Carolyn Sue?

Did Aaron and Ben punch each other in the back of the room like they always seem to do? And, didn't kids whisper in the back of the room?" The teacher replies, "Well, yes, they did that." The second teacher asks, "Aren't those discipline problems?" "No," the teacher says, "That is just teaching."

There is a world of difference between a teacher who sees his or her job as including the teaching of appropriate social relationships and one who sees discipline as separate and apart from the regular job. One smoothly and appropriately teaches in those times when inappropriate behavior happens and the other treats students as interruptions who prevent the actual job from being completed. This is also true in psychotherapy. Counselors who understand that the intake form is psychotherapy and that termination is psychotherapy are able to flow from one moment to the next without jarring transitions. The experience from beginning to end is one of a single cloth woven with consistency and without rents or tears in the fabric. The process of ending is attended to with the same concern with which all other phases and processes of psychotherapy are governed. It is a time for summary, cementing gains, planning ahead, review, and, perhaps, referral.

The Ethics of Termination

Psychotherapists are not in the business of "stringing people along" for monetary or power needs. It is within our ethical guidelines that therapy be as time efficient as possible without a slavish commitment to brevity. Our task is to enter the relationship without guile and move toward a collaborative end as smoothly and expeditiously as possible. Ethically, counselors do not "abandon" clients because they are difficult, troublesome, or inconvenient. Much of the help we are able to provide stems from our willingness to "stick it out" when others might have quit. It is equally important to recognize that if we are unable to be of help, for whatever reason (competence, personal conflicts, intrapersonal dilemmas), then therapy should be ended. There are a number of appropriate ethical reasons for bringing therapy to a close.

1. The client is no longer benefiting.
2. It seems clear that the client no longer needs therapy.
3. The therapy is no longer serving the client's needs.
4. The client no longer seems invested in counseling.
5. The counselor believes that a referral to a more experienced or specialized therapist would be appropriate.
6. Agency limits or other external considerations force an end. In such a situation an appropriate referral should be made, if necessary.

Often these consideration have been previously discussed at the beginning of therapy in a client rights statement or a disclosure form that was given to all clients in the first session (see, e.g., Lauver & Harvey, 1997, p. 249, and Appendix 3).

Practical Considerations

In a review of goals, accomplishments, and unfinished business remember that perfection is not the goal. In the review process it is not necessary to "dot every 'i' or cross every 't.'" Consider this advice—you don't have to be perfect, you just have to be "good enough" (Winnecott, 1993). The task of psychotherapy is not to send a perfect human being into the world but merely to do our best to send one out of therapy more able to cope than when he or she came in. We should, of course, do what we can to ensure that the client's newly found, newly discovered, or newly created coping strategies have a reasonable chance of success in the world. Given that, then we have done our job.

Preparing for Termination

As it becomes clear that the clients' abilities to cope with their lives are growing and approaching the point where they no longer need to be in therapy, it is important to begin the process of considering terminating

253

therapy. Some issues to consider as the process approaches its end might be:

1. Review the intake session, the treatment plan, and progress notes to get a firmer grasp on the evolution of change as it has occurred in therapy.
2. Make a note of gains and plan an opportunity for discussing how those gains can be maintained once therapy ends.
3. Be aware of work that still needs to be done—what might be called "unfinished business."
4. Make a note of the times in therapy when it was a struggle and how those moments were ultimately transcended or overcome.
5. Plan to reassure the clients about any concerns they may have about how records are stored and maintained, especially around issues of security and confidentiality.
6. Be prepared to reassure clients that while therapy is ending, the possibility of future contact is open and, if necessary, be prepared to offer appropriate referrals.

The Taxonomy of Termination

When all things go well, the counselor and the client mutually decide that the time has come to end the therapeutic relationship. Frequently, however, all things do not go well and rather than a planned and timely end, the therapy might begin to sputter. Clues might begin to appear that the therapy is no longer fully serving the needs of the client, but the client might not feel comfortable bringing up these concerns directly. We think that termination in psychotherapy falls into two types—planned and unplanned. When things go well, then termination conforms to our expectations and can be structured and managed. When things slip outside our expectations, then termination may be quick or, unsatisfyingly, may not occur at all.

Planned Termination

Even when the therapy is proceeding well, it is sometimes difficult to appropriately determine when to end. This is especially true if the psychotherapy is open-ended and the client's issues, problems, or dilemmas are vague and undifferentiated. In such a case, a good deal of time may have to be devoted to exploration and determining clear and precise outcome goals will be difficult. In such a situation, the following considerations may help determine when to bring the therapy to an end.

1. Has the presenting problem been sufficiently addressed?
2. Has any crippling stress been alleviated?
3. Is the client coping more efficiently?
4. Have the client's relationships improved.
5. Has the client's work or school performance improved?
6. Overall, does the client report that he or she is enjoying life more?
7. Does the client feel that he or she can manage without psychotherapy?

Given such general guidelines, we believe that there are two major types of planned termination. These are time limited and natural.

Time Limited. Psychotherapy is limited for several reasons. One, of course, is that the practitioner uses a form of psychotherapy that is purposefully brief. Such a solution-focused approach would be explained to the client in the beginning and termination would be included in the planned number of sessions. Another reason is that a client is employed in a company with an existing Employee Assistance Program (EAP) that permits a contracted number of sessions. After those sessions, the client might be referred to another psychotherapist outside the EAP. In another case, clients who see counselors in training have their therapy limited by the nature of the academic process. A therapist's practicum might be a 3-to-5 month training period in which the counselor in training would see clients and be supervised. When the quarter or semester ends, then typically the therapy would end with either a referral or a closing session. Each of these time-limited models plans a closing session into the counseling experience and both the counselor and the client know the number of sessions and the ending date from the start.

Natural. When the process of psychotherapy moves along at a good and effective clip and both the counselor and client mutually decide that the therapy has served its purpose, then termination can be anticipated and planned collaboratively. We call this ideal situation natural and we mean that the ending is guileless, uncontrived, and unforced. It ensues and eventuates as a reasonable outcome of the process. Both the counselor and client agree and the end becomes mutually satisfying. This is not to say that all issues have been resolved or that there are no feelings of loss at the end of so intimate a relationship. What we mean is more like the recognition that the purposes of the relationship have been largely met and the simultaneous recognition that continuing the relationship might do more harm than good—creating dependency, for example. In such a complementary situation, the goals of termination outlined later in this chapter will be most effectively accomplished.

Unplanned Termination

Endings are not always planned or even anticipated. Some happen quickly and most unsatisfying of all is a situation in which there is no opportunity to bring closure to the therapeutic relationship.

Spontaneous. Sometimes clients come to a session knowing that their work is finished. In the normal flow of the session it may become clear that the client is ready to end and the counselor may fully agree. In such a situation the ending is mutual even though it has not been discussed prior to that session. This is a case, although not an ideal one, in which the goals of effective termination can be adequately accomplished. The counselor might have to simply throw open the client's folder and say, "Let's look at the goals we set in the beginning and review them together." The outcome can be satisfying and even though accomplished on the "spur of the moment," it can be thorough enough and can provide the opportunity for both a review of gains and a discussion of tasks yet to be accomplished. Spontaneous endings might well signal a client's difficulty with saying good-bye in general and if this has not been a part of the therapy and if the opportunity presents itself it might be worthwhile to talk about this aspect of ending with the client.

Arbitrary. The least satisfying ending for a counselor is one in which the client simply stops coming to therapy without the opportunity for an ending session. Typical clues to arbitrary endings might include:

1. missing sessions
2. failing to complete homework assignments
3. having trouble finding important issues to bring to therapy
4. requesting a lengthier period between sessions
5. showing signs of boredom and withdrawal during sessions

257

When clients begin to show such signs, it may be possible to anticipate an arbitrary ending and make it a planned ending instead. It is important, of course, for therapists to understand that the client is the one who is in charge of termination and that although a mutually decided upon ending may be more satisfying for the counselor, the client may end therapy at any time. It is possible, however, that if the signs of restlessness can be recognized the counselor can request an ending session in which the goals of termination may be accomplished. If the counselor sees signs of "premature termination," then steps can be taken to ensure a more appropriate ending. Counselors typically encourage clients to give thought to assessing progress, discussing the possibility of ending the therapy, and making a purposeful decision. Consider the

Chapter 18

following checklist based on Bruckner-Gordon, Gangi, and Wallman (1988) to help clients in their decision.

_____ I have gotten what I need for counseling and am satisfied.

_____ I keep thinking I am ready to leave.

_____ My family and friends are pressuring me to stop.

_____ I cannot continue because of changed circumstances.

_____ My counselor cannot continue because of changed circumstances.

_____ I don't seem to be gaining or learning anything new.

_____ My counselor and I don't seem to be working well together.

_____ I think I have gained all that I can from working with this counselor.

_____ I think I have gained enough to continue on my own without working with this counselor.

_____ My counselor has suggested that I have gained enough to continue on my own without working with him/her.

_____ Or, _____.

Such a checklist, or a personally generated list of client responses, can help move the psychotherapy from an arbitrary to a natural termination.

Another form of arbitrary ending may come from the counselor. A counselor may, for any number of reasons, find it necessary to end a counseling relationship before it is mutually satisfying to both parties. One of us, for example, recently moved from one community to another. As a result of the move, he had to end the counseling relationships with his clients. Some of these terminations resulted in spontaneous endings and some resulted in referrals. Such situations might be unavoidable, and just as counselors move so do clients.

Sometimes counselors recognize some intrapersonal feelings that interfere with their effectiveness and they ethically feel the need to refer the client to another therapist. For example, one of us received a referral and met with a new client. This client expressed her frustration and irritation at being referred because she did not know the reason. In fact, neither did the new therapist. He asked her permission to speak to the previous therapist to discover why she had been referred. As it turned out, the previous therapist had gone through a divorce and the client bore a striking resemblance to his former wife! He simply felt that he would not be able to get past her physical appearance. He consented to the current therapist informing the client of his reasons and when that was done the client was able to form a relationship with the new therapist and move on. Such things happen. Counselors may find that a client presents with a disorder that demands specialized knowledge and may feel ethically bound to refer to a more competent practitioner. More often than not, clients accept these referrals as being in their best interests, especially when the situation is adequately explained.

In more unfortunate circumstances, death can come unexpectedly in each of our lives and both clients and counselors have to cope when death takes a client or a counselor. When a client ends his or her life by suicide the counselor should seek the support and advice of other psychotherapists to deal with any feelings of guilt or mourning. After the death of a therapist clients are in a more precarious place and unless the counselor happened to work in a group setting there might not be someone immediately available to meet with distraught clients.

The Meaning of Ending and Issues in Termination

Even in the best of circumstances there can be issues in the termination of psychotherapy. Some are simply unavoidable and may even include the natural issues of ending any relationship. Others are peculiar to the therapeutic relationship.

The Meaning of Ending

Psychotherapy is an intimate relationship. Both clients and psychotherapists can be taken off guard at how quickly an intimate and significant relationship can develop. While there is healing potential in such relationships, there can be danger as well. For the counselor, there is the danger of self-aggrandizement, misuse of power, manipulation, and exploitation (e.g., financial, sexual, etc.). For clients, there is the danger of creating dependency, hero worship, and a self-diminishing attitude where they may believe that they are incapable of success in life without the therapist. Even when the dangers are avoided and the relationship is one of empowerment and mutual satisfaction, ending it can bring feelings of loss and a wish for continued contact on a social or more informal level. We are not too far out on a limb to mention that we are a species that has made our way in the universe by togetherness. We are more comfortable coming together than we are at separating. Saying good-bye is a task that many in our culture have reported as troublesome. Tears come easily to some and even ending relationships with brief acquaintances may result in a tearful good-bye. While counselors struggle with the importance of therapeutic distance, the end of a long and intimate relationship may still "tug at one's heartstrings."

For clients, who have not been through the training of managing detached concern (Welch, 1998), these separation issues can be more intense. They might have greater issues with feelings of abandonment and attachment than the therapist and a good termination provides the opportunity to discuss these feelings.

Issues in Termination

Referral presents a different set of issues with which counselors must cope. In termination, it must be made clear that the possibility of returning is open for the client. If for some reason this is not the case, then provide specific information so that clients can continue to receive the help they need. This may involve telling clients that a practicum or volunteer experience may be repeated, for example, or that at a college or a university the counseling center will provide services for students. It may involve providing the client with the telephone number of a local mental health center and the names and telephone numbers of appropriate independent practitioners. In addition, it may include providing clients with ways to contact organizations and/or support groups to continue clients' progress.

A final problem with which counselors must cope in termination is the tendency of clients to begin to withdraw emotional energy from the therapy once termination is mentioned as a possibility. A therapist may find himself or herself as a "lame duck therapist," unable to continue the effective work that was being done as the clients begin to invest less and less energy in the session, anticipating their end to therapy. While we have made much of the point that psychotherapy always anticipates its ending, it is simultaneously true that the premature suggestion of ending can frighten clients and prevent effective work. It is difficult to accurately and collaboratively decide the appropriate time for ending without jeopardizing the therapy. We suggest not presenting the idea of termination until the counselor is firmly convinced that the therapeutic issues have been addressed and then waiting until approximately two weeks before the anticipated final session. An alternative to this procedure is the process in which clients are moved from weekly sessions, to biweekly, monthly, and quarterly sessions until they feel fully comfortable being on their own without the need for the support of therapy. While therapy should include planning for termination, its premature introduction can have a negative effect on therapy and the introduction of the idea of ending should be approached cautiously.

Guidelines for Appropriate Termination

The tasks of termination are straightforward and mirror the summary phase of an individual session. Just as in an individual session, there needs to be a summary, a cementing of gains, a review of goals and progress, a discussion of work remaining and homework, and a referral, if necessary.

Summarize

The termination session is a chance to spend some time looking back. What were the presenting issues? What new issues emerged? What were the highlights, low points, struggles, and interpersonal issues? It is a time to look back over the path that the client and counselor traveled together. This is both a cognitive (intellectual/analytical) and an emotional summary. It is important that the client take the lead in this summary. The counselor's role is to listen to the client's summary and then add anything that the client leaves out that seems important to the counselor.

Cement Gains

The termination session is a time in which clients can reflect upon the changes they have made in therapy. It is a time to measure the space between the starting line and their present position. The counselor can help by being concrete and practical in the movement. It is a time when both the client and the counselor look back and judge the perceived changes. Again the client should lead and the counselor adds what he or she believes the client has neglected.

Review Goals and Progress

It is helpful for the counselor to bring in a written list of the formal goals established in the treatment plan. It might be helpful to also have the client write out the goal, the progress made, and what is left to do with that goal. Table 18.1 provides an example of such a chart.

Discuss Work Remaining and Homework

Psychotherapy is not designed to do everything within the confines of the therapeutic session or, for that matter, within the confines of the

Table 18.1   Goals and Progress

Goal	Progress	Needs

therapeutic encounter. Obviously, much is done by the client outside the time spent in the therapy session. This reasoning extends to the time after psychotherapy has been completed. Welch (1998, pp. 151–154) discusses the need for clients to become "therapist to the self." In a discussion of work remaining, clients and counselors can talk about what the clients need to do to continue their progress as they continue their lives. This is a time for encouragement and support as the counselor helps the clients begin the transition from having a supportive climate they can visit each week to a sense that they are increasingly capable of coping with the issues and problems of their lives. Again, it is important for the client to lead and for the counselor to add what seems necessary.

Offer Referrals

The issue of referral has been previously discussed, but just as a review, clients need to know that they can return if they feel the need. The counselor's job here is to be encouraging without giving clients the impression that if they come back they have somehow failed. It is, as is much in psychotherapy, a delicate time and task. Clients need to be encouraged to move out on their own and be reassured that the counselor is there to be of assistance if necessary. One way to do this is to make a statement that recognizes psychotherapy as one of the tools the client now has to cope with life issues. A counselor might say, for example, "You know something now that you didn't know before and that is that when you are facing the stresses of your life you have this place to come to if you wish." This statement implies that psychotherapy is just one more way in which to cope and is not a sign of failure.

It may also be a time to refer clients into a different modality of psychotherapy such as marriage and family or group therapy rather than individual sessions. It is a time to help clients become aware of community resources that might be appropriate and, if necessary, a time to refer the client to a therapist who specializes in the client's concern.

It is also a time to reassure clients, if appropriate, that in the counselor's opinion, a referral is not needed and that the issues they came with and those they identified in exploration have been sufficiently dealt with and that further psychotherapy does not appear to be necessary. This can be a powerful statement for clients.

Summary

Termination is not merely the end of psychotherapy, it is psychotherapy. It should not be treated as something that counselors do that is separate from the process of therapy. Termination is ideally presented as one more therapeutic process in the counselor's effort to be of service to the client.

It is important to note that ending psychotherapy both efficiently and effectively is an ethical matter for psychotherapists; we are not in the business of unnecessarily extending the time a client spends with us.

Psychotherapy concludes with either planned or unplanned endings. Planned endings include time-limited psychotherapy and what we call natural, mutually satisfying endings. Unplanned endings include spontaneous and arbitrary endings. It should be noted that time-limited, natural, and spontaneous endings all have the possibility of accom-

264

plishing the tasks of termination and may be viewed as positive. Only the arbitrary category is viewed as negative.

The goals of termination are to summarize the therapy in a cognitive, intellectual, and analytical way as well as to make an emotional summary of the path taken in the therapy. It is important to review the gains made in therapy as well as to review the presenting problem(s), formal goals, progress, and work yet to be done. Finally, clients need to know that they can return to therapy without guilt if they feel it necessary, and the counselor may make a referral to help the client continue the work he or she has initiated in the present therapy.

References and for Further Reading

Bruckner-Gordon, F., Gangi, B. K., & Wallman, G. U. (1988). *Making therapy work*. New York: Harper & Row.

Cormier, L. S., & Hackney, H. (1993). *The professional counselor: A process guide to helping* (2nd ed.). Boston: Allyn & Bacon.

Egan, G. (1994). *The skilled helper* (5th ed.). Pacific Grove, CA: Brooks/Cole.

Fordham, M. (1994, March). Ending psychotherapy. *Group Analysis, 27,* 5–14.

Kramer, S. A. (1990). *Positive endings in psychotherapy: Bringing meaningful closure to therapeutic relationships*. San Francisco: Jossey-Bass.

Lauver, P., & Harvey, D. R. (1997). *The practical counselor: Elements of effective helping*. Pacific Grove, CA: Brooks/Cole.

Omer, H. (1991, Fall). Writing a post-scriptum to a badly ended therapy. *Psychotherapy, 28,* 484–492.

Penn, L. S. (1990, October). When the therapist must leave: Forced termination of psychodynamic therapy. *Professional Psychology: Research and Practice, 21,* 379–384.

Roberts, J. (1994, October). Time-limited counselling. *Psychodynamic Counselling, 1,* 93–105.

Schlesinger, J. J. (1996, Fall). The fear of being left half-cured. *Bulletin of the Menninger Clinic, 60,* 428–448.

Schmukler, A. G. (Ed.). (1991). *Saying goodbye: A casebook of termination in child and adolescent analysis and therapy*. Hillsdale, NJ: Analytic Press.

Sommers-Flannagan, J., & Sommers-Flannagan, R. (1993). *Foundations of therapeutic interviewing*. Boston: Allyn & Bacon.

Tudor, K. (1995, July). What do you say about saying goodbye?: Ending psychotherapy. *Transactional Analysis Journal, 25,* 228–233.

Welch, I. D. (1998). *The path of psychotherapy: Matters of the heart*. Pacific Grove, CA: Brooks/Cole.

Winnecott, D. W. (1993). *Talking to parents*. New York: Addison-Wesley.

265

Appendix One

Affective Vocabulary List

Developing an affective vocabulary may begin with four large categories: mad, bad, sad, and glad. Of course, this is the beginning of an affective vocabulary and not the end. Each of these four categories divides into the richness, fullness, and subtlety of our language.

Consider the many ways in which each of these words may be expanded. By studying this list, and by forcing yourself to generate other words when you discover yourself overusing a particular word, you will increase your own affective vocabulary. By increasing your affective vocabulary, you will be better able to demonstrate your understanding of the subtlety of feelings clients might express.

We invite you to play with words. One way to do this if you have a word processing program is to simply use the thesaurus function and increase your affective vocabulary. "Sad," on our program for example, reveals "unhappy," "melancholy," "sorrowful," "downhearted," "rueful," "dispirited," "dejected," and "disappointed." "Dispirited" and "downhearted" are words that might not ordinarily come to mind but that capture a good bit of meaning in the lives of sad people.

MAD

aggravated
aggressive
agitated
angry
annoyed
antagonistic
aroused
austere
bad tempered
belligerent
biting
bitter
bloodthirsty
blunt
boiling
bristling
broiling
brutal
bullying
burned
callous
cantankerous
cold-blooded
combative
contrary
cool
corrosive
cranky
critical
cross
cruel
deadly
dictatorial
disagreeable
discontented
displeased
enraged
exasperated
ferocious
fierce
fighting

fired up
frenzied
fretful
fuming
furious
gruesome
hard
hard-hearted
harsh
hateful
heartless
hellish
hostile
hot
ill-tempered
impatient
incensed
inconsiderate
indignant
inflamed
infuriated
inhuman
intolerant
irked
irritated
malicious
mean
murderous
nasty
obstinate
oppressive
out of sorts
outraged
perturbed
poisonous
provoked
pushy
quarrelsome
raving
ready to explode
resentful
rude
ruffled

ruthless
sadistic
savage
spiteful
steamed
stern
stormy
strung out
unfriendly
unmerciful
vicious
vindictive
violent
wrathful

BAD

Confused
anxious
awkward
baffled
bothered
crazy
dazed
depressed
disorganized
disoriented
distracted
disturbed
embarrassed
frustrated
hopelessly lost
mixed up
panicky
paralyzed
puzzled
stuck
surprised
trapped
troubled
uncertain
uncomfortable
unsure
upset
weak

Scared
afraid
awed
chicken
fearful
frightened
horrified
insecure
intimidated
jumpy
nervous
shaky

Scared (cont'd)
stunned
tense
terrified
threatened
timid
uneasy
unsure
worried

Weak
ashamed
defenseless
discouraged
fragile
frail
helpless
ill
impotent
inadequate
insecure
lifeless
lost
overwhelmed
run-down
sick
vulnerable
wishy-washy
worn out

Distressed
afflicted
anguished
at the mercy of
awkward
badgered
bewildered
clumsy
constrained
disgusted
disliked
dissatisfied
distrustful

disturbed
foolish
futile
grieving
hindered
impaired
imprisoned
lost
nauseated
offended
pained
perplexed
puzzled
ridiculous
sickened
silly
skeptical
speechless
strained
suspicious
swamped
tormented
touchy
ungainly
unlucky
unsatisfied

Fearful, Anxious
afraid
agitated
alarmed
anxious
bashful
desperate
dreadful
embarrassed
fearful
fidgety
hesitant
ill at ease
insecure
intimidated
jealous

jittery
jumpy
nervous
on edge
overwhelmed
panicky
restless
scared
shaky
shy
strained
tense
terrified
terror-stricken
timid
uncomfortable
uneasy
worrying

Belittled, Criticized, Scorned
abused
belittled
branded
carped at
censured
criticized
defamed
defined
deflated
deprecated
depreciated
derided
diminished
discredited
disdained
disgraced
disparaged
humiliated
ignored
jeered
lampooned
laughed at

made fun of
made light of
maligned
minimized
mocked
neglected
not taken seriously
overlooked
poked fun at
pooh-poohed
pulled to pieces
put down
ridiculed
roasted
scoffed at
scorned
shamed
slammed
slandered
slighted
underestimated
underrated

Impotent, Inadequate
anemic
broken
broken-down
chicken-hearted
cowardly
crippled
debilitated
defective
deficient
demoralized
disabled
exhausted
exposed
feeble
flimsy
fragile
frail
harmless
helpless

Impotent, Inadequate (cont'd)

impotent
inadequate
incapable
incompetent
indefensible
ineffective
inefficient
inept
inferior
infirm
insecure
insufficient
lame
maimed
meek
nerveless
paralyzed
powerless
puny
shaken
uncertain
unimportant
unqualified
unsound
unsubstantiated
useless
vulnerable
weak
weak-hearted

Miserable, Troubled, Hurt, Frustrated

aching
awful
battered
bruised
burdened
crabby
cramped
cut to the heart
deprived

desolate
despairing
desperate
destitute
disagreeable
dismal
displeased
dissatisfied
distressed
disturbed
divided
dreadful
futile
harassed
hassled
hemmed in
hindered
imprisoned
jammed up
loaded down
lousy
mistreated
oppressed
pathetic
peeved
perturbed
pitiful
pressured
pulled apart
rotten
ruined
sore
stabbed
strained
strangled
suffering
temperamental
terrible
threatened
thwarted
tormented
tortured
trapped

uneasy
unfortunate
unhappy
unsatisfied
unsure
wiped out
wounded
wretched

Ashamed, Guilty, Embarrassed

apologetic
awkward
blamed
branded
chagrined
cheapened
condemned
conscience stricken
contrite
degraded
denounced
disapproved of
disgraced
dishonored
disreputable
doomed
embarrassed
evasive
exposed
foolish
humbled
humiliated
in a bind
in trouble
judged
punished
put down
rebuked
red faced
regretful
remorseful
ridiculous

roasted
shamed
sheepish
silly
slammed
sorry
wicked
wrong

Confused, Surprised, Astonished

aghast
amazed
appalled
astonished
astounded
awed
awestruck
baffled
bewildered
bowled over
breathless
dazed
dismayed
disorganized
distracted
doubtful
dumbfounded
emotional
forgetful
gripped
horrified
in doubt
jarred
jolted
mixed up
muddled
mystified
overpowered
overwhelmed
perplexed
rattled
ruffled

Confused, Surprised, Astonished (cont'd)

shocked
speechless
staggered
startled
struck
stunned
taken aback
torn
trapped
tricked
uncertain

Lonely, Forgotten, Left Out

abandoned
alienated
alone
betrayed
bored
cast aside
cheated
deserted
discarded
disliked
disowned
empty
excluded
forsaken
friendless
hated
hollow
homeless
homesick
ignored
isolated
jilted
left out
lonesome
lost
neglected
ostracized
outcast
overlooked
rebuffed
rejected
scorned
secluded
shunned
slighted
snubbed
stranded
ugly
uninvited
unimportant
unwelcome

Disgusted, Suspicious

arrogant
callous
cynical
derisive
despising
detesting
disgusting
displeased
distrustful
dogmatic
doubting
envious
grudging
hesitant
jealous
loathing
mistrustful
nauseated
offended
queasy
repulsed
revolted
sickened
skeptical
sneering
wary

SAD

Depressed

alien
alienated
angry
annihilated
apathetic
awful
bad
below par
blue
burned out
cheapened
crushed
debased
defeated
degraded
dejected
demolished
desolate
despairing
despised
despondent
destroyed
disappointed
discarded
discouraged
disfavored
dismal
disturbed
done for
down
downcast
downhearted
downtrodden
dreadful
embarrassed
estranged
excluded
forlorn
forsaken
gloomy

glum
grim
hateful
hopeless
hurt
in the dumps
jilted
kaput
loathed
lonely
lost
low
miserable
mishandled
mistreated
moody
mournful
painful
sorry
stranded
tearful
terrible
turned off
unhappy
unloved
valueless
washed up
wrecked

GLAD

Happy
alive
amused
calm
cheerful
content
delighted
ecstatic
excited
fantastic
fine
fortunate
friendly
glad
good
great
hopeful
loving
motherly
optimistic
peaceful
pleased
proud
relaxed
relieved
satisfied
thankful
thrilled
turned on
up
warm
wonderful

Strong
active
aggressive
assertive
alert
bold
brave
capable
confident

determined
energetic
happy
healthy
loved
open
positive
potent
powerful
quick
secure
solid
super
tough

Elated, Joyful
amused
blissful
brilliant
cheerful
comical
delighted
ecstatic
elated
elevated
enchanted
enthusiastic
exalted
excellent
excited
fantastic
fine
glorious
grand
gratified
great
happy
high-spirited
inspired
joyful
jubilant
magnificent
majestic

marvelous
overjoyed
splendid
superb
terrific
thrilled
tremendous
triumphant
wonderful

Potent
able
adequate
assured
bold
brave
capable
competent
confident
courageous
daring
determined
durable
dynamic
effective
energetic
fearless
firm
forceful
gallant
hardy
healthy
heroic
important
influential
intense
lionhearted
mighty
powerful
robust
secure
self-confident
self-reliant

sharp
skillful
stable
stouthearted
strong
sure
tough
virile
well-equipped
well put together

Curious, Absorbed
analyzing
attentive
concentrating
considering
contemplating
diligent
engrossed
imaginative
inquiring
inquisitive
investigating
occupied
pondering
questioning
reasoning
reflecting
searching
thoughtful
weighing

**Kind, Helpful, Loving,
    Friendly, Thankful**
adaptable
admired
adored
affectionate
agreeable
altruistic
amiable
amorous
appreciative

Kind, Helpful, Loving, Friendly, Thankful (cont'd)

aroused
benevolent
bighearted
brotherly
caring
charitable
cherished
comforting
compassionate
compatible
congenial
conscientious
considerate
cooperative
cordial
dedicated
dependable
devoted
diligent
empathic
fair
faithful
fatherly
fond
forgiving
gallant
generous
genuine
gentle
giving
good
gracious
grateful
honorable
humane
idolizing
indebted to
involved
just
longing for

mellow
merciful
mindful
motherly
neighborly
nice
obliging
open
optimistic
passionate
patient
praiseful
respectful
rewarded
sensitive
sharing
sincere
sisterly
softhearted
straightforward
sympathetic
tender
thoughtful
tolerant
treasured
trustful
unassuming
understanding
unselfish
warmhearted

Interested, Excited, Peaceful

active
alert
aroused
attracted to
bubbly
bustling
busy
challenged
delighted
eager

enchanted
enthusiastic
exuberant
fascinated
impatient
impressed with
interested in
involved
keyed up
quickened
resourceful
responsive
spurred on
stimulated
tantalized
thrilled

Peaceful

accepted
at ease
calm
carefree
clear
comfortable
complete
fulfilled
gratified
lighthearted
pleasant
pleased
poised
refreshed
relieved
renewed
revived
safe
satiated
satisfied
serene
settled
soothed
sweet
wholesome

wonderful

Playful

agreeable
amusing
breezy
cleaver
frisky
frolicsome
fun loving
funny
genial
good-humored
hearty
hospitable
joking
lighthearted
lively
mirthful
mischievous
original
quick-witted
sociable
spontaneous
sportive
sprightly
spry
uninhibited
vivacious

Counseling Techniques

1. Empty Chair
2. Role Playing
3. Talking to Parts of the Self
4. Ask the Expert
5. Mirroring the Body
6. Mirroring the Language/ Metaphor of the Client
7. Visualization
8. Fantasy
9. House of Control
10. Whose Face Is That? Whose Voice Is That?
11. Wise Old Man/Wise Old Woman
12. Empowering Language
13. Body Scan
14. Homework
15. Put Yourself on the List
16. Body Language/Work
17. Self-Talk
18. Lifeline
19. The Five Worst Things a Human Being Can Be
20. Paradoxical Intention
21. Charting
22. Put It in the Box
23. Card Sort of Emotions

Empty Chair

This technique employs a bit of imagination. It asks the client to bring a person into the room with whom the client needs to speak one-on-one. The process involves a number of steps. (1) You need an empty chair. (It is recommended that four chairs be used—two for the client and two for the therapist.) (2) Ask the client to identify , describe, and reach out with a hand and touch the person in the empty chair (this is to personalize the experience). (3) Begin the exercise with a stem— for example, the therapist might say (speaking as the client), "Dad, I need to talk to you about something important to me." Then, let the client do the speaking unless the client has trouble and needs to be "prompted." Then, as in the theater, give the client a line to speak— for example, "I'm having trouble getting started." Giving the client a line is more concrete and direct and seems more effective than urging the client to speak, as in, "Say anything you want." (4) After the client has spoken to the empty chair for a few sentences, the counselor faces the decision of whether simply to allow the client to say whatever he or she wishes or to move toward some resolution. If a resolution appears necessary, or even close, then move the client into the other chair where the client will assume the role of the person to whom he or she has been speaking. When the client moves into his or her other chair, the therapist moves simultaneously into the other chair provided for the therapist. In this situation, the client may move back and forth between the chairs in a dialogue fashion. (5) When the episode is finished, which requires a judgment from the therapist, ask the client to move back into his or her original seat, say "good-bye" to the person to whom the client has been talking, move the empty chairs aside, and ask the client, "What did you learn in that exercise?" It is important at this point to ask what has been learned rather than what the client feels, because the purpose of this step is to promote a cognitive processing of the experience. (6) The therapist might also have learned something in the dialogue and it is acceptable to introduce that information at this step.

Usefulness. The empty chair is an excellent technique for dealing with anger, unresolved issues, and death and dying (see page 293 where this technique is repeated as a reminder of its usefulness in grief work) and it can also be used as a behavioral rehearsal technique for some upcoming difficult situation in the client's life.

Role Playing

This technique asks the therapist to assume the role of some person with whom the client has unresolved issues or to assume the role of the client himself or herself. The therapist may choose any sort of role (helpful, argumentative, insulting) as a way of understanding how the client responds in a particular situation and/or as a way of helping the client have some insight into his or her own behavior. This technique may be used as a method to teach the client other ways of responding. The therapist acts the role faithfully until the exercise is finished, when the therapist stops role playing. This unambiguous stoppage is necessary to make clear to the client the distinction between the "role" and the therapist. When the exercise is finished, ask the cognitive, processing question, "What did you learn from that experience?"

277

Usefulness. This technique is particularly useful for a dramatic understanding of how a client may actually be responding as opposed to a verbal description of how the client says he or she is responding. This technique can offer a client an insight into ineffective behavior and it can teach other ways of responding. It is also possible to use role playing as a behavior rehearsal technique.

Talking to Parts of the Self

This technique is a variation on role playing and the empty chair. The therapist asks the client to identify a part of the self (either in general or a specific part that has become the source of some problem—e.g.,

"Can you get in touch with that part of yourself that is so condemning of you?" "Can you get in touch with that part of you that believes in you?"). The purpose here is to place that part of the self in a chair for an interview so that it may be questioned for information about causes of behavior, motivations, dynamics, or underlying beliefs that are either hindering or helping the client. The steps in this exercise are straightforward: "Let's do something here. Close your eyes and get in touch with that part of you that _____. Let me know by a nod of the head or some gesture that you are in touch with that part. Ask if it will talk to us." (If the client says no, ask the client to find another part that will talk for the original part that you want to interview.) Then, have the client ask questions or enter into a dialogue with the part. The therapist may ask questions as well. When the exercise is over ask the client to slowly come back to the session and ask the cognitive, processing question, "What did you learn from that experience?"

Usefulness. This technique is particularly suitable for exploring unknown influences in the client's life. It is a good exploratory technique that can help clarify for the therapist and client sources of influence in the client's life.

Ask the Expert

This technique is used in response to a direct question. The client might ask about what to do in a specific situation or why he or she acts in some particular way. The process may involve a story to set up the exercise or it may be entered into directly. The story format involves setting up the situation as follows: "You need to know why you don't stand up to your father. What you need is an expert on family relations who can answer your question. Luckily, we have an expert right here in this office. I'll bring him/her in in just a minute. What exactly do you want to ask him/her?" Have the client formulate the question. Then, say to the client, "Come, sit in this chair" (the therapist's chair). Switch seats with the client. The therapist then asks the exact question formulated by the client. The therapist may role play if other questions occur as the client speaks in the role of the expert. (If the client says that he or she doesn't know, then the therapist should prompt the client by saying, "You must know. You are the expert. You have written a book on the subject!") When the exercise is finished, switch seats again and ask the client, "What did you hear the expert say?"

If the therapist sees no reason to create a story, then simply say, "Come sit here. You are the expert. Why doesn't a person stand up to a father?"

Usefulness. This technique is useful in avoiding direct questions and for helping clients explore areas of confusion. It is also an empowering technique in which the client is allowed to discover his or her own solutions to personally felt issues.

Mirroring the Body

279

Mirroring the body simply means that the therapist uses the gestures, posture, and physical attitude of the client as a way to nonverbally demonstrate that the therapist understands the client. It comes from the discovery that at high levels of empathy therapists tended to "mirror" the actions of the client. This was discovered, in part, from analysis of videotapes that permitted slow-motion replay and delayed studies of therapist-client interaction. Mirroring the gesture or posture of a client may be done as a part of a verbal interaction (where when the therapist speaks he or she would make the gesture noticed in the client) or simply as a nonverbal behavior indicating that the therapist is with the client.

Usefulness. The usefulness of this idea is, of course, limited. It is merely another way of demonstrating empathic understanding and allows a variation in sitting postures for the therapist in addition to the classic attending posture. A note of caution should be introduced here: It is not appropriate to "mirror" postures that are closed or defensive in nature.

Mirroring the Language/
Metaphor of the Client

This technique is similar to mirroring the body except that it is used to match the language style and metaphor of the client. Some clients are visual ("I'm in a fog"; "I just can't see my way through this problem"); some clients are auditory ("I just said to myself, 'I'm going crazy'"; "It just sounds bizarre, even when I say it out loud"); some clients are kinesthetic ("I just can't seem to get the jump on life"; "Wham! Life just punched me in the nose"). The intent is to match the client so that a statement demonstrating understanding matches not only content but feelings in a language style that is used naturally by the client (e.g., "I just seem to be in a fog" is not well matched by a therapist phrase such as "I hear you saying," because the former is visual and the latter is auditory. It would be mirroring the language to use a phrase such as, "You just can't seem to see your way clear.").

> *Usefulness.* This technique is somewhat more useful than mirroring the body because conceptually it offers more opportunity for genuinely demonstrating that what has been said has truly been understood by the therapist.

Visualization

This technique asks the client to visualize metaphors used or implied in the therapeutic discussion. A client might say, "I'm blocked from reaching a solution." The therapist would say, "Close your eyes and visualize the block you see. Describe it for me." Or, the client might say, "I just feel like I am being attacked from all sides." The therapist would say, "Close your eyes and visualize what or who is attacking you." The therapist dialogues with the client during the visualization. The therapist has the freedom to suggest different aspects of the visualization and even to intervene to alter an ending or event in the visualization if it is therapeutically suggested.

Usefulness. This is a helpful and widely useful technique. Visualization may be used in the exploration, understanding, action, or problem-solving stage of therapy. It allows a client to use a metaphor brought up in therapy to actually explore, understand, or take action on a concrete life issue. The therapist must have a creative imagination to quickly overcome any obstacles presented by the client in the visualization. The therapist can encourage the client to bring in people or objects necessary to overcome any obstacle.

Fantasy

Fantasy differs from visualization in that it may involve a story begun by the therapist and ended by the client. It can begin with a metaphor suggested by the client or it can come from some concrete event in the client's life that the therapist wishes to explore, understand, or problem solve with the client through fantasy. The therapist begins by saying, "Close your eyes. I want you to imagine . . . " and then begins a short story that the client will finish. The therapist might even ask before beginning the fantasy, "What do you want to have happen in this situation?" For example, a client with a negative self-concept might profit from a fantasy in which the self is nurtured and grown. The therapist might say, "Close your eyes. I want you to imagine that you are a flower in a garden. In fact, at this point, see yourself as a seed newly planted in rich, loving soil. Now imagine the budding plant just emerging from the ground. The flower is small, tender at this point, perhaps not very strong. Now see a warm, bright light shining on the flower. Imagine that rich, pure water is being poured around the earth in which the flower is growing. Even as you watch, you can see the flower respond to the light and the warmth and the water. The flower is growing stronger and stronger. Now, every day I want you to imagine the flower and the light and the water and the warmth. Watch as the flower grows stronger and stronger."

Another fantasy might involve a client who feels blocked from some goal or understanding. The therapist might say, "Close your eyes. I want you to visualize the block. What does it look like? . . . What is it made of? . . . What do you need in order to knock it down or drill a hole in the wall? . . . Now, drill a hole in the wall. Look on the other side and tell me what you see. Now, when you are ready come back slowly to this room and tell me what you learned from that experience." This last fantasy allows the therapist and client to metaphorically explore what the block might be hiding, thus presenting the possibility of deeper understanding. (Note: this technique is repeated on page 296 as a reminder of its usefulness in grief work.)

Usefulness. Fantasy is another technique that offers a wide range of uses. It is particularly useful with situations that have occurred in the past and that seem to have no solution in the present. It becomes metaphorically possible to solve some problems in fantasy that cannot be solved in reality. For example, this technique is especially helpful when the client feels powerless to do something about an event that occurred in the past yet still troubles him or her. Perhaps the client was raped or physically abused and the rapist or abuser cannot, in fact, be confronted. In fantasy the outcome can be very different from what happened in reality. In fantasy the rapist can be defeated, captured, frightened, or beat up, whatever is necessary for the client to reclaim strength, dignity, and/or power over his or her own life. Problems can be solved in fantasy in the hopes that there will be some carryover into actual life. There is no issue, problem, or dilemma that cannot be conquered in fantasy.

House of Control

The house of control is a specific guided fantasy to help clients gain control over decisions that directly affect their lives. In this fantasy the therapist must be creative and quick in order to overcome block, suggest alternatives, and be ever mindful that the purpose of this technique is to give power to the client. The name is derived from the notion that the center of control in every person must be housed, metaphorically, somewhere. The house metaphor is one of many that may emerge. The fantasy begins with the therapist saying, "Close your eyes. Find that place inside yourself where things are controlled. When you find it give me a signal that you can describe it to me. Describe it to me." When the initial description is completed, the therapist must help direct the fantasy. "Now describe the inside to me." (In this description the therapist is listening for evidence of some device or mechanism by which messages are sent out to the self.) In the description of the exterior and interior of the house listen for the condition, the upkeep of the house. If it is shabby, then in fantasy some repairs are going to have to be made so that the house of control is attractive both on the outside and the inside.

Next, have the client explore the control room. "Look inside the control room. Tell me what you see. Next, I want you to make sure that there is no other person in the control room with you. If there is, then do whatever you need to do so that that person or those persons leave. Now lock the door so that no one can get in. This is your control room and no one has any right to be in there except you. Look around. Does the room need to be redecorated? Bring in rugs or flowers or paintings so that this room is yours and yours alone. Now, look at the door. There is a picture on the wall beside the door. Underneath the picture there is a title—'Person in Charge'. Whose picture is that?" (If it is not a picture of the client, have the client remove the picture that is there and replace it with his or her own picture.) "There may be various levers, dials, knobs, or other devices by which a message is sent out of the control center. I want you to look at those and see if they have labels. Read the labels to me. Now, do you want to send a message?" (If the client sends a message, ensure that it is a positive message.) "Now we are going to leave your house of control. Go outside and lock the door so that no other person can get in and slowly return to this room in this place and time." The therapist then asks, "What did you learn from that experience?"

283

Usefulness. The house of control is designed for one purpose—to help clients, through fantasy, move toward control of their own lives. It is meant to empower the client with an attitude of control in which the client sees himself or herself as able to make decisions, cope with stress, and deal with life crises. He or she is the one who makes the decisions that rule his or her life.

Whose Face Is That? / Whose Voice Is That?

This is a quick intervention aimed at determining whether decisions in the client's life are being unduly influenced by some outside agent. It is triggered by negative statements the client makes about his or her life. For example, a client might say, "I'm just hopeless." Then the therapist asks, "Whose face do you see?" (If the client says, "I don't see anything," then repeat the phrase and say, "Whose voice is that?") Because some clients are more visual or more auditory, be prepared to switch from one stimulus to the other. Typical responses are parents, grandparents, the client, or the therapist. Each of these cases allows the client and the therapist to explore undue influence in the client's life.

Usefulness. This technique is useful for discovering what person or persons in the client's life may be the source of negative feelings and/or the source of influence that robs the client of a central role in self-determination.

Wise Old Man / Wise Old Woman

When clients seem genuinely confused about what direction to take, this exercise is helpful in allowing them to give advice to themselves. After some appeal for advice or an expression of being stuck around some decision, the therapist might say, "Close your eyes. I want you to go inside yourself and search until you find the wisest part of yourself from where you can seek advice. When you find that part give me a signal. Describe what you see." (What the therapist is looking for in this description is a wise old man or wise old woman figure—a sage, saint, wizard, medicine woman, etc. It should be an image that avoids youthfulness, a parent, or some representation of mere authority.) "Ask that part for advice about the dilemma you are facing." (Listen to the client talk to the wisest part of himself or herself.) "Now, slowly return to this room in this time and place knowing that you can return to this wise part whenever you like for advice. What did you hear the wisest part of yourself say?"

It is important to listen closely to advice that comes from a part of the self that is spontaneously described as an old man or woman. It is important to downplay advice that comes from a part described as the self, a parent, or some figure of authority such as a professor, minister, or rabbi.

Usefulness. This is an effective way to have clients give advice to themselves and to keep the therapist out of advice giving. It allows the therapist to have a good idea of what level of advice the client is able to give to the self. It also permits the therapist to appraise the advice in order to understand its usefulness in the life of the client and emphasize or downplay the advice as necessary.

Empowering Language

To some extent, the language used by people may be a part of the problems they are having in living. In a larger context, the thoughts we express to ourselves may profoundly influence the actions we take in life. This concept, of course, lies at the heart of many therapeutic interventions. This technique is less profound than that conception and yet akin to it. The language changes are meant to teach clients. First, "you to I" is meant to teach the concept of ownership of thoughts and emotions. Second, "but to and" is meant to teach the concept of contradictory language. Third, "can't to won't/don't" is meant to teach the concept of empowerment and personal responsibility for decisions. The change is made in a gentle way and without confrontation. For example, "I heard you say 'You know how people are, they just hate to be lied to.' I think it's clear to me that you hate to be lied to. Is that right? Yes. Could you just say it that way, 'I hate to be lied to'?" Follow the same model for the other two language changes.

Usefulness. This clarification of language, which is a way of teaching clients to be more clear in their thinking and expression, has only limited usefulness. That in itself, of course, is helpful.

285

Body Scan

This is an exploratory technique designed to identify the source of some emotional upset in a client. It is a form of body work. When the client is discussing some issue in his or her life but cannot seem to identify the emotion that accompanies the issue, this technique can be helpful. The technique involves a short description of what the client is to do and an identification of the emotion involved. The therapist identifies the issue with the client—for example, "I can't talk to my wife." Then, the therapist might say, "I want you to do something. I'll describe it for you and then I want you to use your hand as a scanner for feeling in your body. You know how a computer might scan a photograph for a particular image or object. I want you to scan your body for feelings about this issue. Close your eyes and move your hand from the top of your head across your body down to your feet. When you feel something, a catch or any feeling, stop and then move on. Do you have any questions? Do it now." The therapist observes the scan and notes any stops. Ask the client to touch the places where the scan stopped. Label that part of the body.

There are common places clients touch and each has a fairly literal interpretation of meaning. Here are some examples: Head = intellectual/cognitive—they may feel stupid about the situation. Shoulders = heavy load—they are carrying a burden. Mouth, Throat = communication—they may not feel comfortable talking about the issue. Throat = choking—they may feel suffocated by the issue. Heart = love—they may feel unloved. Chest = armor, box—they may feel defensive, trapped, or that something is hidden from them. Stomach = nurturance, guts—they may feel unloved; they may lack courage to face the issue. Genitals = sexual—the issue might be infidelity; they are being "screwed." Back = pain—the issue or person is a pain. Feet = running—they want to get out of the situation. The secret of interpretation here is to be as literal as possible. Consider the first impression that comes to mind or a common cliché. It is important to have the client identify the part of the body touched and the symbolic meaning given to that part of the body. Then, the therapist can add any additional thoughts.

Usefulness. This technique is a quick way to identify the emotion attributed to an issue in the life of a client. While the description is long, the actual technique is short and is meant to quickly provide an insight for the client and therapist.

Homework

Not all the work clients do in therapy is, nor should it be, done in the session itself. Homework is a way to have clients do work outside the therapy session. The homework assignment should be concrete and, if possible, something that can be written down so that it may be demonstrated and discussed in the next session. For example, in a grief issue, the therapist may say, "Sometime during the next week, I want you to write a letter to your dead husband explaining the trouble you are having now that you are being asked to go out to dinner with men and how you feel guilty about accepting." The client will bring the homework assignment into the next therapy session for discussion.

Usefulness. Homework can be an effective way to try out new skills to safely express thoughts and feelings that are too threatening when expressed directly. This technique may employ fantasy situations or real situations in the person's life that need to be practiced and discussed later on.

Put Yourself on the List

When a client has an overdeveloped sense of responsibility for others, this technique can point out that the client can be responsible for himself or herself as well. The therapist merely asks the client to provide a list of all the people for whom the client is responsible. The therapist might say, "Tell me all the people for whom you are responsible." If the client does not list himself or herself, then the therapist would say, "Put yourself on the list. I'm not telling you that your name has to be number one, I am just saying that your name can be on the list of those people that you feel responsible to take care of." If the client does list his or her name, then the therapist can say, "I see you are aware that one of the people you have to take care of is you."

Usefulness. This technique is designed to help clients understand that they have some responsibility for taking care of themselves. It is especially useful when clients forget to list themselves.

Body Language / Work

Often clients make gestures or use the body in ways that provide clues to their underlying feelings. There are two essential ways in which the body may be used to better understand a client. First, it may be used as a clue to forming an empathy statement. For example, a client may rub a hand across his or her forehead. The therapist might say, "It is just such a feeling of relief" because that gesture gives a clue of relief. The second method is to directly use a gesture to help a client explore what that gesture means to him or her. The therapist might observe a client place his or her arm out, palm up, with a slight up and down motion. The therapist might say, "Look at your hand. What are you carrying?" in hopes that the attention brought to the gesture will allow the client to arrive at an insight.

Usefulness. The use of body language, gestures, and posture in therapy can be the source of the breakthrough in insight for the client. It is often a powerful tool. The danger is that the therapist may read too much into the gesture or posture without being willing to acknowledge that sometimes the gesture does not carry symbolic meaning.

Self-Talk

This strategy may be used with highly verbal and insightful clients. It simply asks the client to take a question he or she is puzzled about and to talk about it without interruption for 3 to 5 minutes. The client is encouraged to ask the question over and over and to answer it over and over. After the client stops, the therapist can ask, "What did you hear yourself say?"

Usefulness. This technique challenges the client to speak rapidly about an issue of concern, answering it over and over in an attempt to overcome any resistance or reluctance the client may have to answering the question in some meaningful and important way for fear of judgment, embarrassment, or silliness. It is often the source of a breakthrough or an insight for the client.

Lifeline

This method of collecting personal history is more creative than a simple narrative or responding to a number of questions. It may be used as homework. The therapist says, "I want you to draw a long line on this piece of paper." (Use the middle of the paper to allow for variations in how far from average an experience is judged to be. Use a "+" on the top half of the page for positive experiences and a "–" on the bottom half of the page to designate negative experiences.) "The right end of the line is the present. The other end is as far back as you wish to go. Place everything you think is important in your life and development on the line. Positive up above and negative down below. The line represents an average experience." When the client has finished, use the lifeline as a reference for material in therapy.

Usefulness. This technique provides the therapist with a quick way of obtaining a developmental history that is meaningful to the client without a lengthy question-and-answer session. It is also useful with nonverbal clients as a way to generate material for discussion in therapy.

The Five Worst Things a Human Being Can Be

The therapist asks the client to list the five worst things a human being can be. Then, immediately after the client responds, the therapist asks, "Are you any of those things?"

The point here is that when a client is very condemning of himself or herself, this quick intervention should show that he or she is not the worst thing in the world. It is a way of gaining some perspective for the client.

Usefulness. This strategy is used for a quick intervention for self-concept purposes and for highly self-condemning clients. It is meant to provide the client with some perspective on the self. The client may have self-doubts and still recognize that he or she is not the worst imaginable human being.

Paradoxical Intention

This technique, which should be used carefully so as not to violate the dimension of genuineness, essentially means that the opposite of what is intended is reflected. It may take the form of purposeful naiveté or over-reflecting/exaggerating the intention of the client. The therapist might say, "So, if I understand you correctly, your husband is the crummiest human being alive and ought to be tortured to death." What usually happens is that the client is forced into a more moderate position than he or she originally stated. The therapist might say, "So the situation is hopeless," when the client is expressing difficulty. The outcome might be that the client would say, "Well, it is not hopeless. There is some hope."

Usefulness. This technique may be used to shock a client into a different way of thinking and may be thought of as a form of confrontation. It is useful when rapport is highly established and a good deal of trust exists between the client and therapist.

Charting

This simple technique involves merely having the client write on a wall sheet (or a table sheet) a list of desires, needs, shortcomings, or any other range of topics that lend themselves to writing. The technique may also involve listing the issue on one side of the page and listing solutions or feelings on the other. It can be used to help clarify and separate a number of issues presented confusingly by a client. The purpose of the technique is to help both the client and the therapist clarify something vague or confusing in the client's thinking.

Here is a suggested format. "Topic" means the overall concern of the client (e.g., self-doubt, relationships). "Issue" means the specific concern within the overall topic (e.g., in relationships the client might report an issue with social ineptitude, shyness, or lack of conversational ability). "Feelings" equals the affective state associated with the issue (e.g., anger, sadness). "Wish" means what the client wants to have happen. "Stopping" means what is getting in the way of the wish. "Settle for" means what the client would accept if what is truly desired is not possible. "C/NC" means is it within the client's control or not. "Priority" under "Issues" means that after the list of issues is completed, it is important to put the items in their order of importance for the client so that they can be processed accordingly. It seems to work best to complete each line (issue, feeling, wish, etc.) rather than making a list of issues and then going down each column (i.e., do each row rather than completing the chart by columns).

Topic
(Relationships)

Issues (Priority)	Feelings	Wish	Stopping	Settle for	C/NC
Shy	Embarrassed	Confident	Doubt	Improving	C
Dates	Greedy	More Dates!	Shyness	A date	?-C

Usefulness. This technique actually provides two useful purposes in therapy. The primary use is to clarify the thinking of the client regarding some blockage or vaguely felt concern. The secondary use is to introduce physical activity into the session by using a wall sheet, which requires the client and therapist to stand. This breaks the ritual of "sitting-talking-listening" that may become too passive.

Put It in the Box

This is a straightforward strategy to help a client deal with some troublesome behavior in therapy. For example, a client who laughs constantly may be asked to take the laugh and "put it in the box" for the therapy session. Or, a client who constantly replies "I don't know" can be asked to take that phrase and "put it in the box" for the session.

Usefulness. This techniques permits a client to talk more seriously about presently felt concerns by symbolically deciding not to use a common defense. It permits more serious and meaningful talk about presently felt emotions and thoughts.

Card Sort of Emotions

In this technique, the therapist prepares approximately 100 3″×5″ index cards with one emotion on each card. The deck of cards should contain a mix of positive and negative emotions. Some attention should be paid to including emotions that the therapist suspects are felt but are not being expressed by the client. The client is then asked to sort the cards into two stacks—those emotions that are felt by the client in the situation being discussed and those that are not (it is possible to have a third stack of "I'm not sure" cards). Once the cards are sorted the stack of emotions that are descriptive of the client may be further sorted or ranked from most to least important.

Usefulness. This technique is useful for clients who have difficulty identifying emotions characteristic of their situation or for clients who have difficulty talking about their life situation. It is a stimulus activity that generates materials for the therapy session.

References

Bellack, A. S., & Hersen, M. (1985). *Dictionary of behavior therapy techniques*. New York: Pergamon Press.

Dyer, W. W., & Vriend, J. (1977). *Counseling techniques that work*. New York: Funk & Wagnalls.

Kanfer, F. H., & Goldstein, A. P. (1986). *Helping people change: A textbook of methods*. New York: Pergamon Press.

Karasu, T. B., & Bellack, L. (1980). *Specialized techniques in individual psychotherapy*. New York: Brunner/Mazel.

Stone, H., & Stone, S. (1993). *Embracing your inner critic: Turning self-criticism into a creative asset*. New York: HarperCollins.

Stone, H., & Winkelman, S. (1989). *Embracing ourselves: The voice dialogue manual*. Mill Valley, CA: Nataraj Publishing.

Vriend, J. (1985). *More counseling techniques that work*. Alexandria, VA: Association for Supervision and Development.

Techniques of Grief Therapy

1. Empty Chair
2. Letter to the Deceased
3. Obituary
4. Eulogy
5. Poetry
6. Drawing/Painting
7. Reality Testing
8. Fantasy
9. Memorabilia
10. Trip to the Cemetery

Empty Chair

This technique employs a bit of imagination. It asks the client to bring a person into the room with whom the client needs to speak one-on-one. The process involves a number of steps. (1) You need an empty chair. (It is recommended that four chairs be used—two for the client and two for the therapist.) (2) Ask the client to identify, describe, and reach out with a hand and touch the person in the empty chair (this is to personalize the experience). (3) Begin the exercise with a stem—for example, the therapist might say (speaking as the client), "Dad, I need to talk to you about something important to me." Then, let the client do the speaking unless the client has trouble and needs to be "prompt-ed." Then, as in the theater, give the client a line to speak—for exam-ple, "I'm having trouble getting started." Giving the client a line is more concrete and direct and seems more effective than urging the client to speak, as in, "Say anything you want." (4) After the client has spoken to the empty chair for a few sentences, the counselor faces the decision of whether simply to allow the client to say whatever he or she wishes or to move toward some resolution. If a resolution appears necessary, or even close, then move the client into the other chair where the client will assume the role of the person to whom he or she has been speak-ing. When the client moves into his or her other chair, the therapist moves simultaneously into the other chair provided for the therapist. In this situation, the client may move back and forth between the chairs in a dialogue fashion. (5) When the episode is finished, which requires a judgment from the therapist, ask the client to move back into his or her original seat, say "good-bye" to the person to whom the client has been talking, move the empty chairs aside, and ask the client, "What did you learn in that exercise?" It is important at this point to ask what has been learned rather than what the client feels, because the purpose of this step is to promote a cognitive processing of the experience. (6) The therapist might also have learned something in the dialogue and it is acceptable to introduce that information at this step.

Usefulness. The empty chair is an excellent technique for dealing with anger, unresolved issues, death and dying, and grief and loss. The empty chair is particularly useful for any sort of "unfinished busi-ness." It may be used to say good-bye, resolve some conflict, deal with guilt, or advance the grief process.

Letter to the Deceased

Writing a letter to the deceased is another method of confronting "unfinished business." It is assigned as homework. The therapist sim-ply says, "Before next week's session, I want you to write a letter to _____ about the feelings you are having. Bring it with you next week and we can talk about the letter then."

Usefulness. Writing a letter is useful in advancing the grief process, asking for advice, confronting conflict, and saying good-bye.

Obituary

Similar to writing a letter, writing an obituary is a method of confronting grief. The therapist says, "Before next week's session, I want you to write an obituary for _____. Bring it with you to the session and we will talk about it then." (An obituary is a notice of a person's death with a short biographical account of that person's life.)

Usefulness. This technique is useful in the early part of the grief process or when clients are having trouble accepting the reality of the death. It is meant to advance the grief process. It allows the grieving person to relive some of the memories of the deceased by recounting a biographical account of the deceased's life.

295

Eulogy

Similar to writing a letter and an obituary, the client is asked to write a eulogy for the deceased. Be prepared to define what a eulogy is and to talk about the feelings it brings up for the client. This technique is also used early in the grief process. (A eulogy is a formal statement of praise for the deceased.)

Usefulness. The purpose is to advance the grief. It is a way for the grieving person to acknowledge the valuable contribution the deceased made to his or her life.

Poetry

The purpose of having the client write poetry about the loss is to help the client in the exploration of grief and to help the therapist understand the process the client is going through. It is an especially effective way to help clients who are not highly verbal bring important emotional material into the session.

Usefulness. This technique is meant to advance the grief process and to bring more personally meaningful material into the sessions. It is useful for persons who are highly literate but not particularly verbal. Poetry may be used at any point in the grieving process.

Drawing / Painting

It is possible to use techniques such as drawing and painting with adults as well as with children when dealing with death. You may have the client draw or paint scenes that are personally meaningful to stimulate memories and feelings for discussion in the session.

Usefulness. This technique is useful for nonverbal clients and clients who have trouble expressing their emotions. It allows important material to be brought into the session and can be used to stimulate verbal interaction as well as previously unexpressed feelings.

Reality Testing

This strategy is meant to be somewhat confrontational in that it asks the client the same question several times. For example, "What did you do? What else? What else?" It is meant to challenge the irrational thoughts that somehow the client could have done something to have saved the life of his or her loved one or that the client did something that caused the death.

Usefulness. This technique is helpful in dealing with guilt after rapport has been established with the client.

Fantasy

Fantasy differs from visualization in that it may involve a story begun by the therapist and ended by the client. It can begin with a metaphor suggested by the client or it can come from some concrete event in the client's life that the therapist wishes to explore, understand, or problem solve with the client through fantasy. The therapist begins by saying,

"Close your eyes. I want you to imagine . . . " and then begins a short story that the client will finish. The therapist might even ask before beginning the fantasy, "What do you want to have happen in this situation?" For example, a client with a negative self-concept might profit from a fantasy in which the self is nurtured and grown. The therapist might say, "Close your eyes. I want you to imagine that you are a flower in a garden. In fact, at this point, see yourself as a seed newly planted in rich, loving soil. Now imagine the budding plant just emerging from the ground. The flower is small, tender at this point, perhaps not very strong. Now see a warm, bright light shining on the flower. Imagine that rich, pure water is being poured around the earth in which the flower is growing. Even as you watch, you can see the flower respond to the light and the warmth and the water. The flower is growing stronger and stronger. Now, every day I want you to imagine the flower and the light and the water and the warmth. Watch as the flower grows stronger and stronger."

Another fantasy might involve a client who feels blocked from some goal or understanding. The therapist might say, "Close your eyes. I want you to visualize the block. What does it look like? . . . What is it made of? . . . What do you need in order to knock it down or drill a hole in the wall? . . . Now, drill a hole in the wall. Look on the other side and tell me what you see. Now, when you are ready come back slowly to this room and tell me what you learned from that experience." This last fantasy allows the therapist and client to metaphorically explore what the block might be hiding, thus presenting the possibility of deeper understanding.

Usefulness. Fantasy is another technique that offers a wide range of uses. It is particularly useful with situations that have occurred in the past and that seem to have no solution in the present. It becomes metaphorically possible to solve some problems in fantasy that cannot be solved in reality. For example, this technique is especially helpful when the client feels powerless to do something about an event that occurred in the past yet still troubles him or her. Problems can be solved in fantasy in the hopes that there will be some carryover into actual life. There is no issue, problem, or dilemma that cannot be conquered in fantasy. Using fantasy is another way of advancing the grief process, saying good-bye, and

297

having a conversation with the deceased. It is especially useful in resolving conflicts, seeking advice, and seeking permission for future behavior.

Memorabilia

Using memorabilia is a way of getting the client to talk about feelings of grief when the client is somewhat reluctant or confused about what to talk about in therapy. The therapist says, "Next week why not bring something that is important to you that reminds you of _____. It can be pictures or anything that holds special memory for you. We will talk about these items when you bring them in."

Usefulness. Bringing memorabilia into the therapy session promotes talk which advances the grief process. It is another technique that is especially good for less verbal clients and for children.

298

Trip to the Cemetery

At some point, in very difficult deaths especially, the therapist may learn that the client has not visited the cemetery. The therapist may either suggest to the client that going to the cemetery is an important thing to do or that he or she accompany the client on the visit. Such an act is important and can signal the beginning of a healthy grief process.

Usefulness. This strategy is useful for the early stages of the grief process or for any stage where it is clear that the client is in denial and is not dealing with the reality of the death.

References

Childs-Gowell, E. (1992). *Good grief rituals: Tools for healing.* Barrytown, NY: Station Hill Press.

Rando, T. A. (1984). *Grief, dying, and death.* Champaign, IL: Research Press.

Welch, I. D., Zawistoski, R. F., & Smart, D. W. (1991). *Encountering death: Structured activities for death awareness.* Muncie, IN: Accelerated Development.

Worden, J. W. (1982). *Grief counseling and grief therapy.* New York: Springer.

Appendix Three

Some Common and Useful Counseling Forms

The number of pages for each item is given for convenience.

Item	*Number of Pages*
Individual Intake Forms	
Initial Intake Form (Simple)	(1)
Initial Interview With a Child	(2)
Family Therapy Intake Form	(2)
Family Information Survey	(2)
Progress Note Forms	
Case Notes	(1)
Suggestions for Writing Client Progress Notes	(1)
Clinical-Behavior Diagnostic Matrix	(1)
Progress Notes (SOAP)	(1)
Progress Notes (Narrative)	(1)

Appendix 3

Item	Number of Pages
Counseling Forms	
Sample Patient Rights Form for In-Patient Facility	(2)
Authorization to Request/Release Information	(1)
Treatment Plan 1	(1)
Treatment Plan 2	(1)
Termination Summary	(1)
Referral Form	(1)
Insurance Claim Form	(1)
Client Billing Worksheet	(1)
Assessment Forms	
Psychological Report Form	(2)
Mental Status Checklist	(4)

300

COMMUNITY COUNSELING SERVICES

1234 EMPATHY RD.

ANY TOWN, ANY STATE USA

INITIAL INTAKE FORM (SIMPLE)

Counselor_____ Date _____

Client_____ Date of birth _____ Age _____

Address_____ City/State/Zip_____

Telephone_____ Sex_____

Marital status: Married_____ Single_____ Divorced_____ Widowed_____

Occupation_____ School_____

Last educational grade level completed _____

Number of years of college completed _____

Please specify trade schools or special training _____

Referral source: Self_____ Other_____ (Please specify) _____

Previous or current treatment (medical and/or psychological) (kind and by whom?)

_____

Are you currently on medication? _____ No _____ Yes What? _____

Are you in good health? ____ Yes ____ No If not, please describe your condition:

_____

Family data:

	Name	Age	Living/Deceased
Parents:	_____	_____	_____
	_____	_____	_____
Brothers:	_____	_____	_____
& Sisters:	_____	_____	_____
Children:	_____	_____	_____
	_____	_____	_____

Any significant family history or past event I should know about?

What are your expectations/wishes for counseling?

COMMUNITY COUNSELING SERVICES

1234 EMPATHY RD.

ANY TOWN, ANY STATE USA

INITIAL INTERVIEW WITH A CHILD

(COLLECT THE INFORMATION BELOW FROM PARENTS)

Counselor_____ Date _____

Child's full name_____ Nickname _____

Address_____ City/State/Zip_____

Telephone_____ Sex_____

Date of birth_____ Age_____ Primary language _____

Ethnic group_____ School_____ Grade _____

Father_____ Age _____

Address_____ City/State/Zip_____

Telephone_____ Education _____ Occupation _____

Mother_____ Age _____

Address_____ City/State/Zip_____

Telephone_____ Education _____ Occupation _____

Siblings

(Name)	Sex	Age	Grade	at Home
_____			_____	_____
_____			_____	_____
_____			_____	_____
_____			_____	_____
_____			_____	_____

(cont'd)

For the purposes of the intake report, describe the child:
(Establish rapport, relieve fears, and stress confidentiality with child.)

1. What is your name? _____ What do you like to be called? _____

2. How old are you? _____ When is your birthday? _____

3. Where do you go to school? _____ What grade are your in? _____

4. Have you been to other schools before this one? _____ What were their names?
   _____

5. How are you doing in school? _____

6. Do you like/get along with your teacher? _____

7. Do you like/get along with the other kids in class? _____

8. Do you have any problems at home getting along with:

   Brothers   Sisters   Mother   Father   Grandparents   Others

9. Do you feel that your mom or dad is stricter with you than with the other children?
   _____

10. Are you free to have friends come over to the house? _____

11. How well do you communicate with your parents? Can you talk to them about problems?
    _____

12. Why do you think your parents wanted you to come to the clinic?

COMMUNITY COUNSELING SERVICES

1234 EMPATHY RD.

ANY TOWN, ANY STATE USA

FAMILY THERAPY INTAKE FORM

Counselor(s) _____ Date _____

_____ Supervisor _____

Referral source_____

Family name_____ Number of members _____

Address_____ City/State/Zip_____

Telephone_____

1. Family data:

Name	Relationship	Age	Status (living with, living away, deceased)

2. Schematic diagram of family structure:

3. Identifying information (length of relationship, previous marriages/relationships, employment, level of education, socioeconomic status, identified client, geographic stability):

(cont'd)

4. Family's perception of problem (description and history of problem, precipitating event, previous medical/psychiatric history):

5. Family status (dynamics, communication patterns, roles, dominance/submissiveness of each member, involvement of each member in family interaction, family insight into problem):

6. Clinician's observations (brief description of each family member; significant items regarding each person's general appearance and behavior, affect, mental status, and insight):

7. Recommendations:

COMMUNITY COUNSELING SERVICES

1234 EMPATHY RD.

ANY TOWN, ANY STATE USA

FAMILY INFORMATION SURVEY

Counselor(s) _____   Date _____

_____   Supervisor _____

Referral source_____

Family name_____ Number of members _____

Address_____ City/State/Zip_____

Telephone_____

Please complete the following survey in an effort to help us understand your family and any special problems you may be dealing with as efficiently and effectively as possible.

1. Within the past year has your family experienced any of the following? Check all that apply.
   a. _____ death of a family member
   b. _____ birth of a child
   c. _____ major illness
   d. _____ unemployment
   e. _____ change of residence
   f. _____ child leaving home

2. Does anyone in your family suffer from a chronic health problem or disability? If yes, please describe briefly:

3. Does anyone in your family regularly use prescription drugs? If yes, who and what drugs?

4. Does anyone in your family use drugs recreationally? If yes, who and what drugs?

(cont'd)

5. Has drug use ever caused a problem at home, school, or work?

6. Check the answer that most accurately describes your alcohol use, your spouse's, your children's.

Others Living at Home	Self	Spouse	Children
a. do not drink alcohol	_____	_____	_____
b. 0–1 drinks per day	_____	_____	_____
c. 2–3 drinks per day	_____	_____	_____
d. over 3 drinks per day	_____	_____	_____
e. 0–1 drinks per week	_____	_____	_____
f. 2–3 drinks per week	_____	_____	_____
g. over 3 drinks per week	_____	_____	_____
h. drink on occasion	_____	_____	_____

7. Is drinking ever a source of problems at home, school, or work?

8. During childhood did you experience any emotional, physical, or sexual abuse? If yes, what was your relationship to the abuser?

9. Was your spouse the victim of emotional, physical, or sexual abuse? If yes, what was the relationship to the abuser?

10. Is there any additional information about you or your family that would be useful for us to know?

COMMUNITY COUNSELING SERVICES

1234 EMPATHY RD.

ANY TOWN, ANY STATE USA

CASE NOTES

Counselor_____ Date _____

Client _____ Date of birth_____ Age _____

Beginning issues _____

Themes _____

Insights _____

Techniques _____

Future direction_____

Homework _____

Summary questions: 1. What goals did you have for today's session? _____

2. How well were those goals addressed? _____   3. What was effective for you

today? _____ 4. What was ineffective? _____ 5. What goals

can be set for our next session?_____

Counselor_____ Date _____

Client _____ Date of birth_____ Age _____

Beginning issues _____

Themes _____

Insights _____

Techniques _____

Future direction_____

Homework _____

Summary questions: 1.What goals did you have for today's session? _____

2. How well were those goals addressed? _____   3. What was effective for you

today? _____ 4. What was ineffective? _____ 5. What goals

can be set for our next session?_____

COMMUNITY COUNSELING SERVICES

1234 EMPATHY RD.

ANY TOWN, ANY STATE USA

SUGGESTIONS FOR WRITING CLIENT PROGRESS NOTES

The suggestions that follow have been proven effective in providing sufficient information for the counselor while limiting writing time.

Beginning Issues: It has proven important to record how clients typically begin sessions. After a few sessions, this information can provide clues about the client's style that would be helpful should the client deviate from the pattern.

Themes: Themes occur both within and among sessions. It is helpful to keep track of themes in individual sessions so that a quick review can reveal any themes that repeat themselves.

Insights: Insights gained by either the client or the counselor are recorded. This is also reviewed from time to time so that any larger, more comprehensive insight that might be gained from reviewing insights from individual sessions can be seen.

Techniques: Many counselors are creative, spontaneously generating useful techniques. If these are recorded, they can be recovered later for discussion with other counselors and can be shared in the profession. It is also important to know which techniques are being used so that they are not overused.

Future Direction: Used to remind the counselor of any unfinished business or points to be followed up.

Homework: This reminds the counselor to take a quick glance at the notes to see if there is any need for discussion or follow-up of an assignment given in the previous session.

Summary Questions: These serve two purposes. One is to allow the client to move from a perhaps highly emotional state to a less emotional state. It also gives an action aspect to counseling. Present and future goals are addressed as well as the effectiveness, from the client's point of view, of the strategies used in the session.

CLINICAL-BEHAVIOR DIAGNOSTIC MATRIX

"A CLASSIFICATION OF INFORMATION"

	Individual	Family	Community

SUBJECTIVE

History _____

Profile of symptom(s) _____

Explanation of problem(s) _____

Perception of resources _____

OBJECTIVE

Signs _____

Quantitative observations _____

ASSESSMENT

"The diagnostic process" _____

PROGNOSIS

Knowledge of natural history _____

PLAN

Education _____

Intervention _____

Additional data collection _____

COMMUNITY COUNSELING SERVICES
1234 EMPATHY RD.
ANY TOWN, ANY STATE USA

PROGRESS NOTES (SOAP)

Client_____ Counselor_____

Date _____ Client motivation ___ High ____ Medium ___ Low

Subjective report (content covered, feelings):

Objective report (behavioral observation, appearance, affect):

Assessment (significant material, insights, dynamics, immediacy concerns):

Plan (homework, treatment plan, goals/strategies for next session):

. . . .

Date _____ Client motivation: ___ High ____ Medium ___ Low

Subjective report (content covered, feelings):

Objective report (behavioral observation, appearance, affect):

Assessment (significant material, insights, dynamics, immediacy concerns):

Plan (homework, treatment plan, goals/strategies for next session):

COMMUNITY COUNSELING SERVICES

1234 EMPATHY RD.

ANY TOWN, ANY STATE USA

PROGRESS NOTES (NARRATIVE)

Client _____ Counselor _____

Supervisor _____ Intern _____

Date/Length   Nature of Contact, Persons Involved, Essential Description

_____

_____

_____

_____

_____

_____

_____

_____

_____

_____

_____

_____

_____

_____

_____

_____

_____

_____

_____

_____

_____

_____

COMMUNITY COUNSELING SERVICES

1234 EMPATHY RD.

ANY TOWN, ANY STATE USA

(STATE OF COLORADO USED AS AN EXAMPLE)

Your Rights as a Client:

The practice of both licensed and unlicensed persons in the field of psychotherapy is regulated by the Colorado State Department of Regulatory Agencies. Any questions, concerns, or complaints regarding the practice of mental health may be directed to the State Board listed below.

You are entitled to receive information from your counselor about methods of counseling, the techniques used, and the duration of counseling, if known.

Your counselor, who is in training in professional psychology, will consult with the supervisor on treatment issues. As part of the training requirements for your counselor, all counseling sessions may be audio- or videotaped and observed. You are encouraged to discuss your progress in treatment and are reminded that you may end treatment at any time. You may seek a second opinion if you wish to do so. The fee for these sessions has been set at _____ per session.

The information provided by you during counseling is legally confidential except as required by law. There are exceptions that can be discussed and will be identified should any such situations arise during counseling. (Exceptions to confidentiality include "threat of serious harm to self or others," as in the case of child abuse, suicide, or grave disability.)

Sexual contact between client and counselor is not a part of any recognized psychotherapy. Sexual intimacy between client and counselor is illegal in Colorado and should be reported to the grievance board.

All records of your counseling will be maintained in locked files during your time in treatment. Only authorized persons (your counselor and his or her supervisor) will have access to them. At the completion of your counseling, these records will be summarized and placed on file in Denver, Colorado, for a period of 10 years, after which they will be destroyed. Copies of your file can be sent to a qualified professional only by a written request from you.

If you have any concerns or complaints about licensed or unlicensed psychotherapists, you can contact the State Grievance Board at: State Grievance Board, 1560 Broadway, Suite 1340, Denver, CO 80202, (303) 894-7766.

I have been informed of my counselor's degrees, credentials, and licenses. I have read the preceding information and understand my rights as a client.

_____   _____

Client's Signature (Parent or Guardian for a Minor)   Date

_____   _____

(Counselor's Signature)   Date

SAMPLE PATIENT RIGHTS FORM FOR IN-PATIENT FACILITY

TO: _____, (Patient)

1. Your Treatment: You will be examined to determine your mental condition. We believe that if you understand and participate in your evaluation, care, and treatment, you may achieve better results. The staff has a responsibility to give you the best care and treatment possible and available and to respect your rights.

2. No Discrimination: You have the right to the same consideration and treatment as anyone else regardless of race, color, national origin, religion, age, sex, political affiliation, financial status, or disability.

3. Your Lawyer: You have the right to retain and consult with an attorney at any time. If you are here involuntarily, the court will appoint an attorney for you (at your own expense, if you are found able to afford one).

4. Telephones: You have the right to ready access to telephones, both to make and receive calls in privacy.

5. Letters: You have the right to receive and send sealed letters. No incoming or outgoing letters shall be opened, delayed, held, or censored by the personnel of the facility.

6. Writing Materials: You have the right to have access to letter writing materials, including postage. They will be provided, if needed. If you are unable to write, members of the facility will assist you to write, prepare, or mail correspondence.

7. Visitors: You have the right to frequent and convenient opportunities to meet with visitors. The facility may not deny visits at any time by your attorney, clergyman, or physician.

8. Refusal of Medications: You have the right to refuse to take medications, unless you are an imminent danger to yourself or others or the court has ordered medications.

9. Certification: If you are an involuntary patient, you have the right to a review of your certification or treatment by a judge or jury, and you may ask the court to appoint an independent professional person (psychiatrist or psychologist) to examine you and to testify at your hearing.

10. Clothing and Possessions: You have the right to wear your own clothes, keep and use your own possessions, and keep and be allowed to spend a reasonable sum of your own money.

11. Signing in Voluntarily: You have the right to sign in voluntarily, unless reasonable grounds exist to believe you will not remain a voluntary patient.

12. Least Restrictive Treatment: You have the right to receive medical and psychiatric care and treatment in the least restrictive treatment setting possible, suited to meet your individual needs.

(cont'd)

13. Transfers: If you are certified, you have the right to 24-hour notice before being transferred to another facility unless an emergency exists. You also have the right to protest to the court any such transfer, the right to notify whom you wish about the transfer, and the right to have the facility notify up to two persons designated by you about your transfer.

14. Confidentiality: You have the right to confidentiality of your treatment records except as required by law.

15. Access to Medical Records: You have the right to see your medical records at reasonable times.

16. Fingerprints: You have the right not to be fingerprinted, unless it is required by law.

17. Photographs: You have the right to refuse to be photographed except for hospital identification purposes.

18. Voting: You have the right to the opportunity to register and vote by absentee ballot with staff assistance.

19. Restrictions: If you abuse the rights regarding telephones, letters, writing, materials, visitors, or clothing and possessions, these rights may be restricted by the professional person (physician or licensed psychologist) providing treatment, but you must be given an explanation as to why the right is to be restricted. Restricted rights shall be evaluated for therapeutic effectiveness every 7 days.

20. Grievances: Grievances or complaints may be submitted to the Colorado Department of Health, the Colorado Division of Mental Health, or the Legal Center Serving Persons with Disabilities. Your patient representative will help you select the proper agency for your complaint or grievance and assist you in preparing the complaint or grievance if you wish.

COMMUNITY COUNSELING SERVICES

1234 EMPATHY RD.

ANY TOWN, ANY STATE USA

Authorization to Release/Request Information

I, _____, _____
   (First   Middle   Last)   (Date of birth)
hereby authorize the Community Counseling Services to (check one or both):

/__/ Release the following   /__/ Request the following
information to: information from:

_____   _____
     (Person/Agency)   (Person/Agency)

_____   _____
       (Address)   (Address)

_____   _____
    (City/State/Zip)   (City/State/Zip)

Information to be released/requested: _____

Purpose of release/request: _____

I understand that I may revoke this authorization at any time by giving written notice to the Community Counseling Services. Without such a revocation, this authorization shall expire on ____/____/____. (If no date is specified, this authorization shall expire one year from the date of my signature.) I also herewith release Community Counseling Services from all liability for releasing such information.

_____   ____/____/____   _____
(Client's Signature)   (Date)   (Witness)

If the client is under the age of 15 years*, or has a legal guardian appointed by the Court, this authorization must be signed by the client's parent or legal guardian. (*Parents or legal guardians of minors aged 15–18 may have access to information without the authorization of the minor.)

_____   ____/____/____   _____
(Parent/Guardian's Signature)   (Date)   (Witness)

Notice to Whom Information Is Given: The information disclosed by this authorization comes from records whose confidentiality is protected by federal law. Federal regulations prohibit you from making further disclosure of it without the specific written consent of the person to whom it pertains.

COMMUNITY COUNSELING SERVICES

1234 EMPATHY RD.

ANY TOWN, ANY STATE USA

TREATMENT PLAN 1

Date_____

Client_____ Counselor_____

Symptom 1_____ Client's objective_____
Goal:

Symptom 2_____ Client's objective_____
Goal:

Treatment plan—Method of treatment_____

_____

_____

Frequency_____ Estimated length of treatment_____

Options to be used in addition to counseling: 1. _____ 2. _____

3. _____ 4. _____ 5. _____

Supervisor's comments and review:

_____   _____
(Counselor's Signature)   (Date)

_____   _____
(Supervisor's Signature)   (Date)

COMMUNITY COUNSELING SERVICES

1234 EMPATHY RD.

ANY TOWN, ANY STATE USA

TREATMENT PLAN 2

Date _____

Client _____   Counselor _____

1. Nature of the problem/crisis:

2. Goals:

3. Objectives (what the client will do):

4. Methods (what counselor/agency will provide):

COMMUNITY COUNSELING SERVICES

1234 EMPATHY RD.

ANY TOWN, ANY STATE USA

TERMINATION SUMMARY

Counselor _____ Date _____

Client_____ Date of birth_____ Age _____

Address_____ City/State/Zip_____

Telephone_____ Sex _____

Referral sources (if applicable)_____

Reason(s) for service _____

Total sessions _____ Date of first session _____ Date of last session _____

List of all sessions by date_____

_____

Major theme(s) of counseling   1. _____

    2. _____   3. _____

Tests administered (if applicable):

    Date   Test   Administered by:

Referrals and consultations:

    Date   Name   Purpose   Outcome (if known)

Reports (e.g., suspected child abuse, State Grievance Board, etc.)

    Date   Name and Address of Report Recipient   Substance of Report

Reason for termination: _____

_____   _____

(Counselor's Signature)   (Date)

_____   _____

(Supervisor's Signature)   (Date)

COMMUNITY COUNSELING SERVICES
1234 EMPATHY RD.
ANY TOWN, ANY STATE USA

REFERRAL FORM

To _____

Client _____ Date _____

Address _____ City/State/Zip _____

Telephone _____

Referral request: _____

_____

_____

_____

_____

Referred by: Name_____ Supervisor _____

Disposition:

Clinician assigned _____ Date _____

Comments:

_____   _____

(Therapist's Signature)   (Date)

Appendix 3

COMMUNITY COUNSELING SERVICES

1234 EMPATHY RD.

ANY TOWN, ANY STATE USA

INSURANCE CLAIM FORM

Client_____ Date of birth_____ Sex _____

Address _____ Relationship to Insured _____

City/State/Zip _____ ID# – – Group # _____

Insured party_____ Accident related: Yes _____ No _____

Address_____ Work related: Yes _____ No _____

City/State/Zip _____

I affirm that I was provided the services listed   I authorize the payment of benefits to
below and authorize release of the information   the undersigned supplier for the
necessary to process this claim.   services described below.

Signed_____ Date_____ Signed _____

Supplier Information

Date of onset_____ Date first consulted_____ Symptoms before? _____

Total disability?_____ Partial?_____ Hospitalized?_____ Hospital dates _____

Referring physician_____ Site (if not office) _____

Diagnosis code #1 (DSM-IV)_____ Diagnosis code #2 _____

Date	Location	Procedure	Service	Minutes	Dx Codes	Charges
_____	_____	_____	_____	_____	_____	_____
_____	_____	_____	_____	_____	_____	_____
_____	_____	_____	_____	_____	_____	_____
_____	_____	_____	_____	_____	_____	_____
_____	_____	_____	_____	_____	_____	_____
					Total	_____

_____   _____
(Therapist's Signature) (S.S. #)   (Date)   (Supervisor's Signature) (Licence #) (Date)

COMMUNITY COUNSELING SERVICES

1234 EMPATHY RD.

ANY TOWN, ANY STATE USA

CLIENT BILLING WORKSHEET

Client_____   Insurer _____

Address_____   Address _____

Date of birth _____   Group #_____

Telephone _____   Policy # _____

Insured's Name _____   Full Fee $ _____

Therapist _____   Adjusted Fee $ _____

DSM IV DX: 1. _____   2. _____   Date of Intake ____/____/____

Date	Charges Comments*	Client Payments	Insurance Payments	Balance

*CB—Client Billed; IB—Insurance Billed; NC—Noncoverage; OD—Overdue; PD—Paid; WO—Write Off

COMMUNITY COUNSELING SERVICES

1234 EMPATHY RD.

ANY TOWN, ANY STATE USA

C O N F I D E N T I A L

PSYCHOLOGICAL REPORT FORM

Counselor_____ Date _____

Client_____ Date of birth _____ Age _____

Address_____ City/State/Zip_____

Telephone_____ Sex_____

Marital status: Married_____ Single_____ Divorced_____ Widowed_____

Occupation_____ School_____

Last educational grade level completed _____

Number of years of college completed _____

Trade schools or special training _____

Identifying data:

Presenting problem:

Mental status examination: Appearance (behavior, speech, mood/affect); Thought Content (associations, perceptions, insight); Cognitive Testing (orientation, attention, memory, concentration, abstract reasoning, insight, judgment); Vegetative Signs (sleep, appetite, energy, sexual); Drugs and Alcohol (use, overuse, abuse); Suicidal and/or Homicidal Ideations

History of presenting problem:

Past psychological/psychiatric history:

Family and social history:

Developmental history:

Assessments (instruments and outcomes):

Diagnosis (Axis I, Axis II, Axis III, Axis IV, and Axis V):

Differential diagnosis (diagnoses considered and ruled out):

Recommendations:

(cont'd)

Treatment plan:

    Immediate:

        1.

        2.

        3.

        4.

        5.

    Long term:

        1.

        2.

        3.

        4.

        5.

_____   _____

(Therapist's Signature)   (Date)   (Supervisor's Signature) (Licence #) (Date)

COMMUNITY COUNSELING SERVICES

1234 EMPATHY RD.

ANY TOWN, ANY STATE USA

Mental Status Checklist

Counselor_____ Date _____

Client_____ Date of birth _____ Age _____

CODE: Hx = Described but not observed

Nd = No data and not inferred

If you have checked column 2 or 3, please explain in comments section.

1 = Not Present; 2 = Slight or Occasional; 3 = Marked or Repeated

Appearance:　　　　　　　　　　　　　1　　　　2　　　　3
   1. physically unkempt, unclean
   2. clothing disheveled, dirty
   3. clothing atypical, unusual, bizarre
   4. unusual physical characteristics
Comments:

Behavior/Posture:　　　　　　　　　1　　　　2　　　　3
   5. slumped
   6. rigid, tense
   7. atypical, inappropriate
Comments:

Facial Expression Suggests:　　　　1　　　　2　　　　3
   8. anxiety, fear, apprehension
   9. depression, sadness
   10. anger, hostility
   11. decreased variability expression
   12. bizarreness, inappropriateness
Comments:

(cont'd)

1 = Not Present; 2 = Slight or Occasional; 3 = Marked or Repeated

General Body Movements: 1   2   3
  13. accelerated, increased speed
  14. decreased, slowed
  15. atypical, peculiar, inappropriate
  16. restless, fidgety
Comments:

Amplitude and Quality of Speech: 1   2   3
  17. increased, loud
  18. decreased, slowed
  19. atypical, slurring, stammering
Comments:

Doctor-Client Relationship: 1   2   3
  20. domineering
  21. submissive; overly compliant
  22. provocative
  23. suspicious
  24. uncooperative
Comments:

Feeling (Affect and Mood):   1   2   3
  25. inappropriate to thought content
  26. increased lability of affect
Comments:

Predominant Mood Is: 1   2   3
  27. blunted, absent, unvarying
  28. euphoria, elation
  29. anger, hostility
  30. fear, anxiety, apprehension
  31. depression, sadness
Comments:

(cont'd)

1 = Not Present; 2 = Slight or Occasional; 3 = Marked or Repeated

Perception:	1	2	3

32. illusions
33. auditory hallucinations
34. visual hallucinations
35. other hallucinations

Comments:

Thinking (Intellectual Functioning):	1	2	3

36. impaired level of consciousness
37. impaired attention span
38. impaired abstract thinking
39. impaired calculating ability
40. impaired intelligence

Comments:

Orientation:	1	2	3

41. disoriented to person
42. disoriented to place
43. disoriented to time

Comments:

Insight:	1	2	3

44. difficulty in acknowledging the presence of psychological problems
45. mostly blames others or circumstance for problems

Comments:

Judgment:	1	2	3

46. impaired ability to manage daily living activities
47. impaired ability tomake reasonable life decisions

Comments:

Memory:	1	2	3

48. impaired immediate recall
49. impaired recent memory
50. impaired remote memory

Comments:

(cont'd)

1 = Not Present; 2 = Slight or Occasional; 3 = Marked or Repeated

Thought Content:	1	2	3
51. obsessions			
52. compulsions			
53. phobias			
54. derealization, depersonalization			
55. suicidal ideation			
56. homicidal ideation			
57. delusions			
58. ideas of reference			
59. ideas of influence			
60. associational disturbance			
61. thought flow decreased, slowed			
62. thought flow increased			

Comments:

Diagnosis (DSM-IV):	1	2	3
Axis I:			
Axis II:			
Axis III:			
Axis IV:			
Axis V:			

Treatment Planning:	1	2	3
1.			
2.			
3.			
4.			
5.			

General Comments:

Appendix Four

Crisis Management and Crisis Intervention

Crisis Management

The following is a suggested five-step approach to handling crises. People are unique, of course, and no "approach" can be expected to be completely satisfactory in every situation. This approach does, however, provide a framework to begin to understand how to interact with persons in crisis.

Step 1. Present yourself as a person who cares and is understanding and calm. Essentially, you are saying to the person, "Tell me what is going on for you."

Contrary to conventional wisdom, people influence the sequence of reactions to crisis, the crisis does not influence the reactions of people.

Step 2. Invite the person to talk. You might ask a question such as, "How can I be of help?"

It is better for the person to volunteer information than for you to ask a series of probing questions. If the person does not volunteer, you might ask some information-gathering questions—such as, "What happened?" "Have you talked to anyone about it?" "Do you want to talk now?"—as a way to get started.

329

Avoid telling the person what they need. For example, avoid "What you need is cognitive restructuring." "What you need now is to vent some feelings." "You just need to calm down." "What you need now is to call upon your religious beliefs."

Step 3. Get some help. Involve other people. Don't rely on yourself alone.

Step 4. Propose action for the client. Perhaps a question such as, "What can you do outside this room that will help reduce your crisis and provide a little light at the end of the tunnel?"

People in crisis have what is called *tunnel vision* and are unaware of the people and resources that can help them. Your calm approach and involving other people can lessen the "threat" and open up resources to the person.

Step 5. Follow up. Keep checking in with the person from time to time. Continue to check in for about 3 months.

330

Crisis Intervention Principles

1. Immediacy. A crisis is a time of danger, and there is a limited opportunity for intervention. When a person (client) asks for help, you try to determine if there is a crisis. If there is, intervene immediately.

2. Action. In crisis intervention, there is an immediate need to act. Determine the crisis, assess the situation and in collaboration with the client, build a plan of action to deal with the crisis.

3. Restricted Purpose. The minimal purpose of crisis intervention is to prevent disaster. The goal is to restore the client to a sense of self-control again.

4. Instilling Hope. The helper must initially work to instill hope into the situation and for the client. This is done from the first contact through one's attitude about the client and about the situation.

5. Empowerment. From the first contact, the helper must work to foster self-control, self-reliance and combat dependency in the client. Empowerment is balanced with the need for support.

6. Enhanced Self-Concept. The helper seeks to understand the client's self-image, self-worth, and sense of personal adequacy as a way of determining the effect that any intervention might have. The helper works to protect and enhance self-concept in the client.

7. Support. The helper provides support and encouragement during the crisis period mostly by staying in contact and "staying with" the client during the crisis and by being available to go through the process with the client.

8. Solution-Focused. This is the bedrock principle of crisis intervention. Determine "the problem" (the unresolved issue(s) that led to the crisis) and then work with the client to plan and put into action steps aimed at resolving the problem. Keep attention focused on the problem-solving process, and avoid being sidetracked.

Appendix Five

Responding to the Suicidal Person

I. Important Questions to Ask a Potentially Suicidal Person
   A. Have your problems been getting you down so much lately that you've been thinking about suicide?
   B. How would you kill yourself?
      (S) 1. How (S)pecific is the plan?
      (A) 2. Is the method (A)vailable to the person?
      (L) 3. Is the proposed method (L)ethal?
   C. Do you have the means available?
   D. Have you ever attempted suicide before?
      (C) 1. (C)hronology—how long ago was it? The more recent, the greater the risk.
      (A) 2. (A)wareness of lethality—did the person believe the method was lethal?
      (R) 3. (R)escue—did the person assist in the rescue or attempt in a place where he or she would likely be discovered?
      (L) 4. (L)ethality (actual)—how lethal was the method?
   E. Has anyone in your family ever attempted or completed suicide?
   F. What are the odds that you will kill yourself?
   G. What has been keeping you alive so far?
   H. What do you think the future holds in store for you?

II. Intervention with a Suicidal Person
 A. Establish a relationship with the person.
  1. Reinforce the person for making contact.
  2. Be accepting and nonjudgmental.
  3. Try to sound calm, confident, and concerned.
  4. If it is a telephone call, try to get as much information as possible: name, location, age, is someone close by (who, how to contact)? Are drugs or alcohol involved?
 B. Assess the degree of risk.
  1. Use the SAL system.
  2. If it is an emergency:
   a) Act decisively and with determination.
   b) Try to remove the weapon or method but not physically.
   c) Do not leave the person alone.
   d) If a telephone call—obtain help of paramedics and police.
  3. If it is not an emergency:
   a) Try to identify the major problem.
   b) Assess available resources. Ask about friends, neighbors, relatives who might be helpful.
   c) Ask about previous successful coping skills.
   d) Find out what has been keeping the person living so far.
   e) Mobilize the person's resources—surround the person with a wall of caring people (clergy, if the person is religious; neighbors; friends, family; physician).

III. Do's of Suicide Intervention
 A. Try to be positive and emphasize the most desirable alternatives.
 B. Try to be calm and understanding.
 C. Use constructive statements to help separate confused feelings and define problems.
 D. Mention the person's family, friends, clergy, neighbors as sources of strength and help. If any of these are rejected, back off quickly and move on to others.
 E. Emphasize the temporary nature of the person's problems. Explain how the crisis will pass in time.

334

IV. Don'ts of Suicide Intervention
   A. Don't sound shocked by anything the person tells you.
   B. Don't stress the shock and embarrassment that the suicide will be to the family before being certain that this is not exactly what the person hopes to accomplish.
   C. Don't engage in philosophical debate on the moral aspects of suicide because you may not only lose the debate, but also the suicidal person.

Remember:

1. Most suicidal people are in crisis for very brief periods of minutes, hours, or days—keep them alive and don't try to solve all their problems at once.
2. Most suicidal people have chosen a particular method, place, or date once they have decided to take action. If you can keep them from acting out with the method they have chosen, they are unlikely to use alternative methods.

Index

Index